THE HISTORY OF EMOTIONS

Manchester University Press

❦ HISTORICAL APPROACHES ❦

Series editor

Geoffrey Cubitt

The Historical Approaches series aims to make a distinctive contribution to current debate about the nature of the historical discipline, its theory and practice, and its evolving relationships to other cultural and intellectual fields. The intention of the series is to bridge the gap that sometimes exists between learned monographs on the one hand and beginners' manuals on the other, by offering works that have the clarity of argument and liveliness of style to appeal to a general and student readership, while also prompting thought and debate among practising historians and thinkers about the discipline. Titles in the series will cover a wide variety of fields, and explore them from a range of different angles, but will have in common the aspiration of raising awareness of the issues that are posed by historical studies in today's world, and of the significance of debates about history for a broader understanding of contemporary culture.

Also available:
Geoffrey Cubitt   *History and memory*
Joanna de Groot   *Empire and history writing in Britain c.1750–2012*
Matthew Kempshall   *Rhetoric and the writing of history, 400–1500*

THE HISTORY OF EMOTIONS

Rob Boddice

Manchester University Press

Copyright © Rob Boddice 2018

The right of Rob Boddice to be identified as the author of this work has been asserted by him in accordance with the Copyright, Designs and Patents Act 1988.

Published by Manchester University Press
Altrincham Street, Manchester M1 7JA
www.manchesteruniversitypress.co.uk

British Library Cataloguing-in-Publication Data
A catalogue record for this book is available from the British Library

ISBN 978 1 7849 9428 0 hardback
ISBN 978 1 7849 9429 7 paperback

First published 2018

The publisher has no responsibility for the persistence or accuracy of URLs for any external or third-party internet websites referred to in this book, and does not guarantee that any content on such websites is, or will remain, accurate or appropriate.

Typeset by
Servis Filmsetting Ltd, Stockport, Cheshire
Printed in Great Britain by
TJ International Ltd, Padstow, Cornwall

For Blueberry, whatever you may become

CONTENTS

Acknowledgements	*page* viii
Introduction	1
1 Historians and emotions	8
2 Words and concepts	41
3 Communities, regimes and styles	59
4 Power, politics and violence	84
5 Practice and expression	106
6 Experience, senses and the brain	132
7 Spaces, places and objects	168
8 Morality	190
Conclusion	205
Select bibliography	218
Index	242

ACKNOWLEDGEMENTS

This book is the product of years of exposure to different ways of doing the history of emotions. I was fortunate enough to be in one of the major centres of research as the field exploded, and was present as many of its core ideas either took shape or had their shape changed. In Berlin I was part of both the Languages of Emotion Excellence Cluster at Freie Universität and the Center for the History of Emotions at the Max Planck Institute for Human Development. Without those five years of conversation, of listening, of reading and of writing, I could not have written this book.

There are far too many individuals to thank from these institutions, but I reserve mention for Jan Plamper (now of Goldsmiths) and Ute Frevert, who more than any others facilitated debate in the crucible of disciplinary formation. Because of my Berlin ties I was able to make connections to historians of emotion around the world. This book has its origins in the mind of Rhodri Hayward at the Centre for the History of Emotions at Queen Mary University of London, and fell to me to write it presumably because he thought I would not mess it up. I hope it passes muster! Thomas Dixon at the same institution has been a regular correspondent and sounding board. After meeting Javier Moscoso in Berlin he was most gracious in inviting me to Madrid and in being fantastically enthusiastic in his engagement with my work. I am certain there has never been a more hospitable host, and I am also certain that, in his army of graduate students, some of whom have become friends, the future is bright for the history of emotions and the history of experience. The Melbourne node of the Australian Research Council Centre of Excellence for the History of Emotions was kind enough to host me, listen to my thoughts on where we were all going and discuss with me their teaching strategies and future plans. Special thanks to

Charles Zika – another wonderful host – and Stephanie Trigg, for making it a memorable month. And just as I continually reached out to historians of emotions around the world, so they reached out to me. For kind invitations and collegial engagement I must thank Joanna Bourke at Birkbeck, Karen Vallgårda at Copenhagen, Ville Kivimäki at Tampere and George Weisz at McGill. Matthew Milner heightened my senses. Special thanks, for help along the way, go to Susan Matt, Peter Stearns and William Reddy. One could not wish for better pillars of inspiration in this field.

Some sections of chapter 1 have been adapted from 'Medical and scientific understandings', in S. Matt [ed.], *A Cultural History of the Emotions* (London: Bloomsbury, forthcoming). Some parts of chapter 3 have been adapted from 'The affective turn: Historicizing the emotions', in C. Tileagă and J. Byford [eds], *Psychology and History: Interdisciplinary Explorations* (Cambridge: Cambridge University Press, 2014) © Cambridge University Press 2014, reprinted with permission. Parts of chapter 6 inevitably overlap with work produced at the same time as this volume, for the chapter 'Neurohistory', in P. Burke and M. Tamm [eds], *Debating New Approaches in History* (London: Bloomsbury, forthcoming).

Naturally, I owe great debts to the individuals and institutions who support me in my research and writing. Much of the work for this book was done under the auspices of a research grant from the Deutsche Forschungsgemeinschaft. Family and friends are unswerving in backing me to do what I feel I must. Tony Morris is a positive force. And my wife, Stephanie Olsen, as always, has influenced every sentence. As a historian of emotions herself, with more than a small claim to being a leading scholar of the field in its intersection with the history of childhood, I could not have wished for a better sounding board, disputant and emotion modifier.

INTRODUCTION

History departments around the world appear to have taken the 'emotional turn'.[1] In the last decade, an astonishing number of books and articles, as well as centres for research, have appeared specifically to address emotions in history.[2] There are already a number of theoretical and methodological tools, generated by historians, that address what emotions are and what historians should do with them. Historians of emotions have engaged with – sometimes borrowing, sometimes abusing – other disciplines, most notably anthropology and the neurosciences, in the process of carving out a space in which the history of emotions can exist.

At the heart of this process are a series of radical claims that this book aims both to describe and, in many ways, defend: 1) Emotions

---

[1] Tracking who is teaching the history of emotions is not straightforward, but I have found history of emotions programmes for undergraduates at the University of York, London School of Philosophy, Rutgers, Duke, Berkeley, Georgetown, Memorial (Newfoundland), Toronto, Chinese University of Hong Kong and Tampere, and for graduates at Goldsmiths, Max Planck Institute for Human Development, Newberry (Chicago), Loyola, Carleton (Ottawa), Lethbridge and Melbourne.

[2] The principal centres of research are the Centre for the History of Emotions at Queen Mary, University of London; Center for the History of Emotions, Max Planck Institute for Human Development in Berlin; the Australian Research Council Centre of Excellence for the History of Emotions (across Australia); the Hist-Ex (History and Philosophy of Experience) group, based at the Centro de Ciencias Humanas y Sociales del CSIC, Madrid. Many of the field's developments are documented by the project *Les Émotions au Moyen Âge* (EMMA), run between the Université d'Aix-Marseille and the Univeristé du Québec à Montréal. The first strictly historical journal focusing on emotions (*Emotions: History, Culture, Society*) has just been launched, with editorial input from across the world of expertise in the field.

change over time: that is to say, emotions are as much the subject of historical enquiry as anything else; 2) Emotions are not merely the effect of historical circumstances, expressed in the aftermath of events, but are active causes of events and richly enhance historiographical theories of causation; 3) Emotions are at the centre of the history of the human being, considered as a biocultural entity that is characterised as a worlded body, in the worlds of other worlded bodies; 4) Emotions are at the centre of the history of morality, for it is becoming increasingly unlikely that any account of human virtue, morals or ethics can be devoid of an analysis of its historical emotional context. Taken together, the history of emotions is, therefore, putting emotions at the centre of historiographical practice. Emotions cannot be sidelined as another (soft) category of historical analysis, peripheral to the weighty subjects of identity, race, class, gender, globalism and politics. The history of emotions enhances our understanding of all these things.

With the recent proliferation of works in this field, it is extremely difficult for the newcomer to know where to begin. When Jan Plamper wrote in 2012 that the history of emotions is a rocket ship taking off, I doubt even he realised the altitude it would reach in such a short time.[3] His own 'Introduction' to the field necessarily concentrated not on what historians have done with emotions, but on what anthropologists and psychologists did with them, and the way in which the field opened up to historians in the twenty-first century. Now, five years later, there are hundreds of works identified explicitly as contributions to the literature on the history of emotions; a lot of people are actively practising this new discipline, but few have had the chance to take the temperature of the field as a whole as it now stands.

There are a number of general appraisals of what is at stake in

---

[3] J. Plamper, *Geschichte und Gefühl: Grundlagen der Emotionsgeschichte* (Munich: Siedler, 2012). Only seven years prior to this, Peter Burke wrote with a great deal of uncertainty about whether a cultural history of emotions was even possible. Suffice to say that a great many scholars have since answered that it is, but this makes the field particularly difficult to enter at this moment. The unusual rapidity with which it is developing makes a suitable entry point difficult to find. Burke's article, which by ordinary standards might be considered 'recent', has been superseded. See P. Burke, 'Is there a cultural history of the emotions?', in P. Gouk and H. Hills [eds], *Representing Emotions: New Connections in the Histories of Art, Music and Medicine* (Aldershot: Ashgate, 2005), 35–48.

the history of emotions, but the points of reference only get wider, and the *how* of the history of emotions remains in disparate sources, undigested, incoherent.[4] Much of what has been produced in the last few years, as well as numerous conferences and panels throughout the historiographical community, therefore feels the need to ask basic questions of theory and method, going over old ground where it is not really necessary, struggling with conceptual innovations that might already be well developed. This book aims to cut short this kind of unnecessary labour and instead give the field a point from which to move forward and develop. In so doing, it addresses, in one place, the kinds of questions that until now have been answerable only by extensive bibliographical research. How does one *do* the history of emotions? What are its internal debates, challenges and weaknesses? What are its principal theories and assumptions? In short, what does one read first? It is my hope that this book will be the first port of call, not only for students who are new to the history of emotions, but also for established historians of all ranks who wish to find out what the history of emotions can do for them. More importantly still, I hope that this book will reach beyond the discipline of history and, in a substantial and meaningful way, be received and engaged with by psychologists, neuroscientists, anthropologists and philosophers.

Emotions scholarship has, for generations, been fractured along disciplinary lines.[5] It is not an unfair characterisation to say that the emotions in philosophical works are not the same emotions as in psychological works, though they may share some first principles.[6]

---

[4] Recent surveys include B. Rosenwein, 'Problems and methods in the history of emotions', *Passions in Context*, 1 (2010): 1–32; S. Matt, 'Current emotion research in history: Or doing history from the inside out', *Emotion Review*, 3 (2011): 117–24; R. Boddice, 'The affective turn: Historicizing the emotions', in C. Tileagă and J. Byford [eds], *Psychology and History: Interdisciplinary Explorations* (Cambridge: Cambridge University Press, 2014); J. Plamper, *The History of Emotions: An Introduction* (Oxford: Oxford University Press, 2015).
[5] See Plamper's able summary of the distance between anthropological and psychological epistemologies of the emotions, for example, in his *History of Emotions*.
[6] The philosophical literature is legion, but readers could do worse than studying M.S. Brady, *Emotional Insight: The Epistemic Role of Emotional Experience* (Oxford: Oxford University Press, 2013) to see how radically different philosophical approaches are to other humanities disciplines. See also M. Nussbaum, *Upheavals of Thought: The Intelligence of Emotions* (Cambridge: Cambridge University Press, 2001).

These are problems of semantics, but also of fundamental incommensurabilities of purpose. History has long been an interdisciplinary bridge builder, happily borrowing insights and methods from a variety of other fields to suit its own purposes. It is true, however, that the direction of interdisciplinary flow has tended only to be inward. Historiography has projected very few of its own ideas back into those disciplines from which it freely borrows. This is partly because historians themselves see no need to make such contributions, but also because other disciplines have never really seen a substantial value in history for the purposes of their own scholarship and research. In the case of emotions, many historians are beginning to make forceful arguments that this can no longer be the case. Our understanding of what emotions are (and have been), how they work and what they mean, cannot be fenced off from other disciplines in which emotions are thought to be something else, to work otherwise and to mean different things.

Since there are deep convictions among historians of emotions that our findings are far from fanciful, that they are based on strong evidence about emotional experience, expression and practice, it seems imperative to find a way to bring other disciplines to a point of engagement with us. Indeed, historical appraisals of emotional experiences in the past can serve as direct challenges to contemporary scholarship in other disciplines that would narrowly and transhistorically define what emotion is. Happily, recent years have seen the potential for rapprochement between some neuroscientists and anthropologists, with history as the outward-looking bridge.[7] Few people yet recognise the importance of this coming together, but this book's presentation of the potential harmony of constructivist, historicist, genetic and neuroscientific approaches suggests an exciting future, both in terms of research contexts and for our understanding of what makes us tearful, what makes us timorous or amorous, and what makes us tick.

The book is organised in such a way as to represent the diversity

---

[7] See, for example, J. Carter Wood, 'The limits of culture? Society, evolutionary psychology and the history of violence', *Cultural and Social History*, 4 (2007): 95–114, and Barbara Rosenwein's critical response, 'The uses of biology: A response to J. Carter Wood's "The limits of culture"', *Cultural and Social History*, 4 (2007): 553–8. See also W. Reddy, 'Saying something new: Practice theory and cognitive neuroscience', *Arcadia*, 44 (2009): 8–23.

of research being undertaken in the history of emotions. It is at once a review of the field and an appraisal of its varied methods and theories. A grand narrative, or an actual history of the emotions, will have to wait for another book,[8] though this one is coloured and exemplified by histories of emotion across time and from around the world. There are no special instructions for reading this text. It is designed precisely to be an introduction to the field, and therefore is best begun at the beginning. The opening chapter takes a broad overview, looking at the place of emotions in historical writing that pre-dates the formulation of a history-of-emotions project per se. It also looks at the presence of emotional historicism in other fields, tracing the reasons why the emotions failed to be addressed by historians until relatively recently. A brief review of some of the key innovators in the history of emotions is offered at this point, though in-depth analysis will run throughout the book. This, in turn, requires an analysis of the failed psychohistory movement that attempted to apply psychoanalytical methods to the practice of history, as well as relations with the psychological sciences more generally. This leads to an introductory appraisal of the social neurosciences and the possibilities for the history of emotions in this context.

Chapter 2 looks at the long and important history of emotion language, what language can tell us about the concept of types of emotion and, more importantly still, about the historical experience of emotions. The overarching observation here is that a sensitivity to language in a historical context has to be matched with a sensitivity to contemporary language used in historical practice. We are in engaged in a history of the 'emotions'. Is that a satisfactory label for what we do? What does it reveal and what does it obscure? In sum, this chapter suggests that the risks of employing 'emotion' as a master category for our research outweigh the potential rewards; conversely, remaining open to the mutability of language and concepts does not make comparison impossible, or analysis redundant, but enriches them both.

Chapter 3 deals with some of the most important theoretical and methodological innovations in the history of emotions for working out the social dynamics of emotions in the past, putting together

[8] The other book is planned: R. Boddice, *A History of Feelings* (London: Reaktion, forthcoming).

emotional regimes, emotional communities and emotional styles (or emotionologies) in order to compare and contrast their merits. Broadly speaking, these are, respectively, the work of William Reddy, Barbara Rosenwein and Peter Stearns. The influence of each is measured, with suggestions for ways in which the weaknesses of each might be shored up, and their respective strengths united for a common purpose.

Historians tend towards analysis of humans in groups, even where the focus is biography. The history of emotions can challenge this preference by opening up the potential to explore the biological history of individuals. I will come to this shortly. Chapter 4, however, seeks to extend the possibilities for social analysis by exploring the ways in which emotional experience happens dynamically. So much of emotions research in all fields is about the way emotional experiences are part of social interactions and the dynamics of power.[9] This chapter looks at the ways in which emotional prescription is expressed, enforced and reinforced, as well as examining what happens when emotions do not accord with expected norms.

There is a great deal to say here about expression and emotional practice, and therefore there is a good deal of overlap with chapter 5. In this chapter, however, there will be a much greater focus on what individuals go through (or have gone through) in order to emote in different kinds of context. This fills out the picture of dynamic emotional relations, but also re-emphasises the possibilities for a history of the biological individual as a mutable biocultural being. It unites the history of emotions with the history of biology, the history of the body and some key interdisciplinary insights on empathy.

Focus on the body and on biology leads naturally to a consideration of the senses. Generally speaking, the history of the senses has developed separately to the history of the emotions, and it has its own established historiography. Still, there are good reasons for putting the two together, especially when one considers the languages of 'feeling' and of 'sensibility' that intertwine with other emotions concepts. The history of the senses also has in common with the history of emotions a desire to disrupt universalising dis-

---

[9] See, for example, the monumental interdisciplinary collection (though with history excluded), C. von Scheve and M. Salmela [eds], *Collective Emotions* (Oxford: Oxford University Press, 2014).

courses and to explore the endless variety of senses in the past. Chapter 6 serves as introduction and appraisal of this field, with suggestions for fruitful joint efforts in the future that indicate a rich historiography of experience. The emphasis on the historical body/mind invites a fuller appraisal here of the possibilities of neurohistory, and the extent to which historians of emotion must acquire literacy in the neurosciences. Only one sense – the moral sense – is omitted here, for coverage in the last chapter.

For all the talk of social and cultural emotions, we have yet to discuss the spaces and places where socio-emotional interactions take place, or the objects and material culture that are part of the emotional meaning-making process. Chapter 7 discusses these emotional worlds, the ways emotional prescriptions are embodied in architecture and the arrangement of social space, and the ways in which cultural associations with objects are essential to the inscription of emotional wiring in, or the imprint of encounters on, the biocultural brain. This completes the picture of the emotional body, the emotional brain and the emotional society.

This leaves just one key aspect: morality. The final chapter underlines the importance of the history of emotions by attaching it to a category that gives it greater weight. By showing the historical connections between emotions and morals, I am not attempting to force two categories together, but rather to give expression to a dramatically dynamic relationship that has persisted, in many different forms, throughout human history. This is not to assert a universal relationship of emotions and morals, but rather to emphasise that the mutability and historicity of emotions can newly explain and add weight to existing narratives of the historicity of morality. This is the key to what constitutes value in human societies, and makes the history of emotions more than an end in itself. It has the potential to unlock – at the level of experience – that thing that historians have always searched for: namely, what it means to be human.

1

HISTORIANS AND EMOTIONS

Feeling for the past

The purview of historians is change over time. We look for causes and effects in order to explain how and why change happens. Seldom do we look for what *is*. We are focused on what *was*, or on how things came to be. Understanding the complexity of past societies, past cultures and past politics allows us to understand why things happened the way they did. This observation does not merely apply to events, however broadly interpreted, but to experience in general. The historian's role has come to include an appraisal of what it was like to *be* in the past: we have come to ask, what did it *feel* like? Questions of identity, the self, interpersonal relations, relations with institutions, the production and reception of culture, and relations with the environment, the ecosystem and the city: all these have fallen into the realm of historical analysis. The implicit assumption is that such relations and formations in the past were different to what we find in the present. It is not so much that the past explains the present: such a calculation becomes increasingly difficult the further away in time one gets from the here and now. It is more that an analysis of the structure of human experience in the past might help us denaturalise the present.

History challenges our assumptions about what we think we know. It takes common knowledge and common sense and shows them to be situated knowledge and situated sense. What counts as 'normal' or 'natural' is only ever normal or natural under certain circumstances. History disrupts such categories. This is the political edge of historiography. It holds to account those who would proclaim, this is how things *are*. It enables us to ask 'why?' and 'for how long?' It permits us to posit other ways for things to be.

Enter the history of emotions and a curious challenge. In general, and with some notable exceptions, historians have steered clear of historicising the human being itself.[1] Humans have been actors in shifting historical scenery, and it has sufficed to analyse that scenery and the drama within it. This has been at odds with the aforementioned tendency to reject what *is*. If historians have tended to reject transhistorical universals, they nevertheless have also tended until quite recently to assume that the human being, since the beginning of historical time, has been a biological constant. Certainly, histories of the body have shown the ways in which historical understandings of physiology, illness and disease, disability and sex have had profound implications for historical cultures.[2] Moreover, there have long been historical and philosophical works on times, places and cultures in which the boundaries of being biologically human have been blurred for the sake of political or social exclusion.[3] The history of slavery;[4] the history of the Holocaust;[5] women's history:[6] these broad focus areas have highlighted the ways in which boundary lines were drawn around the human being in order to preserve that category for a select group (more often

[1] The notable exceptions include J. Bourke, *What It Means to Be Human: Reflections from 1791 to the Present* (London: Virago, 2011); D. LaCapra, *History and Its Limits: Human, Animal, Violence* (Ithaca: Cornell, 2009); R. Radhakrishnan, *History, the Human, and the World Between* (Durham, NC: Duke University Press, 2008); R. Smith, *Being Human: Historical Knowledge and the Creation of Human Nature* (Manchester: Manchester University Press, 2007).

[2] J. Butler, *Bodies that Matter: On the Discursive Limits of Sex* (New York: Routledge, 1993); C. Gallagher and T. Laqueur [eds], *The Making of the Modern Body: Sexuality and Society in the Nineteenth Century* (Berkeley: University of California Press, 1987); L. Long, *Rehabilitating Bodies: Health, History, and the American Civil War* (Philadelphia: University of Pennsylvania Press, 2004); B.M. Stafford, *Body Criticism: Imaging the Unseen in Enlightenment Art and Medicine* (Cambridge, MA: MIT Press, 1991); R. Cooter, 'The turn of the body: History and the politics of the corporeal', *ARBOR Ciencia, Pensamiento y Cultura*, 743 (2010): 393–405.

[3] G. Agamben, *Homo Sacer: Sovereign Power and Bare Life* (Palo Alto: Stanford University Press, 1998); Bourke, *What It Means*; R. Boddice, 'The end of anthropocentrism', in R. Boddice [ed.], *Anthropocentrism: Humans, Animals, Environments* (Leiden: Brill, 2011), 1–18.

[4] For example, D.B. Davis, *Inhuman Bondage: The Rise and Fall of Slavery in the New World* (Oxford: Oxford University Press, 2006).

[5] For example, D. McMillan, 'Dehumanization and the achievement of *Schindler's List*', in V. Khiterer, R. Barrick and D. Misal [eds], *The Holocaust: Memories and History* (Newcastle: Cambridge Scholars Publishing, 2014).

[6] For example, R. Boddice, 'The manly mind? Re-visiting the Victorian "sex in brain" debate', *Gender and History*, 23 (2011): 321–40.

than not, white men). The point of such narratives, however, is implicitly to point out that such boundary lines were falsely constructed for political ends. Human beings, ultimately, are human beings. These kinds of stories remind us of our own politics, and they cause us to reflect on where lines might be being (falsely) drawn today.

In short, things have always been done on the basis of what humans thought they knew, leaving deep social, cultural and political traces in the historical record. But for all that epistemology – whether high or vernacular – has left its mark, still the assumption remains that, beyond wayward thinking, there was a body and a mind of a being that for all intents and purposes had not changed much in thousands of years. For all that focus on change, the biological human behind all the politics was remarkably fixed as a stable historical category. If we challenge that fixity, it does not mean that we undermine all those aforementioned books and articles that have pointed to the historical injustices wrought by people in power. On the contrary, there is an opportunity to explore further the historical experience of exclusion, from both sides. The history of emotions offers such a new venture for the historian of an interdisciplinary disposition.

At the core of this project is an understanding that human beings – human bodies/minds – are made, and make meaning, in the world. This should not be read as a radical statement aligning the history of emotions solely with the adherents of social constructionism. On the contrary, the once distant disciplines of anthropology and neuroscience are rapidly being bridged: on the one hand by the observation that cultural context undoubtedly prescribes, delimits and influences experience; and on the other hand by the neuroscientific insight that humans are neurologically plastic, writeable pieces of hardware. Instead of a nature/nurture dyad, more of which below, neuroscientists and anthropologists alike are pointing us in a biocultural direction for our research. There is no culture-free or value-neutral context to the study of human 'nature', and there is no 'nurture' without framed biology; that is, the human. I will say much more about this in chapter 6, but it is essential to hold this premise in mind throughout.

Ancient precursor

Emotions research in other disciplines pre-dates the development of a professional discipline of history, and for most of the life courses of those distinct fields of research there was not only no overlap, but apparently no chance of any. In some ways this is surprising, because at a crucial juncture in the nineteenth century there was a clear moment of rapprochement; an opportunity not taken. This is the first of two aborted beginnings for the history of emotions. But before coming to history as a discipline, it is worth reflecting on some earlier works of history that clearly found a place for emotional analysis, even if later historians either did not notice or pretended it was of no importance.

Where better to begin than with the father of historiography, Thucydides (c.460–c.400 BCE)? Much has been made of the Thucydidean method, as it tends to be called, but the principal focus of historiographical engagement with Thucydides has been on his so-called objectivity, his weighing of evidence in context and his checks for bias and reliability. The passages in *The Peloponnesian War* in which Thucydides discusses method are indeed fascinating and repay many readings and re-readings.[7] But I have long harboured doubts that the history unfolded by Thucydides has any real bearing on the debates about truth and/or objectivity that occupied historians from the 1820s onwards. On the contrary, the work is fiendishly cleverly emplotted, and at the centre of the plot is the way in which men (usually men) are driven by passions in strict conformity to prescribed expressions in given contexts, or else on breakdowns of those prescriptions. The first history of emotions, I venture here, was by Thucydides. We could do worse than to re-visit it.

At the core of Thucydides' account of the war is an explanation of what drives men to do what they do. There are ideas of duty and of courage, and indeed we can generally map the ebbs and flows of success and failure among the Athenians onto the extent to which virtues were kept up or allowed to lapse. Thucydides is by no means distinctive in hitching virtuosity to the passions. The virtue of courage, for example, is to fight *despite* fear, not in the

---

[7] Thucydides, *Peloponnesian War*, 1:21–22. Direct quotations are from the translation by Rex Warner (London: Penguin, 1972).

absence of fear.[8] Virtuous vengeance is the result of controlled and purposeful anger, not a lack of control. Fear and anger are ever-present features of the war. It is from what happens when these passions overcome the virtuous intentions of Athenians that the story becomes dynamic.

There are any number of clear illustrations of this, but a single example will suffice to make the point that the history of emotions is as old as the concept of writing history itself. In Pericles' funeral oration to honour the virtuous dead of Athens, he praises the Athenians for their courage and their sense of duty. Central to this praise is an assessment of the state of feeling of the population. Athenians are neighbourly, striving to avoid hurting 'people's feelings'. They are law abiding, both in terms of written code and unwritten custom, for to break laws was an 'acknowledged shame'.[9] After hard work, Athenians enjoyed the 'recreation' of their 'spirits', and 'cares' were driven away by domestic beauty and 'good taste'.[10] The 'love of what is beautiful' was a contained love, not a softening love. It kept them manly. Moreover, poverty did not arouse shame, but those who did not strive to get out of it were shameful. Overall, Athenians marked themselves out against others for their 'general good feeling', which made their 'friendship more reliable'. Indeed, Athenian altruism was, according to Pericles' speech, 'unique'.[11] These dispositions added up to an extraordinary courage in the face of a threat to the city. The city's population did not reflect on the chance of success or failure, which they left in 'the doubtful hands of Hope', and reached 'the climax of their lives' with 'a culmination of Glory, not of fear'.[12] Driving them was a sense of shame connected to falling 'below a certain standard' and a notion of the value of Athenian freedom. 'Happiness depends on being free', Pericles concluded, 'and freedom depends on being courageous'.[13] Thus, fear, courage and happiness are the essential markers of the successful city state.

In and of itself we might dismiss this as so much political rheto-

---

[8] See also Aristotle, *Nichomachean Ethics*, 1115a6–1117b28.
[9] Thucydides, 2:37.
[10] Thucydides, 2:38.
[11] Thucydides, 2:40.
[12] Thucydides, 2:42.
[13] Thucydides, 2:43.

ric. History is littered with speeches that inflame or incite, exaggerate or boast. We might think of it as idealising or romantic, even. But Thucydides directly demonstrates the substantial truths of the Periclean view by immediately following the speech with his narrative account of the plague that ravaged the city. As the city unravels in chaos, it is precisely the failure of all the qualities enumerated by Pericles that are blamed. The narrative sequence mocks Pericles' insight into the depths of Athenian courage and neighbourliness, showing that the population was as wont to be overcome by passions as any other. In the process of failing to overcome the worst of passions in the worst of circumstances, Athens went to the wall. There was a state of 'unprecedented lawlessness', 'self-indulgence' and hedonism. 'As for what is called honour, no one showed himself willing to abide by its laws,' Thucydides wrote, noting that honour became conflated with pleasure and immediate gratification, such was the fear that one might be dead by tomorrow. The same fear made people feel immune to the system of justice, and the abundant death and desolation shook their faith in the gods: 'No fear of god or law of man had a restraining influence.'[14] Thus, the passions made history, one way or another. When controlled and applied to virtuous ideas and love of the city, they brought about success and honour. When they ran rampant and virtuous ideas were lost, they brought shame, dishonour and death. Circumstance dictated what emotions practically implied.

It is only in recent years that analyses of historical causation in works such as Thucydides' could take at face value the account of emotional prescription, control and rupture as having directly influenced and characterised events. Thucydides' highly esoteric conception of human nature was often taken in its most simplistic sense by historiographers who, according to a certain reading of the Greek text, thought that it provided a justified and entirely appropriate concept of the universality of human nature in times of war and adversity. The orthodox idea was that any reader might find himself, or be able to place himself, in this story, and observe that, yes, he too would feel the same and act the same. This is not the place to enter into a lengthy discussion of what the 'human thing' really is in Thucydides, but at the very least Pericles might be taken at his word when he tells us that the passionate dispositions

---

[14] Thucydides, 2:53.

of Athenians were unique.[15] In direct comparison to Sparta, Athens relied on 'real courage and loyalty'. Spartans were subjected to 'the most laborious training in courage', whereas Athenians had no need of 'state-induced courage', for they met 'danger voluntarily, with an easy mind'.[16] An anthropologist might look at these differences of political culture and social and cultural experience between two different places and point to the cultural construction and variability of emotions. Historians might look at such passages afresh and determine that actually the emotional experiences here are not readily entered into. This is not a general account of human nature, but a highly particular one. The passions were experienced differently in Athens than they were in Sparta, and responses to them were differently conditioned as well.

Modern precursor

Thucydides has perhaps received the most attention of all the historians before Leopold von Ranke (1795–1886), who formulated the academic and methodological principles of disciplinary history, beginning in the 1820s. That historiographical blueprint became the pivot point around which the discipline of history debated. Is history an art or a science?[17] Is history a re-creation or an invention of what is found in the archive?[18] How can one be objective, tell things *as they actually happened*, without factoring in the historical imagination?[19] What is the subject of history, and what is its mode?[20] The biography of great men?[21] The narration of change

---

[15] See M. Cogan, *The Human Thing: The Speeches and Principles of Thucydides' History* (Chicago: University of Chicago Press, 1981), for a thorough summary.
[16] Thucydides, 2:39.
[17] For both sides of this debate, see J.B. Bury, 'The science of history', and G.M. Trevelyan, 'Clio, a muse', both in F. Stern [ed.], *The Varieties of History* (New York: Vintage, 1973).
[18] H. White, 'The historical text as literary artifact', *Clio*, 3 (1974): 277–91.
[19] The first allusion is to the famous Rankean method, from *Histories of the Latin and Germanic Nations, 1494–1514* (1824), excerpted in Stern, *Varieties*, 55–8; the second allusion is to R.G. Collingwood, *The Idea of History* (Oxford: Oxford University Press, 1946), 232–49.
[20] The question of mode was most famously raised by Hayden White in his *Metahistory* (Baltimore: Johns Hopkins University Press, 1973).
[21] This was the approach of T. Carlyle, *On Heroes, Hero-Worship and The Heroic in History* (London: James Fraser, 1841).

over time, of the ebb and flow of power?[22] Such were the debates inspired at first by the Rankean vision.

Yet a contemporary of Ranke, another historian whose methods and vision of historical practice have bequeathed apparently little to contemporary historiography, saw things differently. Jules Michelet (1798–1874), leading historian of the French Revolution until events in France saw the demise of his vision of the nation, understood that great stories of social and political upheaval were not about individuals of great import, or about minutiae of causes and effects, but rather they were about the movement of humanity itself, its spirit and its expression of fraternal love (or the inhibition of that expression).[23]

Hayden White gave Michelet his due in his seminal historiographical work, *Metahistory*, in 1973. White was interested in demonstrating that all historical narratives, however they were framed, were constructed according to a limited number of plot devices and modes. Michelet was among the Romantics. The analysis, for Michelet as much as for every other historian in White's sights, was designed to demonstrate the extent to which histories really say something about historians and the context in which those historians produced their works. There were far-reaching implications of this thesis, which had shaken the very core of historical practice by the 1990s. If histories were, to employ another of White's phrases, 'as much invented as found', and if the only truth they revealed was the truth of the historian, and not of the past per se, then what was the justification for continued historical practice?[24] The challenge here ultimately benefited historians, for it made them more self-reflexive writers and researchers, more up-front about their assumptions and plot devices; but it also made them focus increasingly on the value of empiricism and on the fact that, however partial their reconstructions might be, certain things could be said that were demonstrably true.[25] Just as in a court case a judge

[22] Under this rubric one might imagine both unreconstructed histories of nation states and monarchies, as well as Foucauldian approaches to the question of power.
[23] The key works in question here include Michelet's *Le Peuple* (1846) and his six volumes of *Histoire de la Révolution française* (1847–53).
[24] White, 'Historical text': 278.
[25] This was the basis of Richard Evans' famous 'defence' of history, *In Defence of History* (London: Granta, 1997).

can assemble evidence – however partial or disparate – and arrive at a reasonable sense of who did what to whom and for what reasons, so the historian could appeal to the archival record. The meanings and implications of historical truths are there to be debated, but we have generally moved on from the crisis of post-modernity with the faith that we are not, to modify a criticism of Clifford Geertz, pulling thick descriptions out of thin air.[26]

One of the side effects of the debate was that the likes of Michelet, with his demonstrably Romantic emplotments, were not necessarily restored to the pantheon of historians worthy of emulation. I propose a brief return to this *other* father of modern historiography to see if there are any insights we might actually find useful in contemporary practice. In short, what did Michelet know about the history of emotions that we did not, at least until recently? I propose that we look for the answers, not so much in a thorough scouring of Michelet's works themselves, but, for brevity, just those parts of them that White characterised as history 'explained as Metaphor and Emplotted as Romance'.[27]

At stake here is whether White's characterisation of Michelet as a plot maker does justice to Michelet's own characterisation of what people were like, what they thought and felt, in the French Revolution. White paints Michelet as a dualist, his understanding of historical forces being limited to vice and virtue, 'tyranny or justice, hate and love, with occasional moments of conjunction'.[28] But perhaps this is also a reasonable appraisal of how historical actors also felt, acting accordingly. Michelet's *History of the French Revolution* (1847–53), published, according to White, 'in the heat of passions which the years 1847–53 generated among Frenchmen of all parties', described 'the spirit of France' in the first year of the Revolution, with its 'triumph of the "natural" impulse toward fraternity over the "artificial" forces which had long opposed it'. White casts a raking light over Michelet's account, analysing only Michelet's spin on the qualities of fraternity and not pausing to

---

[26] Linda Connor, comment on P. Shankman, 'The thick and the thin: On the interpretive theoretical program of Clifford Geertz', *Current Anthropology*, 25 (1984): 261–80, at 271. The reference point is C. Geertz, 'Thick description: Toward an interpretive theory of culture', in C. Geertz, *The Interpretation of Cultures* (New York: Basic Books, 1973), and other essays in that collection.
[27] White, *Metahistory*, 149.
[28] White, *Metahistory*, 150.

reflect on whether this is an accurate portrayal of how people (on one side, to be sure) actually felt about the triumph of fraternity. Michelet characterises longing in this period as the transition from a 'vague love of liberty' to a 'unity of the native land'. Pure fraternity breaks all barriers in a miraculous 'return to nature'.[29] For White, these are metaphors. Yet Michelet is telling us about the hearts of men in the throes of revolutionary ardour and the moment of liberation, when *égalité* and *fraternité* were on everyone's lips and in everyone's hearts, and we might learn something from him:

> Men then behold one another, perceive they are alike, are astonished to have been able to remain so long ignorant of one another, regret the senseless animosity which had separated them for many centuries, and expiate it by advancing to meet and embrace one another with a mutual effusion of the heart.[30]

The 'pure love of unity' annihilates all barriers – social, geographical, temporal, spatial: 'Such is the power of love'.[31] All these passages from Michelet are quoted in White. Apart from a brief mention that Michelet spoke in 'a voice which was at once his own and that of the people who believed in the Revolution on that day', the analysis is focused on Michelet himself and his historiographical purpose.[32] Yet the suspicion that Michelet had divined the voice – the sentiments, the emotions too – of the people of the Revolution ought not to be so readily overlooked. Here we have a pointer to the history of love in a most precise context. Michelet reaches into the experience of it and conveys it as something that *had not been experienced before.* Implicitly, given the events in France that unfolded in Michelet's lifetime, it was an experience that was at risk of being *lost*, if it had not been lost already. Here, then, is the essence of a history of emotions. Methodologically, Michelet did not have to set out how he was constructing this analysis as we might want to, but his histories were not pure articles of the historical imagination. He knew something, from his learning and his research, about how it felt to be there, then.

The importance of human experience, of what it felt like, is clear

---

[29] White, *Metahistory*, 151.
[30] White, *Metahistory*, 151.
[31] White, *Metahistory*, 151.
[32] White, *Metahistory*, 152.

enough from Michelet's own introduction to his *The People* (1846), in an extended dedication to Edgar Quinet. Michelet remembers himself, in 1814, in misery:

> I well remember that in the midst of that thorough misery, privations of the present, fears for the future, the public enemy being at the gates (1814!), and my own enemies daily deriding me, one day, one Thursday morning, I sat ruminating about myself, without fire (the snow lay deep), not well knowing whether I should find bread at night, fancying it was all over with me. I had within me, but without any mixture of religious hope, a pure stoic sentiment. With my frost-bitten hand I struck my oaken table (which I have always preserved), and felt a powerfully joyous impulse of youth and future prospects. Tell me, friend, what should I fear now? I, who have suffered death so many times in myself and in my reading? And what should I desire?[33]

Such candid recall of the complexities of historical emotions in context makes for both a wonderfully rich historical source in its own right as well as a style of historiography that foregrounds these things as important. Emotions are at once the effects of historical circumstances and a cause of their change. Far from being mere fleeting passages of irrational behaviour, they were central to the experience and the course of revolutions and counter-revolutions.

Psychological historicism

The first false dawn for the history of emotions coincided with the emergence of the professional discipline of comparative psychology in the middle of the nineteenth century. The historical impetus, curiously, came from the psychologists themselves. Alexander Bain's (1818–1903) magnum opus, *The Emotions and the Will*, was published contemporaneously with Charles Darwin's *The Origin of Species* in 1859.[34] One of Bain's central premises was that the 'fact, or property, named Feeling, is totally distinct from any physical property of matter'.[35] If he had left it at that, Bain's career would have been completely undercut by the Darwinian turn and the coming primacy of materialism. But Bain carefully laid out the

---

[33] Quoted in Stern, *Varieties*, 114.
[34] A. Bain, *Emotions and the Will* (London: John W. Parker and Son, 1859).
[35] Bain, *Emotions*, 3.

body–mind relationship in which emotions prompt actions, and in which there is a 'connexion of dependence between it [Feeling] and a material organization'.[36] Bain effectively gave new currency to a Cartesian view: 'the physical fact that accompanies and supports the mental fact, without making or constituting that fact, is an agitation of all those bodily members more immediately allied with the brain by nervous communication'.[37] Departing from Descartes, Bain launched a new sophistication in psychological language, combined with a greater understanding of physiological functions, and, most importantly, he did not need to account for the soul. Human bodies and human minds were in and of the world and, as such, subject to the world's influence.

Bain identified a 'cerebral wave', made in part of 'emotional currents'. This wave could be reconfigured through the 'power of education'. In practice, Bain was attempting to account for the cultural differences of emotional expression among different human societies, as well as accounting for the apparent gap between humans and other animals. In a so-called 'primitive' state, an astonished man was marked by an 'open mouth', 'sharp cry', 'vehement stare' and a 'toss of the arms', but the 'civilised' man had the capacity of speech to give 'necessary vent to the feeling of the moment'. Expressiveness is reined in, modified, artificially represented. Crucially, Bain saw that this change in outward comportment fed back into the state of consciousness, altering 'the nature of the resulting mental condition'. Bain thus described an emotional dynamic: a process through which feeling states and expressions were mutually involved and respectively modified each other. The astonishment of the 'primitive' man was not only represented differently to astonishment in a 'civilised' man, but also experienced differently.[38] This gave Bain a clue – echoed by Wilhelm Wundt (1832–1920) – that physiology might be the vital key to psychological understanding.[39]

[36] Bain, *Emotions*, 4.
[37] Bain, *Emotions*, 5.
[38] Bain, *Emotions*, 14–15.
[39] W. Wundt, *Lehrbuch der Physiologie des Menschen* (Enke: Erlangen, 1865). See C. Wassmann, 'Physiological optics, cognition and emotion: A novel look at the early work of Wilhelm Wundt', *Journal of the History of Medicine and Allied Sciences*, 64 (2009): 213–49. For a more general treatment, including Wassmann's

The great range of feelings and variations of 'mental tone' are, according to Bain, no less variously embodied. What was lacking was a developed science of 'tracing the physical outgoings of an emotional wave'. Nevertheless, whatever could be described as the physical affect (and effect) of the diffusion of an emotion would bring us to a closer understanding of that emotion. Bodies *talked* the 'natural language of emotion', opening up the 'character of consciousness' to any observer with the power to understand that language.[40] The basic toolkit of understanding might have been supplied by nature, but changes in emotions caused by civilisation necessitated the acquisition of learnt modes of deciphering expressions. This leads Bain to explain the importance of history in understanding changes in emotions over time, which he calls a 'constructive process'.[41] This idea would burn brightly for a time, before disappearing for a century.

Bain's notion of construction put him among the first in a 'scientific' community of psychologists to uphold association as a key marker of the discipline. The alliance of feelings with the intellect allowed for a relational understanding between feelings sensed and the objects that typically stimulated such feelings: 'Thus, we connect the pleasures of repose with an easy chair, a sofa, or a bed, and the pleasures of riding with a horse and carriage.'[42] Such material objectification helped explain apparent variability in emotional experience, both in different places and over time. Emotional meaning was tethered to the things that surrounded the individual. Emotional signs were *of* the place in which they were produced. It is an insight that historians have only lately rediscovered (see chapter 7). In order to sympathise with the emotions of another, first we had to 'acquire the signs of feeling'. We had to 'learn' the appearances of emotions as well as 'the names that describe them'.[43] Central to this process is a cultivated understanding of emotional expressions of disapprobation or approval. For Bain, there was no absolute morality, only specific contexts of feeling

re-appraisal, see S. de Freitas Araujo, *Wundt and the Philosophical Foundations of Psychology: A Reappraisal* (New York: Springer, 2015).
[40] Bain, *Emotions*, 14–15, 28.
[41] Bain, *Emotions*, 220–1.
[42] A. Bain, *The Senses and the Intellect*, 4th edn (London: Longmans, Green, and Co, 1894), 423–4.
[43] Bain, *Senses*, 432.

where right and wrong were, long before being rationalised or intellectualised, experienced as part of a social emotional dynamic. As such, Bain echoed the works of Adam Smith (1723–90) and David Hume (1711–76) on civilisation and the role of sympathy, as well as according with Darwin on the same subject.[44] A moral 'sense' preceded moral reason.

The psychology of Bain and the evolutionism of Darwin both pointed science to a historical understanding and interpretation of emotions and morality. For a brief period, these ideas had great purchase. The last quarter of the nineteenth century was perhaps the last gasp of the scientist as amateur generalist, or the gentleman polymath. New epistemological configurations of the emotions seemed to become possible and necessary, and yet were fleeting and quickly forgotten. One of the clearest and most profound generalist statements on the importance of the emotions for understanding the human condition came from perhaps the most famous of the polymath radicals, George Henry Lewes (1817–78), life partner of the novelist George Eliot (1819–80).

Lewes is usually labelled a philosopher or critic, but he was deeply immersed in the study of science, particularly biology, physiology and psychology. He was a close reader of Darwin, an experimentalist in his own right and influential in transmitting and translating science for large audiences. Rooting philosophy – the 'Logic of Signs' – in the 'Logic of Feeling', Lewes concluded that a true philosophy had to take account of sentiment as regulative of conduct and knowledge.[45] The moral sense was instinctive but historical, competing with egoistical desires and filtered through conscious judgement. The emotional and the intellectual were mutually involved in the *feeling* of right and wrong. So much had been implied by Adam Smith, but the impetus in this case was to take seriously a science of emotions in order to understand better

---

[44] A. Smith, *The Theory of Moral Sentiments* (1759; London: Penguin, 2009); D. Hume, *A Treatise of Human Nature* (1740; London: Penguin, 1985); C. Darwin, *The Descent of Man, and Selection in Relation to Sex* (1871; London: Penguin, 2004); see R. Boddice, *The Science of Sympathy: Morality, Evolution and Victorian Civilization* (Urbana-Champaign: University of Illinois Press, 2016), 26–42; see also D.M. Gross, *The Secret History of Emotion: From Aristotle's Rhetoric to Modern Brain Science* (Chicago: University of Chicago Press, 2006), 114–27, 169–79.

[45] G.H. Lewes, *Problems of Life and Mind*, 1st series, 1 (London: Trübner & Co., 1874), 455.

their nature and the extent to which they were socialised. Lewes' inspired vision was of brains and bodies in the world, moved by moral instincts formed in the crucible of society and culture.

Unusually, then, in an age dominated in scientific circles by evolutionism more or less marked by questions of heredity and acquired habit, Lewes foregrounded social construction as the key to the way in which evolution happens in civilised societies. In short, none of the new sciences of mind and body that sought to define and explore the emotions could work without history: 'Because Psychology is interpreted through Sociology, and Experience acquires its development mainly through social influences, we must always take History into account.' Lewes understood that while insufficient time had passed for a natural evolution of types of human species within the history of civilisation, there were nevertheless significant divergences in 'the quality of moral feelings and the range of conceptions'. Unlike many of his contemporaries, he was convinced that a good physiologist would recognise that the 'organs and functions' were the same in 'the savage and the civilized, in Greek, Hindoo, old German, or modern European', but could not escape the observation that the 'thoughts and sentiments' were markedly different. The 'brain of a cultivated Englishman ... compared with the brain of a Greek of the age of Pericles, would not present any appreciable differences', he averred, noting that the continuity of the physical stuff of humanity by no means accorded with a continuity of emotional or moral disposition. These changes were wrought by social influences, effectively defining and delimiting the emotional and moral compasses of humans who, in physiological terms, were the same over time.

Lewes put forward a radical scholarly agenda that is only now being picked up in the curious merging of the humanities and biology in 'neurohistory' (see chapter 6): 'while the laws of the sentient functions must be studied in Physiology, the laws of the sentient faculties, especially the moral and intellectual faculties, must be studied in History. The true logic of Science is only made apparent in the history of Science.'[46] Alexander Bain would concur, noting pointedly that the historian's task involved the interpretation of 'extinct modes of feeling'. In effect, to understand the

[46] G.H. Lewes, *Problems of Life and Mind*, 3rd series, 1 (London: Trübner & Co., 1879), 153–4.

strange experiences of the past, or the strange experiences of unfamiliar places, such scholars had to construct new emotions from admixtures of their own experience, as best they could.[47] When William James' (1842–1910) contribution turned psychology on its head and thrust physiology to the forefront of emotions research, the historical element was preserved, if only momentarily. James' *Principles of Psychology* first appeared in 1890, coincident with a rapidly expanding experimental fervour among physiological specialists. Laboratories were well established across Europe and reaching important new levels of influence in the United States. James' assertion that 'the general causes of the emotions are indubitably physiological' was, in effect, a rallying call for physiological experiment. This branch of psychology at least could be subsumed. James gave the physiologists more to go on. His most famous pronouncement on emotions was to reverse what he saw as a central assumption:

> Our natural way of thinking about these coarser emotions is that the mental perception of some fact excites the mental affection called the emotion, and that this latter state of mind gives rise to the bodily expression. My theory, on the contrary, is that *the bodily changes follow directly the perception of the exciting fact, and that our feeling of the same changes as they occur IS the emotion*. Common-sense says, we lose our fortune, are sorry and weep; we meet a bear, are frightened and run; we are insulted by a rival, are angry and strike. The hypothesis here to be defended says that this order of sequence is incorrect, that the one mental state is not immediately induced by the other, that the bodily manifestations must first be interposed between, and that the more rational statement is that we feel sorry because we cry, angry because we strike, afraid because we tremble, and not that we cry, strike, or tremble, because we are sorry, angry, or fearful, as the case may be. Without the bodily states following on the perception, the latter would be purely cognitive in form, pale, colorless, destitute of emotional warmth. We might then see the bear, and judge it best to run, receive the insult and deem it right to strike, but we should not actually *feel* afraid or angry.[48]

[47] Bain, *Senses*, 619–22.
[48] W. James, *The Principles of Psychology*, vol. 2 (1890; London: MacMillan, 1910), 449–50. Danish physician Carl Lange arrived independently at the same point, arguing for the physiological basis of emotions. It came to be known as the James–Lange theory of emotion. See C.G. Lange, *Ueber Gemüthsbewgungen. Eine Psycho-Physiologische Studie* (Leipzig: Theodor Thomas, 1887).

In this configuration, an expression was not a sign of an inner emotion, but the emotion itself. There could be no such thing as a 'purely disembodied emotion'. James examined himself and found that 'whatever moods, affections, and passions' he had, they were 'constituted by, and made up of, those bodily changes which we ordinarily call their expression or consequence'.

The implications were profound. On the one hand, emotions could be made the subject of scientific certainty, for if they were bodily they were presumably also measurable. Blood pressure, temperature and a host of visceral and glandular secretions could be subjected to the mechanical gaze of the laboratory. The discovery of the first hormone, secretin, in 1902 was followed quickly by a theoretical expression of hormonal functions by the London-based physiologist Ernest Starling.[49] Here was the *stuff* of emotions. On the other hand, the possibilities for emotions studies seemed endless. James himself noted the logical consequence of defining an emotion as a reflex action aroused by an object, immediately felt: '*we immediately see why there is no limit to the number of possible different emotions which may exist, and why the emotions of different individuals may vary indefinitely* ... For there is nothing sacramental or eternally fixed in reflex action [emphasis in original].'[50]

In some respects, this analytical insight returned James to the constructivism of Bain. Physiological mechanics notwithstanding, James knew the influence of custom on instinct, and therefore assumed a highly relativistic position that at once gave a history to emotions and to the body: '*any classification of the emotions is seen to be as true and as "natural" as any other*, if it only serves some purpose; and such a question as "What is the 'real' or 'typical' expression of anger, or fear?" is seen to have no objective meaning at all. Instead of it we now have the question as to how any given "expression" of anger or fear may have come to exist.' In a long line of early psychologists and evolutionists, James, too, asserted that this was a question for historians to answer, 'although the answer may be hard to find'.[51]

This part of James' theory did not find any traction among phys-

---

[49] E.H. Starling, 'The Croonian Lectures. I. On the chemical correlation of the functions of the body', *Lancet*, 166 (1905): 339–41.

[50] James, *Principles*, vol. 2, 454.

[51] James, *Principles*, vol. 2, 454.

iologists, who ran instead with the emphasis on embodiment. If emotions were findable and recordable in the body, then science would discover their true essence. Here, then, are the beginnings of Affect Theory (see chapter 5). Experimentation would objectively isolate fear, for example, and establish a universal standard for measuring it. Rather than endless possibilities, there would be an endeavour to pare down emotions until the basic foundations for all varieties were discovered.

The experimental impetus behind the search for the physiological constants of emotion came from observations that the emotions of laboratory animals were adversely affecting the results of physiological studies with other aims. Qualities of the blood, visceral secretions, responses to injury and disease, and animal behaviour in general were the subjects of physiological endeavour, with the aim of finding reliable and repeatable standards or physiological norms. The destabilising influence of emotions led to great efforts to try to eliminate or control emotions in laboratory animals, with the concomitant need to isolate what exactly emotions consisted of.

As Otniel Dror has brilliantly evidenced, the late nineteenth and early twentieth centuries witnessed an attempt to cultivate an emotionally neutral array of 'standard' laboratory animals, in part through investigations into the visceral nature of animal emotion itself.[52] Agitated emotional states were not mental or immaterial so much as they were physiological. The secretion of adrenalin, for example, or the boost of blood glucose; a rise or drop in blood pressure: these were not signs of emotion but the emotions *themselves*. As such, given the need for control, universal standards and experimental replication, it was possible to conceive of an evolutionary

[52] O. Dror, 'The affect of experiment: The turn to emotions in Anglo-American physiology, 1900–1940', *Isis*, 90 (1999): 205–37; O. Dror, 'The scientific image of emotion: Experience and technologies of inscription', *Configurations*, 7 (1999): 355–401; O. Dror, 'Cold War "super-pleasure": Insatiability, self-stimulation, and the postwar brain', *Osiris*, 31 (2016): 227–49. Some of the classic studies include A. Mosso, *Sulla paura* (1884), translated as *Fear* (London and New York: Longmans, Green, and Co., 1896); W.B. Cannon, *Bodily Changes in Pain, Hunger, Fear and Rage: An Account of Recent Researches into the Function of Emotional Excitement* (New York and London: D. Appleton and Co., 1915); T.A. Ribot, *La psychologie des sentiments* (Paris: Germer Baillière, 1896); C.S. Sherrington, 'Experiments on the value of vascular and visceral factors for the genesis of emotion', *Proceedings of the Royal Society of London*, 66 (1899–1900): 390–403.

constant of emotional function. James' historical caveat was lost in the noise of the machines that inscribed the emotions being emitted from the viscera of laboratory animals. In the words of Théodule Ribot (1839–1916), who acknowledged the influence of James and Bain, among others, emotions 'plunge into the individual's depths; they have their roots in the needs and instincts, that is to say, in movements'.[53] Thus, at the very moment emotions were being untethered from a universal biology by historicist psychologists, so they were being firmly physiologically grounded according to a literal application of 'emotion' as outward (*e*) movement (*motio*).

The failed impetus of the 1930s

That early psychological works were loaded with historicism was not picked up on by historians, if it was even noticed at all. Moreover, notions of psychological relativism were expunged from the discipline of psychology in short order. It was this categorically clean psychology, replete with a new discursive register of its own that set it out as a science, which Lucien Febvre (1878–1956) encountered in the 1930s. He saw no use for it whatsoever from the historian's point of view.[54] Febvre felt a deep antagonism towards psychological essentialism, for it could have no bearing on the past (nor, presumably, on the future), and spoke only to the *mentalité* of the present moment, for a certain group of people (white men). Febvre understood that emotions not only took place in social context, but also that they were formed and institutionalised in social contexts. When the psychologists of the late 1930s talked of emotions, decisions and reasoning, according to Febvre's assessment of psychological memoirs and treatises, they represented only the emotions, decisions and reasoning of the 1930s. Febvre saw that neither the psychology of his contemporaries nor the psychology of his ancestors was fit for a global application of psychological analysis. *Mentalités* were too intertwined with the peculiarities of space, place and time to ever be fitted into a general scheme. The historian could not, therefore,

---

[53] Ribot, *La psychologie*, ix ['les sentiments ... plongent au plus profond de l'individu; ils ont leurs racines dans les besoins et les instincts, c'est-à-dire dans des mouvements'].

[54] L. Febvre, 'La sensibilité et l'histoire: Comment reconstituer la vie affective d'autrefois?', *Annales d'histoire sociale*, 3 (Jan. – Jun., 1941): 5–20.

make much use of psychological theory to understand the past. If there were to be a history of the emotions, it would have to come from historical reconstruction of past emotions as they were, not as we understand emotions in the present.[55]

The observation holds true, though it was sufficient to ensure that there would be no substantial history of emotions in the time of Febvre, at least not in France. Febvre himself was criticised for having focused the *Annales* school *mentalités* project on 'mental equipment', which circumscribed the history of the body and the mind, just as it promised to open up. As Alain Corbin pointed out long ago, Febvre's interest in the emotions was orientated towards the study of the rise of rational behaviour, as a distinct phenomenon from emotional behaviour.[56] There were some beginnings, such as George Lefebvre's *La Grande Peur de 1789* (1932), which attempted to unpick the burgeoning crowd-psychology theory that the mobilisation of emotions en masse was irrational and therefore not politically functional. Fear was represented as a consequence of the dynamics of social structure and class antagonism, fuelled in particular by hunger. Here, then, an emotion was tied to a bodily sense and a social situation in order to make sense of a sociopolitical movement. Fear itself is not historicised, but the particularities of its appearance and its effects are.[57] Meanwhile, Febvre's *annaliste* comrade Marc Bloch (1886–1944) famously claimed that the 'subject-matter of history' was 'human consciousness', the 'interrelations, confusions, and infections' whereof were 'for history, reality itself'. Peter Gay (1923–2015) later praised Bloch's awareness of the possibilities of histories of the 'secret needs of the heart', and his work on the history of mental styles in *Les rois thaumaturges*, but criticised the historical profession for being too 'nervous' to follow Bloch to his logical conclusions.[58]

Across the border in Germany, meanwhile, another scholar was

---

[55] L. Febvre, 'Une vue d'ensemble: Histoire et psychologie' [1938], *Combats pour l'Histoire* (1952; Paris: Armand Colin, 1992), 213.

[56] A. Corbin, *Time, Desire and Horror: Towards a History of the Senses* (Cambridge: Polity, 1995).

[57] A point picked up later by J. Delumeau, *Le peur en Occident, XIVe–XVIIIe siècles* (Paris: Fayard, 1978); J. Delumeau, *Sin and Fear: The Emergence of a Western Guilt Culture, 13th–18th Centuries* (New York: St Martin's Press, 1990).

[58] M. Bloch, *The Historian's Craft* (New York: Vintage, 1953), 151; P. Gay, *Freud for Historians* (Oxford: Oxford University Press, 1985), 7, 208–9.

experimenting with socio-psychological historicism in a way that would surely have pleased Febvre. Norbert Elias (1897–1990) published the work that would define his career in German in 1939, under the title *Über den Prozess der Zivilisation*. It has become known to a wider audience as *The Civilizing Process*, and has assumed a place of prominence and importance in the historiographical tradition, not least for historians of emotions. Yet the fame of the work came to a large extent with its translation into English, which did not occur until 1982, and the championing of Eric Dunning, Elias' colleague in Leicester. An affordable edition in a single volume did not become available until the 1990s. The reading context for Elias' work therefore changed enormously, and some of its ironic import was lost along the way.

The central thesis was that the monopolisation of violence in the instruments of the State led to ever more tightly controlled emotions across society. This control could be measured by the forms and instruments of etiquette and courtly behaviour in particular, where keeping one's emotions and actions in check was seen increasingly as necessary for survival (figuratively mainly, but sometimes literally) under the nose of power. But even if it contains elements that some would wish to discard – the emphasis on the rise of the nation state as a basic criterion for becoming civilised; the overtly Freudian garb; the sharp division between emotion and reason; the portrayal of the unbridled emotions of medieval actors as child-like – this does not necessarily mean the whole thing should be thrown out.[59] Elias' notion of a dynamic relationship between, in his words, 'sociogenesis' and 'psychogenesis' does in fact fit a persuasive model of biocultural emotional change. The structure of his argument might usefully be retained. Social situations *write* human brains, just the same as human brains (collectively) *make* social situations. In Elias' words: 'The human person is an extraordinarily malleable and variable being'.[60] Elias was already convinced that expressions were inscribed on the face over the course of a life, just as learning to read, write, reason and

---

[59] These criticisms have come, in the main, from Barbara Rosenwein. See the conclusion. Similar criticisms have been levelled at Johan Huizinga's earlier text, *The Autumn of the Middle Ages* (1919; Chicago: University of Chicago Press, 1997).

[60] N. Elias, *The Civilizing Process: Sociogenetic and Psychogenetic Investigations* (1939; Oxford: Blackwell, 1994), 402.

control the emotions materially altered the stuff of the brain. We can reject Elias' central thesis and still make use of the notion of emotional norms being prescribed by individuals or institutions with authority, and the fact that these prescriptions directly effect the experience of living in an 'emotional regime', which some would argue we all do. The fact that Elias has proved so controversial for historians of emotions, a point to which we must return, suggests the magnitude of his influence.

By 1991, when Corbin tried to re-invigorate a history of the senses, the *mentalités* school was obsolete.[61] Corbin is often overlooked by historians of emotions, but he provided a major impetus to the history of the senses, and from the outset he connected the possibilities for such studies to the history of emotions. Despite his reservations about Febvre and the *mentalités* project, Febvre was nevertheless his inspiration. The failed project of the 1930s has therefore produced a lasting and challenging legacy.

Corbin posed the following questions, which still have traction for us today:

> Is it possible to discern retrospectively the nature of the presence in the world of people in the past through an analysis of the hierarchy of the senses and the balance established between them at a particular moment in history and within a given society? Is it possible to detect the fucntions of these hierarchies, and so identify the purposes which presided over this organization of the relations between the senses? Can we envisage submitting this research to diachrony, observing permanences, and detecting open ruptures or subtle differences? Is it helpful to connect modifications to the systems of emotions, which are more easily discernable, to those which operate in the hierarchy and balance of the senses? To respond to such questions is to accept the existence and validity of a history of sensibility, since it implies discovering the configuration of what is experienced and what cannot be experienced within a culture at a given moment.[62]

Psychohistory

The specificity of culture, ultimately, is what killed off psychohistory, but one of psychohistory's leading proponents always argued

[61] Corbin, *Time*, 181.
[62] Corbin, *Time*, 182.

that its murder was unjust. Psychohistory was, in the grand scheme of things, a fleeting illicit romance of historiography and psychoanalysis, of Freudian dreams of social analysis, and of the expansion of biography to social history.[63] At its core, it perhaps goes without saying, was the psychoanalysis of the dead – a project that Peter Gay thought possible – with an acute focus on the emotional drives and anxieties of a historical actor's childhood, as borne out in his or her adult actions. Hence, psychohistory dwelt principally in the realm of biography, but its ambitions were wider. Gay, in particular, saw the potential to psychoanalyse past societies, a theoretical principle that he not only expounded but also practised, voluminously.

Reading Peter Gay's *Freud for Historians* now, long after, I suspect, it has ceased to be read in historiography classes among undergraduates, the extent to which Gay's prescription for psychohistory went beyond Freud is striking. Indeed, Gay was keen to show that the old Platonic adage that 'the individual is culture writ small, culture the individual writ large' could, with sophistication and nuance, be realised as part of historical analysis.[64] Take the following passage, for example, which, if denuded of its Freudian language, might well have spilled from the pen of Barbara Rosenwein or Peter Stearns. Gay is in part quoting Freud himself. It seems to describe an emotional style or an emotional community:

> in modern times, 'each individual is a component part of many crowds, tied in manifold ways by identifications, and has constructed his ego ideal on the most varied models'. He belongs to his race, his class, his religion, his nation, to stable groupings less conspicuous perhaps than those spectacular transient crowds that make most of the noise but no less significant for his mental formation.[65]

---

[63] Some would argue that claims of psychohistory's death have been overstated, but in part this is because psychohistory was never unified in its purpose. What lives on, stubbornly, as a largely discredited part of child studies, has been criticised in extreme terms for its focus on the history of childhood as a history of progress, where the traumas of past ages could be ascribed to the relatively scant regard (or outright cruelty) paid to children in those eras. Mainstream historians of childhood have thoroughly undermined this view. The psychohistory I refer to here is that centred on historical biography and the contribution to social history, led largely by Peter Gay.

[64] Gay, *Freud for Historians*, 148. The analogy of the city and the individual is from Plato, *Republic*, 2: 368c–369a.

[65] Gay, *Freud for Historians*, 153.

The case being built by Gay was that psychohistory did not, or perhaps, ought not, depend on a universal model of human nature that, once culture had been skimmed off the top, always revealed the same anxieties, drives and repressed sexual desires. While the psychohistorical project did retain a notion that societies functioned to ward off things like incest and murder, the particularities of experience were substantial and, importantly, changeable.[66] Observe Gay's allusion to E.P. Thompson's (1924–93) definition of class from *The Making of the English Working Class* (1963), for example:

> Class 'happens when some men, as a result of common experiences (inherited or shared), feel and articulate the identity of their interests as between themselves, and as against other men whose interests are different from (and usually opposed to) theirs'. Class is an experience that masses of men undergo in the 'productive relations' into which they 'are born – or enter involuntarily'. And like class, we may add, other institutions incarnate feelings in rules, buildings, emblems.[67]

The language of feeling and experience is, therefore, imbued with the kind of social identities and prescriptions upon which historians of emotion now focus. Class, in such terms, becomes a *felt* identity. One does not belong, as it were, according to abstract principles (or not wholly), but one must feel a sense of belonging. While the underlying theory of psychohistory might now be obsolete for most, this kind of insight has been carried forward, though hardly acknowledged, into the agenda of the history of emotions. Moreover, Gay's observations about culture more broadly also continue to ring true, and seem to have signalled psychohistory's own theoretical departure from a strictly psychoanalytical foundation. Indeed, Gay was convinced that 'culture is not man's superficial drapery, but integral to the very definition of his humanity', allowing for an analysis that put cultural change at the very core of the investigation of human nature.[68]

These claims notwithstanding, the association with Freud, or with psychoanalysis in general, continued to trouble psychohistory's critics. At the time, this was partly a result of the awkward lack of affinity between Freud and Marx. The theoretical

---

[66] Gay, *Freud for Historians*, 154.
[67] Gay, *Freud for Historians*, 157.
[68] Gay, *Freud for Historians*, 163.

dominance of Marxist historiography in the 1970s and for much of the 1980s blocked psychohistory from making major inroads into the mainstream. As Marxism gave way to the cultural, linguistic and post-modern turns, all meta-narratives were subjected to extreme scrutiny and criticism. Precisely where cultural influence seemed constructive of human nature – including the emotions – was where explain-all theories of human consciousness and behaviour seemed to fail, for cultural forms, and the structures of cultural meaning and practice seemed infinite as a result. The influence of cultural anthropology on historiography at this time put any notion of a universal psyche in jeopardy. More prosaically, an adherence to old-fashioned historicism was still a major sticking point. As Peter and Carol Stearns pointed out as early as 1988, the Freudian architecture of psychohistory, and its association in particular with 'an essentially static psyche', presented the past as 'a simple illustration of a human reality' that essentially never changes.[69] Gay's protestations notwithstanding, this was the mud that stuck.

Astonishingly, the turn away from psychohistory has been so complete that, despite the monumentality of Gay's body of work and the compelling contribution to studies of witchcraft by Lyndal Roper, psychohistory's influence on the emergence of the history of emotions is apparently nil.[70] I do not want to force a connection, but merely state its significance as a precursor and to perhaps encourage a re-visit. Gay's work alone contains enough insight and analysis to make a cultural history of the emotions in its own right, and should surely not be overlooked in its entirety, even if the psychoanalytic moment has passed.

The neuro turn

The assumed fixity of emotional embodiment inspired by twentieth-century physiologists consigned emotions to a place

---

[69] C.Z. Stearns and P.N. Stearns [eds], *Emotion and Social Change: Toward a New Psychohistory* (New York: Holmes & Meier, 1988), 3.

[70] Some of the more noteworthy contributions to psychohistory are as follows: P. Gay, *The Bourgeois Experience: Victoria to Freud*, 5 vols (Oxford: Oxford University Press, 1984–98); L. Roper, *Oedipus and the Devil: Witchcraft, Religion and Sexuality in Early Modern Europe* (London: Routledge, 1994); E. Erikson, *Young Man Luther: A Study in Psychoanalysis and History* (New York: W.W. Norton, 1958); T. Crosby, *The Two Mr. Gladstones: A Study in Psychology and History* (New Haven: Yale University Press, 1997).

within the unchanging human. Whatever it is to love, to fear, to hate or to hope, the appearance of such things in the past were biologically (and presumably experientially) the same as they are now, for 'us', whoever 'we' might be. Emotions happened in history, but did not have a history of their own. With some caveats, this is still the position of a large number of psychologists, evolutionary biologists and neurobiologists.[71]

Offering up a substantial denial to that axiom is still the principal challenge for the history of emotions, but it is absolutely essential that this is carried out. The political importance of history depends on it, in a present defined in part by this emotional essentialism. Certain psychologists have proclaimed emotions to be universal across time and place, among all humans. Some have even posited that emotions in animals are essentially the same as emotions in humans. These never-changing, identifiable emotions can be predicted, interpreted and measured, being put to a number of political uses. Societal happiness is now measured.[72] Facial expressions are 'read' for tell-tale signs of negative emotions that might indicate evil intentions or deceit.[73] Cultural niceties are reduced to their emotional foundations, flattening out the realm of human experience. All of this is typically done in English, using Caucasian expressions as benchmarks and anglophone words as emotional anchor points. Livelihoods depend on this kind of work. Politicians depend on this kind of work. Political ideology depends on this kind of work.[74]

[71] Among the chief popularisers are Antonio Damasio, Joseph E. LeDoux and Paul Ekman.
[72] See, for example, E. Diener *et al.*, 'Subjective well-being: three decades of progress', *Psychological Bulletin*, 125 (1999): 276–302; social happiness and well-being is measured by any number of indices and metrics, from the Social Progress Index to the Life Evaluation Index and the Happy Planet Index, and have been used to compile such things as the World Happiness Report, published by the United Nations Sustainable Development Solutions Network. See T. Hellman, 'Happiness and the Social Progress Index', *Social Progress Imperative*, www.socialprogressimperative.org/happiness-and-the-social-progress-index-2/, accessed 12 December 2016. In general, the field falls under the umbrella of 'happiness economics'. See L. Bruni and P.L. Porta [eds], *Handbook on the Economics of Happiness* (Cheltenham: Edward Elgar, 2008).
[73] See, for example, P. Ekman and M. O'Sullivan, 'Who can catch a liar?', *American Psychologist*, 46 (1991): 913–20.
[74] See D. Bok, *The Politics of Happiness: What Government Can Learn from the New*

The history of emotions, working in tandem with psychologists of a different stripe, as well as neuroscientists, anthropologists, linguists and philosophers, have the opportunity, if not the responsibility, to disrupt this landscape of crude essentialism and emotional reductionism. Though the importance of neuroscience in the history of emotions will be covered in more detail later, especially in chapters 5 and 6, suffice it to say for now that we ignore the neurosciences at our peril. It is not the case that we have to become neuroscientists. We do not have to be competent in running neuroscientific experiments. We do not have to appropriate all of the technical jargon of that discipline. We do, however, have a duty to understand the implications of neuroscience and its variety of research agendas, and not only through its chief popularisers. We are now shifting away from a sense of having to defy the universalising tendencies of the biological sciences in general, towards a sense of rapprochement. Neuroscience is much more open now to biocultural interpretations of brain function and meaning-making. We have entered the age of brain plasticity – the shaping and making of brain patterns in the world – and the possibilities for historians are immense. As neuroscience confirms the contingency of experience, the prospects for historical revisionism become manifest.

Sources and methods

There is no limit to the number or type of sources that can illuminate the history of emotions, and the range of methodological approaches (which will occupy much of this book) is similarly catholic. Nevertheless, we can probably identify the main types of sources that historians of emotions have used up until now, and what they have tended to do with them. An initial impetus might come from a perceived need to revise existing narratives or challenge prevailing orthodoxies. From my own experience with the history of emotional pain, the process was as straightforward as returning to first-person statements about painful experience and taking them at face value instead of as metaphors. Hence, a death that causes great 'pain' in grief can be taken as a literal statement

Research on Well-Being (Princeton: Princeton University Press, 2011); V. De Prycker, 'Happiness on the political agenda: PROS and CONS', *Journal of Happiness Studies*, 11 (2010): 585–603.

of truth, the full ramifications of which are to be worked out, rather than being understood (and quickly dismissed) as a metaphor.[75] The same was true for my research on sympathy, in which I was able to trace clear semantic and experiential distinctions in usage, tracing a genealogy of a new and unfamiliar type to Darwin's *Descent of Man*.[76] The history of emotions is ripe with this kind of opportunity to re-read. Emotion words have tended to be too easy to skip over as self-evident categories, metaphors or as being transparent in their meaning. Contextual analysis of language usage can be most revealing about the meanings and associated experiences of emotion words. This involves jettisoning all preconceived assumptions about what emotion words mean. When reconstructing the world around an emotion word, that word can begin to look unfamiliar, even strange, and so the picture of what it was like to be in and of the past shifts and takes on new meaning. C. Stephen Jaeger, a great pioneer in the history of emotions, said it well in respect of his own work recovering the intricacies of 'ennobling love' (a lost, or largely lost, form of public love of charisma and majesty): 'For the purpose of this study it is good to assume with an anthropologist's distancing that all the rich documentation on ennobling love from antiquity to the nineteenth century are voices from an alien, exotic culture and to study it with minimal contamination from ideas and social practices not its own.'[77] The past is a foreign country. Why should we expect its emotions to be ours?

The more substantiation and cross-referencing that can be carried out in this way, the more the complete the picture will be. Obviously, this gives modernists an advantage over medievalists, especially when it comes to the vernacular. The range of sources is vast: ego documents (diaries, etc.), speeches, non-fiction books and articles as well as more literary accomplishments, newspaper reports, correspondence, company records (minute books, etc.), court records and testimony, legislation, political debates and so

---

[75] R. Boddice [ed.], *Pain and Emotion in Modern History* (Houndmills: Palgrave, 2014); R. Boddice, *Pain: A Very Short Education* (Oxford: Oxford University Press, 2017).

[76] Boddice, *Science of Sympathy*.

[77] C.S. Jaeger, *Ennobling Love: In Search of a Lost Sensibility* (Philadelphia: University of Pennsylvania Press, 1999), 5.

on. The possibilities are endless, but well-defined topics will tend to suggest and also limit what kind of sources will be fruitful.

The linguistic focus is only a beginning. The language of emotions goes beyond words to include facial expressions, gestures, interpersonal body language and positioning. We cannot hope to talk about the history of emotions if we only focus on speech. Historical analysis of drawing, painting and sculpture, as well as photography, is essential in enabling historians to understand the social and spatial contexts of emotional expression, which is, of course, intertwined with what an emotional experience feels like. Research in the cognitive sciences in the 1970s and 1980s steered humanities scholars away from such research because photography in particular was being used to argue that emotional expressions are universal.

Building on Charles Darwin's own experiment of trying to get people to identify emotions by visible signs in the face, Paul Ekman and Wallace Friesen developed a methodology that seemed to prove that 'basic' emotions manifested in the face in much the same way everywhere (this will be discussed in greater detail in chapter 5). Their methodology has been pulled apart by many scholars in different disciplines, but there have been lasting and important effects of their conclusions.[78] Not least of these is the way this universalism is packaged as matter-of-factness in Ekman-influenced projects like Fox TV's *Lie to Me* (2009–11) and Disney's *Inside Out* (2015). There is something deliciously ironic about these significant popularisations of the basic emotions model. At their core is the notion that we can tell what is going on inside, and we can name that process, by what is happening on the outside.

---

[78] P. Ekman and W.V. Friesen, 'Constants across cultures in the face and emotion', *Journal of Personality and Social Psychology*, 17 (1971): 124–9, is the starting point. For criticism, see R. Leys, 'How did fear become a scientific object and what kind of object is it?', *Representations*, 110 (2010): 66–104; R. Leys, 'The turn to affect: A critique', *Critical Inquiry*, 37 (2010): 434–72; L. Feldman Barrett, 'Are emotions natural kinds?', *Perspectives on Psychological Science*, 1 (2006): 28–58; L. Feldman Barrett, 'Solving the emotion paradox: Categorization and the experience of emotion', *Personality and Social Psychology Review*, 10 (2006): 20–46. For an accessible and non-specialist account of Feldman Barrett's opposition to Ekman, see S. Fischer, 'About face: Emotions and facial expressions may not be related', *Boston Magazine*, July 2013, www.bostonmagazine.com/news/article/2013/06/25/emotions-facial-expressions-not-related/, accessed 12 December 2016.

Yet in *Lie to Me*, all the tell-tale signs of basic emotions being betrayed through unconscious micro-expressions are, of course, being consciously performed – acted – by the talented cast. It would not be a straightforward claim to say that the actors were going through anything like the emotional experiences their facial expressions were supposed to indicate. As for *Inside Out*, whatever emotions are supposed to be illustrated in that film are computer generated. We are not looking at emotional expressions at all, but at a programmed representation of them. If it works – that is, if we recognise emotions in these animations – it is by suggestion as much as by our tacit recognition of what is going on. Moreover, if it does work, and we are convinced that we are looking at real emotions in the computer-generated imagery (CGI), then this points to the flaw in our own ability to separate authenticity from dissimulation.

Nonetheless, we can put such televisual media into the pot with other historical sources that say something about what emotions are and what they mean. They can be unpacked and decoded, much like anything else, while being placed in a broader context (in this case, Ekman's contentious research output and the storm of criticism it has generated). Similarly, when looking at visual sources from the past, the depiction of expressions, gestures and positions cannot be read as if what they communicate is transparently obvious; rather they should be interpreted against descriptions of social mores and etiquette, knowledge about social dynamics and power relations, and specific guides to body language and demeanour. For this reason, historians of emotion find advice literature, etiquette books, codes of conduct, accounts of ritual performance and so on extremely useful. Read together, the visual and the prescriptive help us to reconstruct worlds of emotional experience.

This is by no means the limit of possibilities for history-of-emotions sources. A great deal of knowledge about the emotions, and all of the past categories that are related to emotions, has come from the worlds of science and medicine. Scientific and medical treatises, replete with diagrams and illustrations, tell us much about the way in which emotions were thought to function in the past. As mentioned above, this directly pertains to how emotions were experienced, for ideas about emotions influenced practices related to emotions. This observation is as valid for Aristotle's passions as it is for Galen's humoral theory, and works for nineteenth-century psychology as well as the world of psychoanalysis. Going further still, within the field of medicine we can turn to patient testimony and the clinical notes and reports of medical personnel to flesh out the dynamics of emotional experience in different settings, marking the changes over time.[79]

Finally, there is a significant material-history component to the history of emotions. If one of the most basic premises of the study of emotions in the past is that emotional experience is constructed in context, then not only the people, but the *things* of that context, and the spaces themselves, become important. What we feel is often inextricably bound up with the things we feel *about*, and those things – animate and inanimate – derive their meanings and importance from the cultural web in which they are produced and found. We can think of objects as elicitors of emotions, only insofar as we remember that an object does not elicit the same emotions in all people. An old piece of technology – a cassette tape, for example – will arouse different emotional responses in a 40-year-old and in a 20-year-old. Likewise, a dead body can arouse all kinds of emotions, from horror to grief to disgust to remorse, depending on the setting and the context. Clothes, jewellery, domestic goods, weapons, instruments of punishment and torture, and so on, all reveal something about the experiential world of the people who interacted with them, providing we can reconstruct those worlds by cross-reading against other sources. We can extend this analysis to the physical spaces and places in which emotions take place, the types and functions of buildings, as well as the architecture itself. All suggest something about emotional style or emotional prescription, which does not lie intrinsically in the bricks and mortar, but in the rationale behind the placement of bricks and mortar in certain ways, and in people's interactions with them. This *stuff* of emotions will be studied further in chapter 7.

Reading sources against one another, filling in the spaces in between, the past of emotional experience can be reconstructed. The historian of emotions must master discourse analysis, as well as being sensitive to visual and material sources, and aware of dynamics of place, space, race, class, religion and gender. As Alain Corbin

---

[79] See, for example, C. Mattingly and L.C. Garro [eds], *Narrative and the Cultural Construction of Illness and Healing* (Berkeley: University of California Press, 2000); B.J. Good, *Medicine, Rationality and Experience: An Anthropological Perspective* (Cambridge: Cambridge University Press, 1993).

noted in the early 1990s, 'The historian needs to know that the banal is frequently silent, like the perception of a new emotion, awareness of which is not yet very clear, or a means of expression not yet fully worked out.'[80] But we can be more sanguine than Corbin about the range of our sources, which do indeed stretch well beyond the mere linguistic. The theoretical tools will be described in the coming chapters, along with guidance on how historians of emotions have applied them. But a last word on sources must be given to the neurosciences.

Knowledge of the human brain is increasingly proving to be a key source for historians of emotion. It is not that we can empirically examine the brains of the dead and gone, but rather that we can extrapolate from the living what synaptic development might have been like in the past in order to say something about the way in which culture inscribes the brain as the brain creates experience. We can also speculate on the ways in which experiences were altered by the psychotropic effects of coffee and chocolate, alcohol and opium, as well as by less obvious psychotropics such as reading and writing, new forms of transport and new media, up to and including the Internet.[81] Modern neuroscience provides us insight into what happens to our production and reuptake of neurotransmitters while, for example, surfing the Web or riding a rollercoaster. From this we might extrapolate new significance in the invention of moveable type in the fifteenth century, or the mass distribution of cheap literature and prints in the eighteenth century.

It is no longer the case, therefore, that we turn to the neurosciences to find out the transhistorical and universal qualities of the brain. On the contrary, we turn to the neurosciences to find out what proportion of the brain's development happens in the world, through culture and experience, and the ways in which the things we learn influence what we do. Human encounters with each other, with objects and technology, and with spaces and places, all continually write to the brain and help to constitute the meaningfulness of who and what we are in the world. This is particularly important in childhood, where the objects of play and learning,

---

[80] Corbin, *Time*, 190.
[81] See D.L. Smail, *On Deep History and the Brain* (Berkeley and Los Angeles: University of California Press, 2008), 157–89.

and the styles and forms of interaction are massively influential on the development of the brain.[82] Armed with this knowledge – the ultimate source – we are better able to interpret the impact of seismic shifts in the everyday practices of populations, caused by new technologies, the ravages of disease, natural disasters and so on. For the historian of emotion, the emergence of the vaccine, the ready availability of cheap novels, the invention of photography or even just the advent of the custom of sending Christmas cards, all say something potentially very important about the emotional repertoire and the world construction of those people who first accustomed themselves to these new practices.

---

[82] For a review of historical research in this direction, see S. Olsen, 'Learning how to feel through play: At the intersection of the histories of play, childhood and the emotions', *International Journal of Play*, 5 (2016): 323–8; for a review of the contemporary importance of play from a pedagogical perspective, see D. Clark, 'Play-based learning within the early years: How critical is it really?', in G. Geng, P. Smith and P. Black [eds], *The Challenge of Teaching: Through the Eyes of Pre-service Teachers* (New York: Springer, 2017), 109–13; for reinforcement from developmental psychology see C. Pesce *et al.*, 'Deliberate play and preparation jointly benefit motor and cognitive development: Mediated and moderated effects', *Frontiers in Psychology*, 7 (2016): 1–18.

2

WORDS AND CONCEPTS

A master category

Debates about certain concepts and their naming are tired and old, and there is no benefit to us in re-opening them here. Instead, we must distinguish between the language and concepts available to historical actors and those of our own that may be useful analytical tools, even if they were unknown to the objects of our study. Nobody doubts, for example, that masculinity is a useful analytical category, even in periods of history where that word did not exist. Debates about late eighteenth-century manliness can happily find a place within the corpus of masculinity studies, for the historian is not only trying to get at what the actors thought, but also at the structural element that the actors could not necessarily see. An essential part of such an approach is the acknowledgement that masculinity is not a fixed category, but a fluid one. Despite this, we should reserve a degree of circumspection with regard to the word 'emotion'. Why?

Some historians of emotion, among them Nicole Eustace and Barbara Rosenwein, have no problem in using the word 'emotion' as a master category. They are happy to allow emotions, passions, feelings, affects and so on to be functionally synonymous, and to make no real distinction among them in their analysis.[1] A fifth-century scholastic might use the term *perturbationes animi*, and an eighteenth-century churchman might talk of the passions of the soul, but, according to these scholars, what they mean is

---

[1] N. Eustace, *Passion is the Gale: Emotion, Power, and the Coming of the American Revolution* (Chapel Hill: University of North Carolina Press, 2008), 3, 76–7; B. Rosenwein, *Generations of Feeling: A History of Emotions, 600–1700* (Cambridge: Cambridge University Press, 2016), 7–8.

'emotions' and we can think of these things as emotions without worrying too much about what we are doing to the analysis in the act of translation.

Rosenwein's ease with such conceptual superimposition shows in some of the back-working she does, noting, for example, that Cicero 'wrote about the *perturbationes*, the Latin word that he chose for the emotions'.[2] This implies that the conceptual category, however we fill it in here, already existed in Cicero's time, and that whatever the specific word choice is, he was choosing it to mean 'emotions'. While on the one hand Rosenwein is committed to a historicism that leads her to 'not rule out *anything* as possibly having affective valence ... as possibly being "an emotion"', and is explicitly aware of the way that expressions, evaluations and experiences of this potential infinity of emotions change, she nevertheless refuses to 'shy away from using words like feeling, emotion, and even passion interchangeably', because 'all of these words formed what we might call the "penumbra" of what we more-or-less mean by the word emotion'.[3] Put another way, there is a category 'we' that understands the category 'emotion', and neither this 'we' nor this 'emotion' is sufficiently subject to change or difference over time or place to have any substantial effect on critical analysis. It is, however, acknowledged that within these stable human universals there is massive scope for variation that nevertheless does not alter the overall framework.

Eustace is more sensitive to categorical differences, although she does not functionally employ such differences in her historical work. What she does do, and this will be explored in greater depth later, is address the significant differences in the experience of emotions that, their degrees of distinction notwithstanding, have lived under single and stable emotional labels: love, anger, sympathy, grief, etc. Rosenwein is also, among other things, a master linguist, carefully negotiating Latin, Old French and Old English to find the nuances and, sometimes, large shifts in the meaning of emotion words and their associated experiences. It is somewhat puzzling that scholars who are so sensitive to the shifting ground of emotion words and concepts in a historical context are not so sensitive to the semantic richness of modernity.

[2] Rosenwein, *Generations*, 17.
[3] Rosenwein, *Generations*, 7–8.

Jan Plamper has also averred that it is essential that 'emotion' becomes the master category for talking about emotions in the past, but Plamper's opinion is more deeply considered and begs us to address the most basic of methodological questions of what we do when we do history. In arguing that we should use 'emotion' as a meta-concept or meta-category, Plamper walks a fine line.[4] On the one hand, he enumerates many of the reasons why using a contemporary label for historical categories does not, or should not, work. Such labels come replete with conceptual and semantic baggage, even when we can assume that contemporary usage is itself stable, which it generally is not. Plamper refers to research that pointed out the ninety-two definitions of 'emotion' that Kleinginna and Kleinginna traced as being current between 1872 and 1980. It is often telling in written debates about the nature of emotions between disciplines that the core of the problem lies in incommensurate definitions of the object of enquiry.[5] Once other words for that object – affect, passion, sentiment – are introduced, the problem is further compounded. A high degree of sensitivity is required if historians are to avoid what Plamper calls 'casual use of conceptions of emotion from their own time', which leads inevitably to the 'trap of anachronism'.[6]

On the other hand, however, Plamper is concerned that history without meta-categories is not much analytical use. In many respects we cannot avoid using master labels for things that would be better off historicised, precisely because one of our aims as historians is to weigh the past against the present or other eras; not to judge

[4] Plamper, *History of Emotions*, 10–12, 38, 296, 299.
[5] Plamper, *History of Emotions*, 11; P.R. Kleinginna Jr and A.M. Kleinginna, 'A categorized list of emotion definitions, with suggestions for a consensual definition', *Motivation and Emotion*, 5 (1981): 345–79.
[6] Plamper, *History of Emotions*, 296. The problem is compounded by some critics of the history of emotions, claiming that historians do not mean the same thing by 'emotions' as it is understood in other disciplines, often an accusation of essentialism by reference to a different essentialism. This is just the kind of reductive semantic disciplinary stand-off that should be avoided. See, for example, H.U.K. Grundlach, 'The fortunes of emotion in the science of psychology and in the history of emotions', in J.C.E. Gienow-Hecht [ed.], *Emotions in American History: An International Assessment* (New York: Berghahn, 2010), 264f; D. Wickberg, 'What is the history of sensibilities? On cultural histories, old and new', *American Historical Review*, 112 (2007): 661–84, at 682; R. Schnell, *Haben Gefühle eine Geschichte?: Aporien einer History of emotions* (Göttingen: V&R unipress, 2015), 30–3.

the past, but to mark change. It is, in some respects, easier to mark change when we compare phenomena under stable labels. Plamper goes as far as to say that an 'impossibility of using meta-concepts ... would mean the end of scholarship', but that seems both an exaggeration and a somewhat reductive appraisal of attempts at conceptual sophistication.[7] I will return to this point shortly, but let us first look at the reasons Plamper gives for retaining the word 'emotion' as a meta-category for historical analysis. First, he argues there is an etymological connection (at least in European languages) that connects emotion to the projection of movement. Second, comparing draft translations (of what, into what and from when are missing details here) is said to be a productive way of analysing conceptual similarities (and differences). And third – a negative reason – if we do not employ a meta-concept then scholarship 'would relapse into a radically random enterprise'.[8]

Taking each in turn, it is difficult to see the merits of the case. One could similarly find etymological commonalities in the Greek *pathos* and *paschein*, the Latin *passio* and the English 'passion', and an in-depth enquiry would doubtless reveal a rich and complex conceptual history that takes us from suffering through pain to enthusiasm, at various points touching on the emotions but never being subsumed by that category. On what basis, stopping short of the absolute nominalism that Plamper fears, can we even casually conflate passions and emotions? That said, it is unlikely that any historian of emotions doubts, even for an instant, that passions fall under the purview of the history of emotions considered as a coherent field of study. To that end, translations are not only good for studying definitional commonalities, but also for studying the extent to which translators flatten out concepts and thereby change meanings.

On the same page that Plamper asserts the necessity of the emotion meta-concept, we see precisely this. Aristotle's *pathé* are rendered as emotions. As historians of emotion, we must stop and consider the work being done to make one category into another here. And of course we should not forget that the English edition of Plamper's book is itself in translation from the German. The footnote refers to Aristotle's theory of *Gefühle*. It is not 'radically random' to insist that these words and concepts are substantially

---

[7] Plamper, *History of Emotions*, 299.
[8] Plamper, *History of Emotions*, 12.

different and can be treated in their own terms and in their own contexts. To do so would suggest a richness of historical investigation, not a diminution. Plamper's own meta-category is complicated by the translation factor, and contains an uncomfortable slippage between the English (and these days functionally German too) 'emotion' and the German *Gefühl*. In the English edition, Plamper states that 'emotion' will be the meta-concept and 'feeling' will be a synonym for it.[9] But 'feeling' in English takes us into different realms: of the senses and of internal states that may or may not manifest as emotions. The confusion lies in the fact that the synonym Plamper had in mind was in fact *Gefühl*, which is one direct translation option for the English 'emotion'. A degree of conceptual confusion is thus introduced.

It may have been better had the translator left the word *Gefühl* in German, and one might entertain arguments that the word is roughly cognate with 'emotion', and could easily stand in for it. But then again, one might also entertain the argument of one strident Victorian anti-Prussianist, the long-time editor of the *Spectator*, Richard Hutton, who was horrified by 'various kinds of sentiment – for which, thank God, we have no terms in our language'. In his opinion, the 'expansiveness of French "effusion" and the sickly conceit of German "Gefühl" have no kindred with genuine feeling'.[10] This historical example demonstrates the point: if the history of emotions is really to penetrate deeply into the ways in which emotions – words, concepts and their associated experiences – have changed over time, then historians of emotion must retain a sensitivity to the vagaries, niceties, politics and slippages of languages.

I do acknowledge that 'emotion' provides a useful shorthand for talking about what we do, and, in particular, for explaining what we do to a lay audience or to emotions researchers beyond the discipline of history. The field itself is now well established as 'the history of emotions', and this book also purports to be about precisely this subject. But beyond a general convenience of labelling we should be cautious not to proceed further without pause. If

---

[9] Plamper, *History of Emotions*, 12.
[10] For a more general appraisal along these lines, and the compound problems of histories of mistranslation, see C. Wassmann, 'Forgotten origins, occluded meanings: Translation of emotion terms', *Emotion Review*, 9 (2017): 163–71.

Plamper's consciously made points, and Rosenwein's casually made ones, are to be conceded, the risks of translation loom large, and the chances of a distortion of analysis at best and outright of anachronism at worst are increased. Indeed, Plamper, as already mentioned, is acutely aware of the problem of lurking anachronism, but it seems difficult to avoid it if we proceed with anything other than an acceptance for convenience's sake of transcendent labels.

Weighing Rosenwein's semantic policy against Plamper's, for example, one could not escape the conclusion that Plamper would find Rosenwein to be anachronistic. They even state directly opposed policies concerning the word 'affect', for example, and the way that it does or does not (depending on the argument) easily fall under the category of 'emotion'.[11] But bracketing this for the present, we might ask whether Plamper's fears of meaninglessness in historiographical practice if we relinquish the meta-category of 'emotion' are well founded. What is to stop us from writing a conceptual history of emotion, limited only to this word? What is to stop us from doing the same with 'affect', 'passion', 'sentiment' or 'feeling'? And once these things exist, what is to stop us comparing them? Unless historians are willing and prepared to concede that each such history would be practically indistinct from the others, it seems inescapable that conceptual and semantic sensitivity have to be our priorities. Such sensitivity does not neutralise historical analysis, but rather empowers it, as Thomas Dixon has substantially demonstrated.[12] Moreover, new insights from the neurosciences seem to encourage it.

Conceptual plasticity

Emotion words are now acknowledged themselves to effect what emotions are like; that is, how they are experienced and perceived.[13] This insight has come in part from a social–scientific turn

---

[11] Plamper, *History of Emotions*, 12; Rosenwein, *Generations*, 7.

[12] T. Dixon, *From Passions to Emotions: The Creation of a Secular Psychological Category* (Cambridge: Cambridge University Press, 2006); T. Dixon, *The Invention of Altruism: Making Moral Meanings in Victorian Britain* (Oxford: Oxford University Press, 2008); T. Dixon, '"Emotion": The history of a keyword in crisis', *Emotion Review*, 4 (2012): 338–44.

[13] M. Gendron, K.A. Lindquist, L. Barsalou and L. Feldman Barrett, 'Emotion words shape emotion percepts', *Emotion*, 12 (2012): 314–25.

towards the neurosciences, and in part from the neurosciences' turn towards the social. The premise is simple enough, but some background is necessary before reaching it over the course of this book. From at least the mid-1980s, psychologists and sociologists/anthropologists argued about whether or not emotions were built in, natural and universal, or else learnt, nurtured and mutable.[14] Historians, with the exception of Peter and Carol Stearns, were seemingly uninterested in this particular aspect of the debate, though they engaged fiercely with it in other respects. As far as the emotions were concerned, they were occupied by the question of how far psychoanalysis belonged in historiography (not much, it turns out). Still, as we shall see, the nature/nurture debate slowly picked up pace within the discipline of history as more historians took up the challenge of studying the emotions. It seemed incumbent on individual scholars to make a judgement call about how far they presupposed an unchanging human nature or to what extent a human was nurtured, enculturated and socialised.

On what basis could historians make that call? Peter and Carol Stearns could only speculate negatively about human nature by pointing positively to the empirical archival material that seemed to leave no doubt that *some* nurturing in a cultural context took place in human societies, and that this nurturing could and did change the nature of experience at the level of the emotions.[15] This was vague, however, and veiled over by a tendency to relegate whatever that 'natural' component might have been to irrelevant background material.

Historians are interested in what changes, not what stays the same. We have no tools to measure biological continuity, but we do have tools to measure what causes it to alter. And in a field where certain biological constants could be assumed, it was only through cultural departures that anything of human interest for historians actually happened. Hence, as long as historians could extract a concession from other disciplines that there was some nurture involved in emotional experience (by no means always a given), then it was safe simply to bracket nature and go in search of the

---

[14] The background to the nature/nurture (or culture) debate on emotions is fully covered in Plamper, *History of Emotions*, chapters 2 and 3.
[15] C.Z. Stearns and P.N. Stearns, *Anger: The Struggle for Emotional Control in America's History* (Chicago: University of Chicago Press, 1986), 15.

causes and effects of change, much like historians do for everything else.[16]

There is something dissatisfying about this. First, it rather self-consciously relegates the discipline of history to a secondary field with fixed boundaries beyond which it cannot really go. Second, and relatedly, it seems to give up too much ground to other disciplines on the subject of what humans *are*. Third, it either implicitly accepts the assumption that the nature/nurture duality exists, or else it posits that there is only nurture and that everything is socially and culturally constructed. In and of themselves, such assumptions are not terrible, but one cannot effectively act on them unless one can find a justification for them.

In the 1990s anthropologist William Reddy theorised a nature/nurture relationship that would demolish the duality. Details of this will be discussed in chapter 3, but suffice it to say for now that the theoretical collapse of a binary opposition pointed the way forward to a rapprochement of humanities and natural science scholars. That has come with particular impetus from neuroscience and genetics, which has demonstrated the extent to which brain development, both overall growth and synaptic complexity, takes place after birth and throughout childhood before reaching an 'adult' level in adolescence.[17] Even then, our brains continue to change. In other words, we are very much formed in, and by, the world.

All of this seems to endorse the approach of Thomas Dixon, and to a certain extent the early conceptual focus of the scholars of the Center for the History of Emotions in Berlin. Those scholars have pursued word histories of emotions on the basis that, while you may have something proximal to the thing even if you do not have the word, whatever words you do have tend to enhance the meaning,

---

[16] This summarises the general approach of Stearns and Stearns. See, in particular, P.N. Stearns, *American Fear: The Causes and Consequences of High Anxiety* (New York: Routledge, 2006), 13.

[17] The literature is large, but the following provide a representative sample: L.A. Glantz *et al.*, 'Synaptophysin and PSD-95 in the human prefrontal cortex and from mid-gestation into early adulthood', *Neuroscience*, 149 (2007): 582–91; R.C. Knickmeyer *et al.*, 'A structural MRI study of human brain development from birth to 2 years', *Journal of Neuroscience*, 28 (2008): 12176–82; P.R. Huttenlocher and A.S. Dabholkar, 'Regional differences in synaptogenesis in human cerebral cortex', *Journal of Comparative Neurobiology*, 387 (1997): 167–78.

and therefore the experience, of the thing so named.[18] On some level we might want to call passions 'emotions', but if we are conducting a deep analysis of the philosophical insights of Spinoza, chances are we are going to need a deep understanding of what he meant by the word 'passion'. If we choose instead to treat Spinoza as a commentator on the emotions, we shall fail to do him justice.

Dixon, in particular, focused on the modern British transition from the world of passions to the world of emotions, arguing that the predominantly nineteenth-century shift in categories was far more than a mere change in preference for one label over another. Rather, the wholesale move of science (biology and the newly framed discipline of psychology) to 'emotions' suggested a completely different understanding of what feelings were, where they were produced and how they were controlled. That shift in understanding necessitated a shift in behaviour and practice to reflect it.[19] Conceptual change equates to experiential change, at least to some extent. The task of the historian of emotions is to recognise it and to measure its extent.

Linguistic intersections

If the dominant trend since the linguistic turn has been to emphasise the contingency of language and the constructedness of experience, there are nonetheless influential linguistic trends which would undermine such views. Anna Wierzbicka, perhaps the most notable linguist dealing with the emotions across different cultures, tries to navigate a middle line between the Anglocentric and ethnocentric essentialism of psychologists such as Ekman (see chapter 5), but ultimately fails for similar reasons.[20] Her work has

---

[18] Dixon, '"Emotion"'; U. Frevert *et al.*, *Emotional Lexicons: Continuity and Change in the Vocabulary of Feeling, 1700–2000* (Oxford: Oxford University Press, 2014); confirmed by Gendron *et al.*, 'Emotion words'.

[19] Dixon, *From Passions*; Dixon, *Invention of Altruism*; see also Boddice, *Science of Sympathy*; Dror, 'Affect'; P. White, 'Darwin's emotions: The scientific self and the sentiment of objectivity', *Isis*, 100 (2009): 811–26; P. White, 'Sympathy under the knife: Experimentation and emotion in late Victorian medicine', in F. Bound Alberti [ed.], *Medicine, Emotion and Disease, 1700–1950* (Houndmills: Palgrave, 2006).

[20] A. Wierzbicka, 'Human emotions: Universal or culture-specific?', *American Anthropologist*, 88 (1986): 584–94; A. Wierzbicka, *Emotions across Languages and Cultures: Diversity and Universals* (Cambridge: Cambridge University Press, 1999).

been particularly influential for those wishing to chart a moderate course, where cultural difference is underwritten by some natural and universal fixity. Despite Wierzbicka's strong emphasis on the conceptual distance between emotion words (and their experience) in different languages, all of these can still be grounded in something more fundamental. She talks of 'universal human concepts' and 'culture-independent concepts', but it is unclear from what neutral position she can arrive at such insights, in order to demonstrate that certain concepts (given in English for the sake of convenience) have correlates everywhere.[21]

Wierzbicka's culturally specific account is persuasive until it contradicts itself. Social neuroscientists would, I think, prevent this slippage into culture-independent concepts, since all concepts are formed and learnt after being born, once the brain is in the world. Since that brain is bound by the conceptual framework of a specific culture or cultures, even the most fundamental concepts, which Wierzbicka argues are universal, such as 'want' or 'feel', come laced with layers of meaning that do not transcend cultural boundaries. The concept of 'want', for example, from an anglophone perspective, has changed in recent times from being a recognition of being without something – as in, I want *for* bread, or, conversely, I want *for* nothing, giving rise to the well-known but seldom understood aphorism 'waste not, want not' – to being a statement of desire akin to 'I would like to have'. Likewise, the concept 'feel' carries an entirely different set of cultural baggage in the world of eighteenth-century sensibility and sentiment than it does in twenty-first-century daytime chat shows. Stripping it bare and trying to find its *essential* universalism seems fraught with all the same dangers and assumptions that Wierzbicka reserves for the word 'emotion' and anglophone projections of so-called universals such as 'anger' and 'fear'. If those words represent a particular language at a particular time in a particular cultural setting, then it remains a mystery why or how her own 'universal' concepts have come by this status. She isolates what she calls a 'Natural Semantic Metalanguage' in order to find these 'universal human concepts', the prime examples of which are 'good', 'bad', 'know' and 'want'. The premise is that *all* human languages 'have words with meanings

---

[21] Wierzbicka, *Emotions across Languages*, 25, 35.

corresponding *exactly* to the meanings of the English words' here mentioned.[22]

I have already mentioned 'want' as having undergone historical changes. One could similarly pursue the spiritual, philosophical, folk and scientific cadences of what it means to 'know' anything, or for anything to have the state of *knowledge* and be accepted or rejected as such. Such a basic concept is not only culturally and historically contingent, but is also loaded heavily with politics, for the expression 'I know' presumes an ability to know, a recognition that this individual is allowed to know, and further recognitions that what this individual knows actually counts as knowledge. If anything, the quality of being good is even more richly complex, involving the entire history of philosophy and endless political, social and moral wrangling about what it means to pursue, be or know 'good'. One only needs to acknowledge that late modernity has seen one of the definitions of 'bad' become 'good' to know that any pretensions to something transcendent in these concepts is doomed to failure.

While it may be true that all cultures have had some concept of bad and good, want and know, and feel too, they are not reducible to a conceptual rule that works equally for all. For such concepts cannot exist outside of the place where they are formulated and practised. To strive to be good, at one point in time, might have meant paying fair prices for slaves. A few years later, in the same place, the purchase of slaves at any price might be re-cast as bad. I posit that to feel good about something is indissociably bound with that something and carries a quality related to that practice. To feel good about paying fair prices for slaves and to feel good about banning slavery cannot be qualitatively the same. Such apparently basic concepts are bound up in the cosmological worlds of those who use them. Because of that, they are not actually basic at all, but as rich and complex and distinctive as more obviously culturally specific labels such as *Angst*.[23]

Such concepts are also only tenuously attached to emotional experience and expression. Wierzbicka suggests that the sentence 'I feel (something) good now' is universally possible across all

---

[22] Wierzbicka, *Emotions across Languages*, 35.
[23] Wierzbicka insists, for example, that *Angst* is a 'cultural creation', *Emotions across Languages*, 128–67, at 167.

languages (and presumably therefore across *time*), and goes on to make the following breathtaking leap of interpretation: it can 'therefore be plausibly proposed as the meaning of a smile'.[24] The relationship here implied, however, is only of any value if the bald conceptual statement and the accompanying emotion can be worked back from the expression. This she demonstrates later in the same text:

> the core meaning of a smile (that is, roughly speaking, of the configuration of facial muscles in which the corners of the mouth are raised, and of the movement which produces this configuration), can be stated as follows: 'I feel something good now'. Various possible interpretations of smiles ... do indeed depend on the context; but they are compatible with the one meaning proposed here as the invariant core meaning of a smile ('I feel something good now'), and can be regarded as context-dependent elaborations of this invariant.[25]

Anyone who has ever seen a citizen of the United States check her grief as a matter of social convention in a public space and *smile* through tears will know that smiles do not necessarily relate to anything good at all. Similarly, Wierzbicka cannot know too much about English people if she thinks that smiles are so straightforwardly connected to a universal root. I have been known to smile when things have gone wrong, when listening to other people talking offensively, when my football team has lost in the last minute of a match. Expressions occur discretely, just as qualitative states and the language to describe them are irreducible to anything 'basic' or 'universal'. As soon as we attempt to filter out context, specifics, culture, detail, relations, associations, inflexions, plurality of meaning, doubt, confusion and so on, we lose a grip on the essential importance of the experience we are trying to describe. What makes human experience and its history so profoundly interesting and important is precisely its irreducibility.

Wierzbicka dismisses the interpretation of Alan Fridlund that there is something categorically different happening in the context of smile when an actor is 'exacting revenge' or 'giving a gift'.[26] They are reducible to 'I feel something good now', according to

---

[24] Wierzbicka, *Emotions across Languages*, 38.
[25] Wierzbicka, *Emotions across Languages*, 173.
[26] Wierzbicka, *Emotions across Languages*, 172–5.

Wierzbicka. Even if we grant that this might be true, and that it were impossible for a smile to indicate 'I feel something bad now', the reduction would be so complete as to render the observation analytically useless. Such banality tells us nothing of the quality of the emotion of the person exacting revenge, or of the person giving the gift. The context, about which Wierzbicka seems much less interested, is the key to understanding this quality, just as the context tells us when a smile betrays something bad, such as grief, cosmic injustice, or fatalistic resignation.[27]

As soon as we think we know how humans will behave under this or that circumstance, humans surprise us. Francis Fukuyama announced 'the end of history' in the hopeful early 1990s, pondering on the ultimate success of Western liberal democracy.[28] How surprised might he be by the global political landscape of the late 2010s and the early 2020s? What seemed and felt good and what were interpreted as universals turned out, as these things always turn out, to be historical passages and specific historical flavours. The announcement of the end of history has become an unintended irony. The only real universal is that everything changes.

Taking a much harder line than Wierzbicka and pursuing the constructivist half of her argument to its logical and, to my mind, inevitable end does not mean that biology and the body have to be rejected into the bargain. Biology is simply subject to history. Bodies are historical. Minds change. Nevertheless, they exist and play a role in how emotions are experienced.

Emotion words

If the difficulties concerning the generic categories of our subject of study are complicated, things become even more so when we begin to consider individual words and concepts for specific experiences. An anecdote will serve as introduction to this point. In a large gathering of curious scholars at the American Historical Association in Chicago in 2012, a panel on the history of emotions that (for once) bridged modern and pre-modern periods as well as

---

[27] For a much more varied, contextually aware linguistic approach, see R. Caballero and J.E. Diz Vera [eds], *Sensuous Cognition: Explorations into Human Sentience: Imagination (E)motion and Perception* (Berlin: De Gruyter Mouton, 2013).

[28] F. Fukuyama, *The End of History and the Last Man* (New York: Free Press, 1992).

the French–English language barrier, introduced the theories and methods of the history of emotions. For many in the room, despite the field's development over nearly three decades by that point, it was their first encounter with the notion. An audience member asked William Reddy if these ideas meant that they could no longer read Jane Austen novels, for example, as exemplary accounts of authentic love. The question itself was phrased in terms that Reddy could not countenance. There is no 'authentic' love, anywhere, any time. We are not, as historians, trying to clear away the dross of culture and politics in order to get at pure forms or timeless expressions of nature. The very notion that we should do this is anathema to everything the principles of historicism hold dear. And yet, the prevailing and most powerful assumption was that some things (emotions, for example) transcended history and could be found, among other places, in novels.

The caveat to Reddy's response is this: instead of looking to see if this or that novelist or philosopher managed to divine the true nature of love, why not investigate the particularities of those expressions of love and weigh them in the context of others? Nobody, certainly not any scholar in the humanities, is the arbiter of true love, but we can investigate what love is like in different times and places. We can begin by introducing an air of circumspection by referring to specific iterations of love as 'love'. We can look at the way love is structured, not merely as a matter of the heart in the abstract, but in terms of its social dynamics, its politics of expression and the effortful attempts of lovers to accommodate themselves and their feelings to prevailing standards and prescriptions.[29]

Nicole Eustace has done this in an exemplary manner for love in eighteenth-century colonial America, describing how courtship in the name of love was about the politics of marriage, where marriage 'changed social roles as much as it did personal relationships', and where 'expressions of love meant as much for community as for identity'.[30] At stake in Eustace's compendious account of the fine-grained distinctions in emotion words, as their usage cut across social class and race boundaries, is a negotiation of competing

---

[29] See, for example, S.G. Magnússon, 'The love game as expressed in ego-documents: The culture of emotions in late nineteenth century Iceland', *Journal of Social History*, 50 (2016): 102–19.
[30] Eustace, *Passion*, 109.

conceptions of the self. Her period of study, up until the American Revolution, saw the gradual emergence of an individualistic understanding of the self, carved out from older conceptions that only saw selfhood in relation to the community as a whole. Such seismic shifts in the most fundamental and, apparently, 'natural' ways of seeing oneself in the world obviously had massive implications for what was meant by being in love. In Eustace's argument, the 'language of love ... worked to elide distinctions between self and society', making passionate unions out of two parties, just as it bound rulers to the ruled and authorities to subjects.[31]

Susan Lanzoni has pursued the slipperiness of emotion words with particular clarity in her research on the word 'empathy'. Given empathy's short history – it is an early twentieth-century neologism – it has developed a rich semantic field.[32] The misleading Greek-sounding label was back-worked from a German coinage, *Einfühlung*, which detained scholars such as Max Scheler at the turn of the twentieth century. Scheler and his contemporaries laboured in their efforts to sort out empathy (*Einfühlung*), sympathy (*Sympathie*, or *Mitgefühl*), compassion (*Mitleid*) and so on.[33] Literally, it refers to 'feeling in', distinguished from its linguistic associates in the following ways. Sympathy and compassion are etymologically cognate. They both mean 'suffering with', where 'to suffer' is taken in the neutral sense of 'undergoing', or 'enduring'. One might 'suffer' love as much as 'pain', perhaps. In German the two terms are distinguished in common usage by reference to *Gefühl* and *Leid*, respectively, where *Mitgefühl* denotes literally 'feeling with' and *Mitleid* denotes 'suffering with' or 'condoling'. These distinctions are not linguistically present in English but they functionally exist. One might express sympathy with someone's joy, but one could not very well feel compassionate about it. At the beginning of empathy's career, however, we can already detect a language slippage

---

[31] Eustace, *Passion*, 109.
[32] S. Lanzoni, 'Introduction: Emotion and the sciences: Varieties of empathy in science, art, and history', *Science in Context*, 25 (2012): 287–300; S. Lanzoni, 'A short history of empathy', *The Atlantic*, 15 October 2015.
[33] M. Scheler, *Wesen und Formen der Sympathie*, 5th edn (1923; Frankfurt: Verlag G. Schulte-Bulmke, 1948). First published in 1913 as *Zur Phänomenlogie und Theorie der Sympathiegefühle und von Liebe und Haß*. The English translation is from 1954: *The Nature of Sympathy*, trans. Peter Heath (London: Routledge & Kegan Paul, 1954).

from *feeling* to *suffering*, from *Fühlung* to *pathé*. In common English usage, if I empathise with you it might be assumed that I empathise with your plight or suffering, or can recognise in advance how certain actions might hurt you. Few people say that they empathise with someone's happiness, yet technically the word ought to be amenable to all emotional experiences. Such are the biographies of individual words that the Germans re-imported (calqued) the pseudo-Greek English construction that had been borrowed from them in the first place. Empathy in German is now *Empathie*.

Semantics aside, the concept itself has had a remarkably unstable history, given its relatively short existence. It began life as an aesthetic category used to explain how the viewer of a work of art *projects* his own feelings into the painting, receiving them back as if emerging from the work itself. It later came to refer to an individual's capacity to enter into the emotions of another person and experience them in a way kindred to the original emotions observed. Latterly, and the thing searched for by neuroscientists, it is a mechanism internal to the brain that makes experience *as if* replicating the emotions of another, but actually being drawn from the individual's own experience.[34] In its first century or so, in other words, empathy has been a projection, a reception and an internal production. And it is not so much that it was one thing, then another, then another, so much as it is that these three meanings and their associated experiences overlap, co-exist and serve to confuse each other. Neuroscientists might come to find exactly how empathy works in the brain, but this will not narrow down what we empathise with, or what it feels like. There will be more to say about empathy in chapter 5, under 'Other people's expressions', but let it suffice for the moment to say that an emotion word is not an end point, a fixed marker of a fixed thing, but a starting point. This is not to make scholarship a random exercise. On the contrary, it is to make it more precise.

One might easily engage in such exercises with all kinds of emotion words, but it is important that the history of emotions does not

---

[34] C. Burdett, 'Is empathy the end of sentimentality?', *Journal of Victorian Culture*, 16 (2011): 259–74; C. Burdett, '"The subjective inside us can turn into the objective outside": Vernon Lee's psychological aesthetics', *19: Interdisciplinary Studies in the Long Nineteenth Century*, 12 (2011). For the 'brain mechanism' see the section 'Other people's expressions' in chapter 5.

begin with its frames of reference pre-established. If we start out with a list of emotion words that we wish to explore, we risk missing those emotion words and concepts that have come and gone, or that linger in our everyday parlance as something not instantly recognisable as emotional. Ute Frevert, for example, traced the semantic and meaningful outlines of honour (*Ehre*) in order to demonstrate that this was once, for all intents and purposes, an emotion.[35] We might readily make similar enquiries of many of the so-called virtues – courage, temperance, etc. – and look at either their emotional composition or the ways in which they were experienced as emotions themselves. Essential here is the connection between action and feeling, of emotions as carried out at the key moment, rather than being experienced passively and beyond one's control. Courage, for example, is not the absence of fear, but rather the action of confronting fear, and the practice of confrontation may modify fear to become a kind of satisfaction for having been faced. Courage looks very different depending on when it is called up, and for what purpose. There are not, perhaps, adequate words in contemporary English to describe such an experience, but it would be surprising if such experiences were not adequately described in historical sources. Indeed, Don Quixote – a parody of courage, but an exemplar of it for all that – talked of having courage awakened by fear, of his 'heart bursting in his chest' (*hace que el corazón me reviente en el pecho*), as if a positive spirit lay dormant only to be sparked by a negative feeling.[36]

We might also connect etymological studies to questions of disposition, especially where there are clear semantic hangovers from Galen's (129–*c.*200 CE) categories of humoral temperament (from the Latin *tempere*, to mix). Knowledge of the four humours – blood, phlegm, yellow bile and black bile (melancholy) – was the cornerstone of medical knowledge until the nineteenth century. A choleric person, for example, might in modern English be thought of as grumpy or bad tempered. The word itself comes from the Greek for yellow bile: *kholé*. Hardly anybody realises that they are using a humoral category here. An imbalance of temperament in

---

[35] U. Frevert, *Men of Honour: A Social and Cultural History of the Duel* (Oxford: Wiley, 1995).
[36] M. de Cervantes Saavedra, *Don Quijote de la Mancha* (1605; Madrid: Edaf, 1999), 145.

the direction of yellow bile was likely to lead to an angry disposition, but would also have had bodily effects, since it was thought to be a physical substance. Hence, in addition to the English 'choleric', for a grumpy disposition, we also have the disease 'cholera', which originally pointed to the same humoral problem, as well as the French word *colère*, meaning 'anger'. When we use these words in different contexts, we do not connect them to Galen, or to the long history of humoral medicine that saw them adapted, translated, transliterated and changed out of all proportion. But the connections are there and can be mapped. This is more than mere semantic or etymological antiquarianism. This is the search for the connection between words and feelings; concepts and experiences; bodies and minds.

3

COMMUNITIES, REGIMES AND STYLES

Emotionology

The beginning of a substantial historiography of the history of emotions can be dated to Peter and Carol Stearns' 1985 article in the *American Historical Review*.[1] The history of emotions, from this point on, was clearly about emotions in society. While more recent innovations have shifted focus to the individual, and the biocultural production of emotions in the individual, by and large the discipline of history has provided insights that locate individuals in meaningful company. When the Stearns began their work, they saw a fundamental problem with the ways in which historians had been confused about their subject matter when talking about the emotions. This was compounded by a suspicion that prevailing winds from the doomed psychohistory, in all its Freudian garb, too strongly emphasised the individual and 'an essentially static psyche' that allowed the past to become 'a simple illustration of a human reality' that does not change.[2] They detected similar shortcomings in the psychological sciences. If emotions were biologically fixed, a stable and universal quality of human beings, then what interest could they possibly hold for historians?

Historiographical intuition suggested that social and cultural change must have some impact on how people feel, and that how people express how they feel must also be in some way circumscribed by circumstances. Moreover, the Stearns were dissatisfied with the ways in which emotions in social contexts had been passed over by historians, who associated emotions with the irrational.

---

[1] P.N. Stearns and C.Z. Stearns, 'Emotionology: Clarifying the history of emotions and emotional standards', *American Historical Review*, 90 (1985): 813–36.
[2] Stearns and Stearns [eds], *Emotion and Social Change*, 3.

Social protest movements – strikes, riots, revolts, marches – had been written up as a kind of group cognition, or a strictly rational or intentional set of group decisions and strategic moves, with the aim of attaining preconceived targets. The Stearns did not reject the cognitive analysis so much as reject the dualism. Emotions and reason were not opposed, but mutually involved. Emotions were a part of cognition. Peter Stearns later stated that emotions 'are not irrational; they relate to the cognitive processes in that they involve thinking about one's own impulses and evaluating them as an intrinsic part of the emotional experience itself'.[3] He wanted, at least in part, to be able to use the word 'emotional' without it being inferred pejoratively.

The Stearns suspected that the specific forms of emotional expression, whether in social movements or in anything else, were representative of social 'feeling rules' about how emotions could be expressed. Here they built on the work of sociologists and anthropologists, in particular the path-finding research of Arlie Russel Hochschild.[4] Individuals were thought to be effortfully grappling 'with conflicts between social demands and feeling'.[5] What a historian could see, when rooting through the archives, were not emotions per se, but the forms of expression that were possible in a given society. Causes could be given for the range of possible expressions, and effects of those expressions in different contexts could be analysed. To that end, these expressive forms seemed no less the purview of historians than anything else. They could be empirically researched, without any great methodological innovation.

The Stearns assigned the range of a society's available forms of expression a new name: 'emotionology'. The neologism was interchangeable with 'emotional style', and was purposefully meant to distinguish the outward forms of expression, what caused them and what social effects they had, from 'actual' emotions. The Stearns were troubled by a category confusion that mixed up expression

---

[3] P.N. Stearns, *American Cool: Constructing a Twentieth-century Emotional Style* (New York and London: New York University Press, 1994), 14.

[4] A.R. Hochschild, 'Emotion work, feeling rules, and social structure', *American Journal of Sociology*, 85 (1979): 551–75; A.R. Hochschild, *The Managed Heart: Commercialization of Human Feeling* (Berkeley and Los Angeles: University of California Press, 1983).

[5] Stearns and Stearns, *Anger*, 14.

with inward feelings. There could be no simple mapping of the language and gesture of expression, and the way it informed social relations, onto a biological appraisal of what emotions actually were and how they changed. In the early days of constructionist influence in the writing of history, such a slippage might have proven damaging indeed. Emotions themselves were, for the meantime, bracketed in favour of a focus on the ways in which social 'agencies and institutions either promote or prohibit certain kinds of emotions, while remaining neutral or indifferent to others'.[6]

Nevertheless, there was clearly a dynamic relationship between emotionology and emotions. The Stearns cautiously probed at that relationship, suggesting that the study of changes in emotional style could give way to new interpretations of real emotional change, providing the methodological approach was of the required standard. After all, 'emotionology, by shaping articulate expectations, does influence actual emotional experience'.[7] As they developed the concept, emotionology's import grew in stature. Emotionology 'affects behavior as well as judgment, and enters into the cognition by which individuals evaluate their emotional experience. In this sense, by producing affect about emotion – judgment, for example, that fear is pleasurable (as on a scary amusement ride) or objectionable – it enters into emotional experience directly.'[8]

The Stearns' prolific output saw the rapid blurring of the lines they had originally set out to demarcate, as emotionology seemed to be a powerful indicator of emotions or experience itself. Not only were emotions like jealousy and anger socially constructed, but any semblance of biological universality, which the Stearns did not necessarily refute, was of little explanatory use. Jealousy, for example, was 'capable of varied definitions depending on cultural context'.[9] Definitions helped delimit expressions, and expressions were dynamically hitched to feelings. Moreover, the meta-narrative of all the works of the Stearns together, and of Peter Stearns alone and with other collaborators, has stressed a shift towards emotional restraint in modern American history, and the assignation of virtue

---

[6] Stearns and Stearns, 'Emotionology': 813.
[7] Stearns and Stearns, *Anger*, 15.
[8] Stearns and Stearns [eds], *Emotion and Social Change*, 7.
[9] P.N. Stearns, *Jealousy: The Evolution of an Emotion in American History* (New York: New York University Press, 1989), 5.

to those who could master restraint.[10] Since restraint is a form of expression, but also inescapably a form of action to change how a feeling feels, the distance between emotional style and something like 'real' or 'actual' emotions collapses. Years of walking a fine line between nature and nurture, and between basic emotions and constructed emotions, seemed to be resolving into an amalgam of the two. Nobody experiences an emotion outside of an emotionology. There is no neutral or value-free experience of emotions: 'the distinction between precept and experience should not be drawn too sharply, for the two are always held in tension; the one is tested against the other, and each is understood only in the context of the other.'[11] They are always taking place somewhere and sometime, and those places and times always exerted some kind of effect. To that end, what was the use in continuing to separate style and substance? Emotions and emotionology were mutually implicated, inseparable and part of the same process.

Emotives

Enter William Reddy. Reddy was sceptical of what had come to be known as the 'basic emotions' model (see chapter 5), yet remained unconvinced by radical constructionists who seemed to throw out biology altogether. He formulated a new model of how emotional expression is intertwined with both social dynamics and inward feelings, so that emotional experience could be said to be the dynamic – that is, always changing and always in tension – product of all three: the 'emotive'. Reddy launched this idea as an anthropologist, and as a response to the constructionism of anthropologists. The title of this particular article, 'Against constructionism', might seem, on the face of it, to have aligned him with the universalists, but Reddy was actually transforming emotions research as a whole.[12] Nature/culture debates and mind/body debates were collapsed as false

---

[10] In addition to the references above, see P.N. Stearns, *Battleground of Desire: The Struggle for Self-Control in Modern America* (New York: New York University Press, 1999).

[11] J. Lewis and P.N. Stearns, 'Introduction', in P.N. Stearns and J. Lewis [eds], *An Emotional History of the United States* (New York: New York University Press, 1998): 1–14, at 2.

[12] W. Reddy, 'Against constructionism: The historical ethnography of emotions', *Current Anthropology*, 38 (1997): 327–51. Reddy developed the concept more fully

oppositions and, importantly, arguments that tried to occupy the middle ground by suggesting a mixture of nature and culture were found equally guilty of subscribing to the same dualist structure. In Reddy's view, there is no nature outside culture, and there is no culture outside nature. We are, as it were, biocultural. This goes beyond saying, as Daniel Lord Smail postulated, that 'there can be no nature without nurture, and vice versa';[13] it instead reconceptualises nature and nurture as a single category of analysis.

At the heart of this theoretical innovation, then, was a desire to put the body back into anthropological narratives and balance out the acrimonious split between radical views across the nature/culture divide. An emotive, in Reddy's terms, is an affective utterance. It represents an individual's attempt to translate inward feelings through cultural conventions in order to try to match the two. It is a process of navigation, finding a way to bring forth what one feels in accord with the expectations one is obliged to meet. Emotives emphasise the effort – the 'emotion work' – that an individual carries out in order to fit in with a given context. This emphasis on effort, context and translation is always, in Reddy's terms, to some extent a failure. Finding a precise accord between inward feeling and conventional expression is not possible, not least because the feeling and the utterance are not of the same order of thing. Every emotive is a failure and a source of suffering to some extent, because inward feelings are not capable of being expressed 'authentically'. As the distance between conventions of expression and inward feeling grows, so a sense of emotional suffering arises accordingly. In Reddy's own terms, emotive failure leads to the 'discovery of something unexpected about one's own feelings'.[14] Emotives feed back onto the body.

We should pause at this point to consider what might be meant by authenticity when it comes to emotional experience, and what it might mean to say that authenticity is impossible. There are, of course, dissenters to this view. In a recent volume on sympathy and

---

in his *The Navigation of Feeling: A Framework for the History of Emotions* (Cambridge: Cambridge University Press, 2001).

[13] Smail, *Deep History*, 119.

[14] Reddy, quoted in J. Plamper, 'The history of emotions: An interview with William Reddy, Barbara Rosenwein, and Peter Stearns', *History and Theory*, 49 (2010): 237–65, at 240.

emotional authenticity in the eighteenth century, it is clear that authenticity refers not so much to the reality, as opposed to the performance, of an experienced emotion, as it does to the validation of emotional expressions in the course of social exchanges.[15] In other words, prescription for emotional expression provides the basis for judging the authenticity of emotions in other people. Authenticity here clearly refers to conformity, and one could easily point to cases where historical actors are *satisfied* by their conformity, and in fact conform seemingly without knowledge of their emotive effort, and without consciousness of the prescribed norm. Socio-emotional harmony might be said to be a sign of authenticity, if we put authenticity in these terms.

Reddy would view this as a more or less successful emotive process. That we, as analysts positioned outside of the social exchange in question, can see the prescriptions that the actors cannot necessarily see allows us to appraise such processes as authentic in context, but not as *authentic* per se. It is the anthropologist's advantage, and the historian's too, to be able to step out to an etic position, the better to understand the emic. The category of authenticity, when used analytically, risks implying that there is an actual or real emotion there somewhere, or some biological constant, free of culture, waiting to be identified. Since emotive processes are always culturally bound, this notion of authenticity ceases to be useful.

This has another consequence, which is to collapse the distinction and/or the identification between authentic and performed display. In Reddy's terms, the emotion work done in an emotive process that aims to match expression to feeling is not performative and cannot be reduced to performance. Since an emotion statement (I would add, an expression or gesture, but I will come back to this) 'has a direct impact on the feelings in question', it cannot be understood as either a performance that in some way takes place irrespective of the inner feeling, or as a performance that essentially enacts the inner feeling.[16] Performing anger, for example, is

---

[15] H. Kerr, D. Lemmings and R. Phiddian [eds], *Passions, Sympathy and Print Culture: Public Opinion and Emotional Authenticity in Eighteenth-century Britain* (Houndmills: Palgrave, 2015).

[16] Reddy, 'Against constructionism': 331; cf. D. Martín Moruno and B. Pichel [eds], *Emotional Bodies: Studies on the Historical Performativity of Emotions* (Urbana-Champaign: University of Illinois Press, 2018); J. Moscoso, *Pain: A Cultural History* (Houndmills: Palgrave, 2012); E. Sullivan, *Beyond Melancholy: Sadness and Selfhood*

not simply equated, as a simplistic representation, to being angry. An anger-type feeling is put into the world according to the more-or-less strict terms and limits that exist for expressing anger at a given time and in a given place.[17] Such terms and limits can and do change enormously. The feeling in question is impacted by these prescriptive circumscriptions, so that one can never be truly said to be performing an emotion, since the performance is a way of measuring a feeling, which duly changes under those conditions. This might even hold good for those people, as in Arlie Russel Hochschild's work, who were under instructions to perform happiness, or another emotion. The effect of this performance was to change the experiential state of the performer, to the point that performance work was constitutive of feeling states, which in turn impacts the performance.[18] This would be better understood as an emotive process, where the employer's imperative to its employees to smile becomes a distinctly tangible emotional prescription.

Reddy is not going as far as to say that naming emotions, uttering them, tells a body how to respond or how to feel, but he does maintain that utterances do things to bodies and, in turn, bodies do things to utterances: 'There is an "inner" dimension to emotion, but it is never merely "represented" by statements or actions.'[19] Central to this process is a continual striving to make meaning out of sensory input, to add signification to stimulation. The more people make

---

in *Renaissance England* (Oxford: Oxford University Press, 2016); K. Barclay, 'Performance and performativity', in S. Broomhall [ed.], *Early Modern Emotions: An Introduction* (New York: Routledge, 2016), all of which emphasise performativity in emotional expression.

[17] Anger has produced a disproportionate number of works. See Stearns and Stearns, *Anger*; B. Rosenwein [ed.], *Anger's Past: The Social Use of an Emotion in the Middle Ages* (Ithaca: Cornell University Press, 1998); R. Barton, 'Gendering anger: *Ira, Furor* and discourses of power and masculinity in the eleventh and twelfth centuries', in R. Newhauser [ed.], *In the Garden of Evil: The Vices and Culture in the Middle Ages* (Toronto: Pontifical Institute of Mediaeval Studies, 2005); W.V. Harris, *Restraining Rage: The Ideology of Anger Control in Classical Antiquity* (Cambridge, MA: Harvard University Press, 2001); Y. Haskell, 'Lieven de Meyere and early modern anger management: Seneca, Ovid, and Lieven de Meyere's *De ira libri tres* (Antwerp, 1694)', *International Journal of the Classical Tradition*, 18 (2011): 36–65; M. Pernau, 'Male anger and female malice: Emotions in Indo-Muslim advice literature', *History Compass*, 10 (2011): 119–28.
[18] Hochschild, 'Emotion work'.
[19] Reddy, 'Against constructionism': 331.

meanings associated with given states, the more readily accessible those meanings become, leading to the *appearance* of effortlessness: a seemingly natural accord of emotion and expression. But since these utterances of emotions are made in conformity to cultural norms that are associated with and imposed by collective practices, there is always scope for the 'natural' emotion to feel 'wrong'. When contexts change, politically, institutionally, interpersonally, a person may no longer know how to give utterance to a feeling. If we think back to the literal meaning of the word 'emotion' as outward movement, here we see how it can make literal sense: in such a situation of contextual doubt, a person might not know how to get the movement *out*. Under such conditions, the effort of emoting suddenly re-appears, where once it seemed so natural.

Elsewhere I have described the potential result of complex changes in convention as leading to 'emotional crisis',[20] which was kindred to Hochschild's description of the 'marginal man', for whom there had been 'a change in the relation of feeling rule to feeling and a lack of clarity about what the rule actually is'.[21] When '[f]eelings and frames are deconventionalised, but not yet reconventionalised', a person may reflect that 'I don't know how I should feel'.[22] This has been explored at length for Renaissance England, in a work that reconceptualises emotional effort and emotives as 'emotional improvisation'. Erin Sullivan combines a language of expression with bodily gestures, where both utterances and bodily practices work to translate the ambiguity of passion concepts into something like meaningful experience. Where concepts were contested, so improvisational techniques varied, so that an individual might translate his feelings differently depending on whether he were faced with an intellectual, a medical man, a priest or a theatrical performance. Encounter and exchange determined what feelings felt like and supplied their social meaning and import. Only through the vagaries of emotional improvisation did historical actors 'find themselves', forge subjectivities and identities, and work out their shifting place in the world.[23]

---

[20] Boddice, 'Affective turn', 158–63.
[21] Hochschild, 'Emotion work': 567.
[22] Hochschild, 'Emotion work': 568.
[23] Sullivan, *Beyond Melancholy, passim*. Introduction of term 'emotional improvisation' at 1.

Hochschild's focus on physical expressions, such as the smile, in emotional labour should give us pause, as should the word 'action' in the quotation from Reddy above, which was under-developed in Reddy's original formulation of the emotive. It is essential to understanding how the field has developed along these lines. The relationship between feeling rules or prescriptions, emotionology in the Stearns' terms, and inward feelings has been extended by cultural theorists who, in turn, have also extended Reddy's limited focus on speech as emotive acts to the whole world of bodily expression and gesture. Sara Ahmed put it thus:

> emotions are not only about the 'impressions' left by others, but that they involve investments in social norms ... Injustice may work precisely through sustaining particular kinds of affective relations to social norms through what we do with our bodies. ... [C]hallenging social norms involves having a different affective relation to those norms, partly by 'feeling' their costs as a collective loss.[24]

This collective loss was described by Reddy as 'emotional suffering', a result of emotive failure (see below). I suggested in 2014 that criticisms of Reddy's speech-centred analysis might simply be resolved by including in his definition of 'utterance' all the bodily practices that come bundled with efforts to emote.[25] Reddy has also indicated the potential of taking this path, but imposed some important caveats. To conclude this section, I will look at the way in which emotives have developed and the potential for their future development, in particular in their intersection with practice theory. There is a great deal more to say with regard to practices and 'unconscious' expression, beyond what must be introduced here, a discussion that I will pick up in chapter 5.

As Reddy developed 'emotives', first through his *Navigation of Feeling*, and afterwards in line with an increasing interest in neuroscience, he accommodated it into practice theory.[26] This can be summarised as an extension of the statement that an emotive is 'an

---

[24] S. Ahmed, *The Cultural Politics of Emotion* (Edinburgh: Edinburgh University Press, 2004), 196.
[25] R. Boddice, review of *The History of Emotions: An Introduction* (review no. 1752), *Reviews in History*, www.history.ac.uk/reviews/review/1752, accessed 13 December 2016.
[26] Reddy, *Navigation*; Reddy, 'Saying something new': 8–23.

attempt to feel what one says one feels',[27] so as to render it thus: 'an emotive is an attempt to feel what one *does*'. Reddy has placed certain limits on the kinds of bodily practices that we might include in a broader definition of emotives. He is comfortable to expand the definition to include all verbal, gestural and facial expressions 'that derive from conscious, intentional "decisions" made in the full light of attention', but distinguishes these from 'other expressions that occur inadvertently or with only partial awareness'.[28] Utterances, however broadly conceived, are, in Reddy's terms, always 'managerial and exploratory', and therefore fall within the realm of 'conscious, direct decision-making', whereas things like shedding tears or blushing do not.[29]

In limiting the extent to which language can be, as it were, *automatic*, and emphasising a universal bodily automation that is or seems to be beyond the direct control of consciousness for most people, other scholars have found grounds for criticism. The tenor of this criticism risks the rejection of emotives altogether, but in reviewing some of this material I want to make a case for retaining emotives, even if it means departing from the limits Reddy has himself imposed on them. The foundation of this criticism is that even unconscious bodily and verbal gestures – what we might call instincts, reflexes and automatic processes – are subject to the world in which they are situated. This is not to re-state a radical social constructionism, but rather to collate empirical observations of bodily responses changing according to context and to formulate the idea that even automatic processes are 'worlded'.

Reddy's example of the blush is a good case in point. It is not up for debate here whether or not the blush is a physiological universal. Let us assume that it is. Nevertheless, the situations that elicit blushing are, quite manifestly, not universal. What causes a sense of embarrassed self-awareness – a state typically but not always associated with the blush – clearly depends on the internalisation of certain cultural norms, manners, customs, etc. That blushing often becomes more severe precisely when the blusher becomes aware of it and tries to manage it does not disqualify this physiological response from being part of an emotive process. The conditions

---

[27] Reddy, quoted in Plamper, 'Interview': 240.
[28] Reddy, quoted in Plamper, 'Interview': 241.
[29] Reddy, quoted in Plamper, 'Interview': 242.

under which a person blushes are directly related to a person's habitus, which refers to the way a person consciously and unconsciously embodies perceptions of their world. The term 'habitus' is most commonly associated with Pierre Bourdieu, and it is from this Bourdieusian perspective that the biocultural understanding of emotions has been extended.[30]

Let me exemplify the point, remaining with the blush, by turning to an example provided by Darwin. We can leave what Darwin thought about the meaning and function of expressions until another chapter, focusing for now on the importance attributed to blushing in context. Darwin was under no doubt whatsoever that the blush was a human universal, but he understood, after a fashion, that the circumstances and extent of a person's blushing depended on cultural habit. It had come, in his estimation, to be associated with moral conduct and shame, both of which could be clearly demonstrated to change over time. He gives the example of a 'sensitive person' who 'will sometimes blush at a flagrant breach of etiquette by a perfect stranger, though the act may in no way concern her', and even though the rules of etiquette were evidently historically transitory.[31] In a given place and time, etiquette appears to be fixed: social mores are loaded with moral qualities, such that breaches of etiquette become, as it were, moral transgressions. That a person might blush at such a breach, where the code itself is evidently constructed and might appear so even to the blusher, demonstrates the effect of habitus.[32]

The blush in such circumstances seems to me exactly to fit the definition of an emotive, for the blusher expresses something bodily – blushing is something a body *does* that can be considered a contextualised, if uncontrollable, bodily practice – that confronts her inner feelings with a social situation. In the process, feelings, embodiments and conscious utterances might be affected. Something managerial and exploratory is happening. And even though the universal blush occurs, it always does so according to

---

[30] The principal reference in question here is M. Scheer, 'Are emotions a kind of practice (and is that what makes them have a history)? A Bourdieuian approach to understanding emotion', *History and Theory*, 51 (2012): 193–220.

[31] C. Darwin, *The Expression of Emotions in Man and Animals* (London: John Murray, 1872), 335.

[32] See D.M. Gross, 'Defending the humanities with Charles Darwin's *The Expression of the Emotions in Man and Animals* (1872)', *Critical Inquiry*, 37 (2010): 34–59.

the kinds of things that make people blush in a given context. Nobody blushes outside culture.[33]

Emotional regimes, refuges, suffering

For emotive processes to make any sense, it was necessary for Reddy to formulate the thing that supplied and enforced the prescriptions for emotional expression: the element of power. Without it, it would not be possible to analyse what precisely was at stake in an emotive process. Inward feelings are checked against something, so what is it and from where does it come? Reddy's answer was the 'emotional regime'.

An emotional regime was variously defined in *The Navigation of Feeling*, according to the type of regime in question. The formal definition was given as follows: 'The set of normative emotions and the official rituals, practices, and emotives that express and inculcate them; a necessary underpinning of any stable political regime.'[34] The secondary clause here does not limit the definition to political regimes, but the word 'any' does give us some clue as to the breadth of emotional regimes possible. 'Strict' regimes 'require individuals to express normative emotions and to avoid deviant emotions'.[35] When such an emotional regime is aligned with a political regime, with its machinery of State, 'a limited number of emotives are modeled through ceremony or official art forms. Individuals are required to utter these emotives in appropriate circumstances, in the expectation that normative emotions will be enhanced and habituated.'[36] The effect for the population could be in one of three directions. The first is as follows:

---

[33] For more on the history of emotions and the contextualisation of the blush in particular, see O. Dror, 'Seeing the blush: Feeling emotions', in L. Daston and E. Lunbeck [eds], *Histories of Scientific Observation* (Chicago: University of Chicago Press, 2010), 326–48; P. White, 'Reading the blush', *Configurations*, 24 (2016): 281–301; A. Kay, '"A reformation so much wanted": Clarissa's glorious shame', *Eighteenth-century Fiction*, 28 (2016): 645–66; C. Castelfranchi and I. Poggi, 'Blushing as a discourse: Was Darwin wrong?', in W.R. Crozier [ed.], *Shyness and Embarrassment: Perspectives from Social Psychology* (Cambridge: Cambridge University Press, 1990), 230–51.
[34] Reddy, *Navigation*, 129.
[35] Reddy, *Navigation*, 125.
[36] Reddy, *Navigation*, 125.

Those who refuse to make the normative utterances (whether of respect for a father, love for a god or a king, or loyalty to an army) are faced with the prospect of severe penalties.[37]

The second possibility is one of emotive compliance, but with a high degree of personal emotive failure:

> Those who make the required utterances and gestures, but for whom the appropriate emotions are not enhanced or habituated, may seek to conceal their lack of zeal. If they are unsuccessful, they, too, face penalties. The penalties may come in the form of torture, aimed at extracting a change through induced goal conflict, or in the form of simple avoidance, confinement, deprivation, exile.[38]

The third possibility is emotive success:

> Many will find that the strict emotional discipline of their regime works well for them, shoring up a personal emotional management style that serves as the core of a coherent, rewarding way of life.[39]

These broad strokes that characterise emotional regimes writ large have proven especially influential for research on the ways in which political regimes, particularly autocratic regimes or dictatorships, ensure conformity not only in form but also in spirit.[40] The emotional regime allows us to understand how indoctrination shapes the reality of populations, so that emotional fealty to a political system feels natural, as it were, or else the penalties for failing emotionally to align with a political system induce such fear as to result in obedient outward displays and expressions of fealty.

---

[37] Reddy, *Navigation*, 125.
[38] Reddy, *Navigation*, 125.
[39] Reddy, *Navigation*, 125.
[40] I include here only a few examples. A delimited search for the term 'emotional regime' in Google Scholar will demonstrate the extraordinary range of use of this term, beyond the level of the State. But for State-related cases, see O. Rozin, 'Infiltration and the making of Israel's emotional regime in the state's early years', *Middle Eastern Studies*, 52 (2016): 448–72; H. Flam, 'The transnational movement for Truth, Justice and Reconciliation as an emotional (rule) regime?', *Journal of Political Power*, 6 (2013): 363–83; A. Tikhomirov, 'The regime of forced trust: Making and breaking emotional bonds between people and state in Soviet Russia, 1917–1941', *Slavonic and East European Review*, 91 (2013): 78–118; M. Caruso, 'Emotional regimes and school policy in Colombia, 1800–1835', in S. Olsen [ed.], *Childhood, Youth and Emotions in Modern History: National, Colonial and Global Perspectives* (Houndmills: Palgrave, 2015).

All of these effects of a strict emotional regime writ large might easily be transferred to a smaller, more tangible emotional regime with similar strictness confined to a certain space, place, time or context. For historians of emotions studying particular schools or school systems, youth groups such as the Scouts, military organisations of various descriptions and sizes, churches (at the local level) and Churches (including the vagaries of confessional differences), this formulation of how a strict emotional regime works has proven and will continue to prove useful. Both an understanding of how power is displayed and applied, and an understanding of how that power is experienced are to be gained from this analytical frame.

The word 'regime', however, tends to arouse images of strictness, to the point where it seems automatically to accord with some form of enforced disciplinary scheme, whether through violence or the implicit threat of violence. Indeed, it was the steady centralising process of the instruments and means of administering violence that lay at the core of Elias' argument about why the civilising process took the course it did. Nonetheless, it was not Reddy's initial intention to associate emotional regimes only with groups where the enforcement of emotional style was strict and resistance was a high-stakes move. On the contrary, Reddy argued that we all live (just as everyone has lived) in emotional regimes, in fact in multiple regimes at the same time. Moreover, he conceptualises 'loose regimes', or regimes of 'emotional freedom',[41] as well as those 'in the middle of the spectrum'.[42] In short, certain kinds of emotional prescription offer a wider latitude for emotives to take place, leading to a greater range of permitted or acceptable expressions in any given scenario.

In Reddy's construction of this landscape of emotional regimes, it is possible to judge what kinds of regime are more or less just, based on the amount of emotional suffering they bring about.[43] This part of the argument has been challenged by other historians, who question whether it makes any sense, on the one hand, to historicise emotions, and on the other hand to make a notion of justice ahistorical.[44] To understand Reddy's argument, and the

[41] Reddy, *Navigation*, 127.
[42] Reddy, *Navigation*, 128.
[43] Reddy, *Navigation*, 122–9.
[44] See especially the extended treatment in Plamper, *History of Emotions*, 261–5.

arguments against it, we must understand the concept of emotional suffering.

'Emotional suffering' does not define suffering in a universal way. It does not attempt to give a value to emotional pain that transcends history. Rather, this kind of suffering is a measure of the distance between the emotional style demanded from a particular regime and the amount of effort it takes to match inward feelings to that prescription. Where emotive failure is met with punishment of one form or another, be it direct physical punishment or indirect social punishment (such as ostracism), the cost of failure is high. Again, this does not determine the exact form of suffering, but merely marks out the consequences of failing to conform. In the example of a strict regime outlined above, there might be assumed to be a large degree of emotional suffering. But emotive failure is by no means limited to extreme political configurations. Indeed, Reddy gives as examples of emotional suffering both 'political torture' and 'unrequited love',[45] and points out that capitalist democracies limit the range of expression through 'contractual relationships (that is, by access to money and property)', where '[t]hose who depend on a single contractual relationship for their income and social identity ... are, in practice, severely limited in the types of emotional management strategies they may adopt – even though these strategies vary widely from one enterprise or household to another.'[46]

Where Reddy takes a more controversial step is to use these conceptual tools to make 'a defensible commitment to liberty'.[47] By liberty, again, he is not espousing a particular type of political configuration for society, but rather a measurement of the amount of emotional freedom an individual has in a particular society. The stricter the emotional regime, the greater the degree of emotional suffering. The more freedom an individual has to explore inward feelings so as to discover something about herself, without concern at the consequences of transgressing expression norms, the lesser the degree of emotional suffering. Or such is the theory. By this measure, Reddy proposes we judge emotional regimes: 'The only questions that need to be asked are, Who suffers? Is the suffering

---

[45] Reddy, *Navigation*, 129.
[46] Reddy, *Navigation*, 127.
[47] Reddy, *Navigation*, 130.

an unavoidable consequence of emotional navigation or does this suffering help to shore up a restrictive emotional regime? That is, is this suffering a tragedy or an injustice?'[48] Where it is unjust, in these terms, Reddy believes we can label it thus.

Historians in general recoil from the suggestion that such judgements can be made in anything other than the historical context of the regime in question. The post-modern turn may have largely collapsed in on itself, but one of the key legacies of constructionism that remains at the core of historiographical practice is that we do not write histories to praise and condemn in our own terms. This is not to advert to an overriding relativism that prevents us from saying anything substantial about anything, but rather to point to the advantages of historicism for assessing historical events, political systems, cultures, etc., according to their standards. By resisting anachronistic analytical positions, historians do not render themselves unable to make historical judgements. They are wary, however, of making judgements that will only serve to historicise *them*, rather than saying anything meaningful about history. As Jan Plamper has argued with reference to Reddy's theories:

> it is ... perplexing that the closest thing to Reddy's idea of emotional liberty is liberal democracy within a market economy and solid protection of minority rights, and that the transhistorical and transcultural position that Reddy has created so that it might once more be possible to establish persuasive political valuations turns out to match precisely the utopia that provides orientation to many progressive forces in Western democracies – namely, Reddy's own contemporary political reality.[49]

Emotional liberty, in short, seems to be too hitched to *liberty* per se, just as emotional suffering seems to call to mind an *anguish* recognisable by a contemporary American who considers himself to be free. In attempting to restore some political substance to anthropological theory in the wake of constructionist devastation, did Reddy not simply reinstate a meta-narrative of the kind that those constructionists would have happily and justifiably taken to pieces in short order?

A further criticism might be applied to the general framework

---

[48] Reddy, *Navigation*, 130.
[49] Plamper, *History of Emotions*, 262.

that ascribes virtue to emotional freedom. If one takes the view that the regime does not simply work on people's conscious or 'managerial' efforts to emote in the 'correct' way, but is cognitively constructive – that is, it forges new synaptic development in the brain and therefore works, as it were, unconsciously too – then even the most liberal regimes will present problems of emotional suffering caused by not knowing how to feel. To some extent, if one takes a neurohistorical point of view, humans have evolved in cultural settings that predispose them to respond to emotional prescription.[50] Where prescription is entirely missing, if one could hypothesise a situation entirely devoid of culture, it is difficult to imagine the humans there being free of emotional suffering. One could make the argument, then, that emotional prescription in stricter emotional regimes might actually lead to less emotional suffering if the prescriptions are largely met with emotive success. Such was the regime imagined by Francis Galton, pioneer of eugenics, who expected the population to succumb to a grand lie that would see them emotionally devote themselves to an ancestor cult that reinforced the precepts of eugenic breeding.[51] Postulating its success, one would be faced with the difficult dilemma of ascribing it a virtuous regime due to the lack of emotional suffering – people who would have suffered would be literally prevented from coming to be – while acknowledging that in the way it drew its national borders it was racist, and that in the way it led its population it was fundamentally corrupt.

The resolution, it seems to me, does not lie in trying to bridge the gap between universalism and constructionism so as to reinstate a plausible political orientation in the humanities. If, instead, we collapse the dualism entirely, then emotional bodies are always in a dynamic relationship with their specific context. Emotional suffering and emotional liberty become relative measures extrapolated from the experience of historical actors, not measures imposed by the historian. Historians do not particularly require a place from which to cast judgements about past regimes, because the history of emotions allows us insight into past experiences, which in turn allow us to judge the past in its own terms. But more to the point,

---

[50] See chapter 6 and Smail, *Deep History*.
[51] Such was the plot of Galton's unpublished novel. See Boddice, *Science of Sympathy*, 124–5.

historians' interest in the past has consistently been about understanding cause and effect, how things happened or came to be, or why things stayed the same or appeared to stay the same. To be able to get at the emotional experience of past actors, to find their motivations and reactions according to *how they felt*, is a great new device for understanding cause and effect, drilling down to things done in the name of feelings. The analysis of emotives in emotional regimes should not principally be about reaching judgement, but about reaching new understandings of past societies, gaining new insights along the way about our own.

The same applies for Reddy's other principal innovation that completes the picture of the elements of an emotional regime: the 'emotional refuge'. Reddy defines this as

> A relationship, ritual, or organization (whether informal or formal) that provides safe release from prevailing emotional norms and allows relaxation of emotional effort, with or without an ideological justification, which may shore up or threaten the existing emotional regime.[52]

In other words, the refuge is a 'place' where the prescriptions for emotional style apply only in their absence. At some level, the emotives that take place in the emotional refuge are still shaped and defined by the prescriptions from which the refuge is a hiding place. The very fact of containment implies the external framework against which this 'free' space is opposed. An emotional refuge might, as in the case of calendrical events like Hallowe'en, or the Shrovetide festivals (Mardi Gras, Carnival, etc.), serve to reinforce the dominant regime by allowing a safe and predictable subversion of it on a given day. Such a singular permissiveness works by the practice of emphasising all the things that are not normally allowed, thereby highlighting in the breach the presence of the established rules. An emotional refuge also allows for the sowing of emotional practices that, in principle, oppose the prescriptions of the larger regime. In either case, it is worth pointing out that refuges themselves fit the definition of emotional regimes.

Refuges can also be characterised by ritualistic practices that define and delimit them, and while they allow a certain release from another emotional regime, they also set terms on the emo-

[52] Reddy, *Navigation*, 129.

tive processes that can take place within them. A gentleman's club in nineteenth-century London might be said to be an emotional refuge from both the emotional regime of domesticity and the emotional regime of public life, but it nevertheless came with rather strict emotive expectations.[53] The emotional refuge of the cabaret in Weimar Germany might have shifted the boundaries of acceptable expressions of sexuality and gender identity, but in its re-drawing of the social frame it did not eliminate the social frame.[54] The church in Lutheran strongholds in Germany might have allowed a certain refuge from Catholic practices and power, but there is no question that reformed practices – such as the new semiology of bell-ringing – not only secured the new regime, but also clearly set into relief common knowledge of prevailing Catholic prescriptions.[55]

Emotional communities

The concept of 'emotional communities' belongs to Barbara Rosenwein, who has written extensively about such communities in medieval Europe.[56] It has been widely adopted, but with some uncertainty or lack of consistency about what is meant by it.[57] It is therefore useful to return to Rosenwein's original contribution and

[53] A. Milne-Smith, *London Clubland: A Cultural History of Gender and Class in Late-Victorian Britain* (Houndmills: Palgrave, 2011).
[54] M.J. Schmidt, 'Visual music: Jazz, synaesthesia and the history of the senses in the Weimar Republic', *German History*, 32 (2014): 201–23; J.S. Smith, *Berlin Coquette: Prostitution and the New German Woman, 1890–1933* (Ithaca: Cornell University Press, 2013).
[55] P. Hahn, 'The reformation of the soundscape: Bell-ringing in early modern Lutheran Germany', *German History*, 33 (2015): 525–45.
[56] Introduced to historians by B. Rosenwein, 'Worrying about emotions in history', *American Historical Review*, 107 (2002): 821–45; developed in B. Rosenwein, *Emotional Communities in the Early Middle Ages* (Ithaca: Cornell University Press, 2006) and Rosenwein, *Generations*.
[57] For its diversity in action, see, for example, A. Chaniotis, 'Emotional community through ritual: Initiates, citizens, and pilgrims as emotional communities in the Greek world', in A. Chaniotis [ed.], *Ritual Dynamics in the Ancient Mediterranean: Agency, Emotion, Gender, Representation* (Stuttgart: Steiner Verlag, 2011), 264–90; S.C. Bolton, 'Me, morphine, and humanity: Experiencing the emotional community on Ward 8', in S. Fineman [ed.], *The Emotional Organization: Passions and Power* (Oxford: Blackwell, 2008), 15–26; M. Jimeno, 'Lenguaje, subjetividad y experiencias de violencia', *Antípoda*, 5 (2007): 169–90.

her subsequent clarifications about what an emotional community is, how it is formed and why it is useful.

Rosenwein defined emotional communities in the clearest terms. They are:

> precisely the same as social communities – families, neighbourhoods, parliaments, guilds, monasteries, parish church membership – but the researcher looking at them seeks above all to uncover systems of feeling: what these communities (and the individuals within them) define and assess as valuable or harmful to them; the evaluations that they make about others' emotions; the nature of the affective bonds between people that they recognize; and the modes of emotional expression that they expect, encourage, tolerate and deplore.[58]

Unlike Reddy, Rosenwein keeps apart experience and representation, being principally interested in developing the Stearns' emotionology. The 'emotional standards' at the heart of that concept are, in Rosenwein's work, shown to be constructed at various social levels, in groups configured in any number of ways, and related to each other at various points of intersection. People live in more than one emotional community at a time, and sometimes in what she has called 'subcommunities'.[59] The norms and standards within each community compete at the individual level, with individuals adapting their emotional expressions according to context. Essential to this, however, is the view that any navigation between one emotional community and another must depend on the 'new emotional community's norms' not being 'radically different from the original'.[60] This makes it difficult to understand emotional navigation when radically different communities overlap (something that clearly happens throughout history), but I shall return to this point presently.

The emphasis on standards allows Rosenwein to keep a theoretical distance between expression (or performance) and experience. The question of authenticity or of experienced feelings are secondary to an exploration of the reasons for historical change in standards of expression in emotional communities.[61] By expression, Rosenwein limits herself almost entirely to the histori-

---

[58] Rosenwein, 'Worrying': 842.
[59] Rosenwein, *Generations*, 3.
[60] Rosenwein, 'Worrying': 842–3; Plamper, 'Interview': 256.
[61] Rosenwein, 'Problems': 1–32, at 21.

cal use of emotion words to track historical change, a criticism that she in turn levelled at William Reddy.[62] Other forms of expression – facial, gestural – are doubtless much more difficult to come by in medieval sources, but this notwithstanding, Rosenwein underlines the importance of words, emphasising that community norms are largely enforced through community vocabularies, and because we 'understand our "true feelings" via these words'.[63] She is, therefore, critically aware of the relationship between experience and expression, and makes a link between performance and the effect thereof on feelings, but the dyad of true feelings and expressed emotions remains implicit.[64]

The importance that Rosenwein ascribes to emotional communities lies in the way the concept opens up the study of emotional expression in ways not linked to politics, narrowly conceived. Rosenwein's career in the history of emotions has been consistently defined by an explicit circumspection about the linkage between emotions and politics, or emotions and the State. It is her principal reason for criticising Reddy's emotional regimes, for she understands the word 'regime' narrowly and literally to refer to the nation state or else strongly to imply such a reference.[65] The basis for this claim perhaps lies in Reddy's statement, in *The Navigation of Feeling*, which introduces emotional regimes for the first time: 'Any enduring political regime must establish as an essential element a normative order for emotions, an "emotional regime"',[66] as well as that secondary clause in his formal definition. The fuller account, however, even as it stands in that book without further clarification or qualification, clearly casts a wider net to include 'regimes that use such strict emotional discipline only in certain institutions (armies, schools, priesthoods) or only at certain times of the year or certain stages of the life cycle'.[67] Clearly then, the kinds of community with which Rosenwein deals were also, potentially, the kinds of regimes with which Reddy could have dealt (even though in the specific case study in *The Navigation of Feeling*, the regimes in

---

[62] See Plamper, 'Interview': 241.
[63] Rosenwein, *Generations*, 5.
[64] Rosenwein, *Generations*, 6.
[65] Rosenwein, 'Problems': 22.
[66] Reddy, *Navigation*, 124.
[67] Reddy, *Navigation*, 125.

question were of the absolutist political type. Rosenwein wants us to cast the net wider, and look at emotional communities at all levels of society.

Rosenwein's criticism of Reddy employs a narrow definition of the word 'politics'. Her works, after all, are shot through with the politics of emotion, by which I refer to the power structures that define and enforce the emotional standards that are the foundation of her analyses. There can be no question that the kinds of communities she principally deals with, which centre on courtly and religious elites, have dynamics of power running through them that provide a rationale for their vocabulary choices and usages. Her criticism of the concept of an emotional regime has, in turn, been countered by Reddy, who has demonstrated the capaciousness of that concept. Seemingly any social situation can have the hallmarks of an emotional regime, so long as emotional styles are enforced 'through penalties such as gossip, exclusion, or demotion'.[68] In Reddy's view, an emotional style becomes an emotional regime 'when the sum of the penalties and exclusions adds up to a coherent structure, and the issue of conformity becomes defining for the individual'.[69] In sum, anything that looks like an emotional community in Rosenwein's terms is probably also an emotional regime in Reddy's. The differences attributed to them pale in comparison to their similarities.

Both concepts could be pushed further, the substantial task of which I reserve for chapter 8 and the conclusion. For now, it remains only to say that what both concepts have in common is a tendency to be used for the analysis of emotives as they take place in social interactions. Whether letters between private correspondents or testimony given in court, what fundamentally unites emotional communities and emotional regimes is the necessity for emotions to be expressed or uttered *to* someone else. In part, this is a result of the way in which historical traces are left. We are not privy to private, solitary moments, unless they are recorded in diaries.

Nevertheless, following a clue left by Peter Gay about the need for history to explore the unconscious,[70] one might contend that

---

[68] Plamper, 'Interview': 243.
[69] Plamper, 'Interview': 243.
[70] Gay, *Freud for Historians*, 209.

an emotional community is not absent when an individual is left alone; an emotional regime does not cease to exert its power just because nobody is looking. Indeed, practice theorists might argue that the barrier between conscious and unconscious should be broken: there is no part of the mind that is not in the world, so there are no hidden recesses not subjected to the world. Habitus does not get switched on and off. Emotive processes – that presence of the social dynamic as we work out what we feel – are not removed, giving us access to something unalloyed or authentic, when we are by ourselves. To argue otherwise would go against much of what the history of emotions has become through the Stearns, Reddy and Rosenwein. The historian of private life, therefore, has the possibility of digging deeper into a literal formulation of those words. For what happens in private – those things we read about in diaries, letters never sent, autobiographical writing and so on – is no less of a social barometer of emotional prescription than what happens in social interactions. Emotional communities are not, therefore, 'precisely the same as social communities', or at least not only so; emotional communities are embodied, internalised, always acting on our efforts to emote. In that way, they share much in common, and might be considered conceptually equivalent to, emotional regimes (when denuded of the value-judgement component that Reddy wants to extract from them).

Emotional communities have proven to be enormously influential among historians of emotion in the last few years, with much uncritical appropriation of the bare label and some critical re-working of it. Mark Seymour, for example, argued that 'apparently divergent emotional communities could overlap in unexpected and alarming ways', illuminated by the institutions of bureaucracy and power exemplified by courts of law.[71] That was part of a wider project demonstrating individual range in emotional styles, where apparent contradictions and incommensurabilities are given their due plausibility.[72] The boundaries of emotional communities are, once one begins to probe them, revealed to be porous, amorphous and might be conceived of differently from one individual to the next.

---

[71] M. Seymour, 'Emotional arenas: From provincial circus to national courtroom in late nineteenth-century Italy', *Rethinking History*, 16 (2012): 177–97, at 192.

[72] B. Gammerl [ed.], 'Emotional Styles – Concepts and Challenges', special issue of *Rethinking History*, 16 (2012).

The emotional community might be more an imagined phenomenon of the historian than at first glance. Susan Broomhall preferred to talk in terms of 'socialities', where emotional prescription defined the experience of those implicated in a given space – physical or conceptual – whether or not they belonged.[73] Work on the history of childhood has also pushed analysis of the unstable contingency of emotional communities, setting out to revise and replace the concept (see chapter 7).

For her part, Sara Ahmed arrived at a different understanding of emotional collectives, attempting to explore 'how feelings make "the collective" appear *as if* it were a body in the first place'.[74] Explicitly, in this case, a community is *forged* on common feelings, which is to say that it appears 'only as an effect' of 'how we feel about others' who may or may not 'belong', but who are nonetheless imagined.[75] Alignments with collectives take people – and this is by no means only a recent phenomenon – beyond their immediate locales. 'Community' loses some of its traction when we think of those emotional collectives that hang together by means other than face-to-face contact, and sometimes because of a lack of such contact.

Putting the analysis this way around begs the question of whether communities are bound by emotional styles in common, or whether emotional styles emerge through a perception and practice of commonality that is formed epistemologically prior to affective ties. Do citizens of the Classical world, or Enlightenment men of letters, or white supremacists in the contemporary United States come together because they partake in a shared emotional experience, or does that shared emotional experience follow assumptions of connectedness and the experience of connection? As with Rosenwein and Reddy, Ahmed puts the individual and the social together in a dynamic relationship, but goes further. Rather than envisaging an internal feeling and an external feeling rule or prescription, she perceives that emotional movement gives effect to 'the very

---

[73] S. Broomhall, 'Introduction', in S. Broomhall [ed.], *Spaces for Feeling: Emotions and Sociabilities in Britain, 1650–1850* (London: Routledge, 2015), 2–3.

[74] S. Ahmed, 'Collective feelings: Or, the impressions left by others', *Theory, Culture and Society*, 21 (2004): 25–42, at 27; cf. Broomhall, 'Introduction', in Broomhall [ed.], *Spaces for Feeling*, 1.

[75] Ahmed, 'Collective feelings': 27.

distinction between inside and outside'.[76] In other words, emotional interaction with others is prior to and causative of distinctions between internal and external. Such concepts are the effect of figuring out what emotional interaction means and feels like. They are a sign of the impression left.

Historians might feel that such a position is less useful for them. After all, the historian of emotions does not typically have emotion itself as the end in mind, but rather what emotions *do* in society. Yet this is the direction in which Ahmed tends. Conceptualisations of inside and outside, of what emotions are based on how they feel, leads to social claims and practices that are the effect of epistemological claims. Put another way, if I 'know' something, I act on that 'knowledge' accordingly. If you understand how I come to 'know' what I claim to know, you can understand my motivations, my movements, my alignments and why I call my 'community' my community. Ahmed explains her theory with a mind on present-day power dynamics and social configurations. Following her method, finding the different effects of interaction and movement on the knowledge claims of past actors, has enormous potential for historical research. Such research would reach beyond the evidence Rosenwein pieces together for different kinds of emotional community at different times and places, to the reasons *why* those communities look like communities. What makes them align, and against whom? What makes them, over time, become unaligned or differently aligned? Ahmed might argue that emotional communities are surfaces, or bounded spaces, and that the real question is through what precise sequence of sensation, evaluation, translation and experience such surfaces appear. Emotional communities, by such a reckoning, are effects. They are not, in and of themselves, analytic entities, but descriptive ones.

[76] Ahmed, *Cultural Politics*, 10.

4

POWER, POLITICS AND VIOLENCE

Historical narratives, if we consider the sweep of historiography from, say, Ranke to Richard Evans, have tended to rely on a stark opposition when dealing with public matters. The remit of history was originally to document the dynamics of public life, and public life was the sphere of reason. There was no place for emotion, which derailed politics. Where it cropped up it was easily identifiable as an aberration: an unwelcome diversion that usually plunged polities into catastrophe. Strictly speaking, historical practice was bound up, for most of the discipline of history's existence, with the search for reasonable thoughts and reasonable practices. Intellectual history was based upon this premise, as were political and diplomatic history and the history of science and/or knowledge. As the discipline of history began to give way, from the 1960s, to new focuses on women, the family and children, so emotions were given due attention. But with the 'domestic' of the private sphere being enshrined as the realm of emotions, the original opposition between reason and emotion was preserved.

These oppositions, between public and private, and between reason and emotion, have been collapsing in on each other for the last several decades of historical research. It is safe to say, however, that the collapse of the former of these two dualities is much more advanced than the latter. The distinct ideological and intellectual separation of public and private, home and work, male and female, has been replaced by more complex understandings of entanglement and social navigation.[1] There remains much to do to bring

---

[1] D. Goodman, 'Public sphere and private life: Toward a synthesis of current historiographical approaches to the old regime', *History and Theory*, 31 (1992): 1–20; for a general review and thoughtful revision, see S. Gal, 'A semiotics of the

the reason/emotion split into line with these new developments, and this involves two distinct projects. The first is the pursuit of a general collapse of the distinction between reason and emotion per se, a project that has attracted significant and long-standing attention in the disciplines of philosophy, phenomenology and anthropology. There is a risk, however, that in asserting the role of emotion in reason – 'cogmotion', or something like 'emotional intelligence' – we nevertheless essentialise this new object of knowledge.[2] Remember that the history of emotions is not searching for a master category that can be universally applied, but rather for both conceptual and experiential flexibility. Any model of the emotions that fixes the object of our research will inevitably limit it.

The second project, therefore, is to examine the ways in which emotional intelligence has worked in context and in practice, to identify it even where historical actors might not have and to demonstrate the extent to which historical understandings of the reason/emotion divide have had a material effect on the experience of both reason and emotion in public and private life.

The model for this approach has been pioneered in the history of science by Lorraine Daston and Peter Galison. At the heart of their book, *Objectivity*, is a claim that the practice of science is affective, even when the claims staked for that practice are antithetical to affect. To clarify, Daston and Galison demonstrate that allusions to the objectivity of scientific practice as a core tenet of scientific *neutrality* are political, masking the affective behaviour of and among scientists, and enabling them to present their procedures and results as morally valueless.[3] Daston and Galison

public/private distinction', *Differences: A Journal of Feminist Cultural Studies*, 12 (2002): 77–95.
[2] For 'cogmotion', see D. Barnett and H.H. Ratner, 'The organization and integration of cognition and emotion in development', *Journal of Experimental Child Psychology*, 67 (1997): 303–16; for a slight revision, see J. Plamper, 'Ivan's bravery', in U. Frevert *et al.*, *Learning How to Feel: Children's Literature and Emotional Socialization, 1870–1970* (Oxford: Oxford University Press, 2014), 191–208, at 204–5. Emotional intelligence has been variously defined. See J.D. Mayer and P. Solovey, 'The intelligence of emotional intelligence', *Intelligence*, 17 (1993): 433–42; D. Goleman, *Emotional Intelligence* (New York: Bantam, 1995).
[3] L. Daston and P. Galison, *Objectivity* (New York: Zone Books, 2007). See also B. Latour, *Science in Action: How to Follow Scientists and Engineers through Society* (Cambridge, MA: Harvard University Press, 1987); P. Bourdieu, *Homo academicus* (Palo Alto: Stanford University Press, 1988); T. Kuhn, *The Structure of Scientific*

demonstrate the influence of context, of assumptions, of exclusions and of emotions throughout scientific recording procedures that, if taken at face value, purport to depend only on reason, detachment and an ethos of recording 'nature' as it is, as opposed to offering an interpretation of it. Science, the arena of reason par excellence, is shown to be shot through with suppressed affective and emotional qualities that help shape and define this particular definition and practice of reason. Moreover, the history of science inevitably contains evidence of the affective nature of reason, for practices carried out in the name of reason change over time; what may once have been justified as reasonable looks, from the vantage point of hindsight, to be its very opposite. In sum, practitioners practise in the name of being right and in the name of being reasonable, even if they are neither.[4] The advantage that the historian of emotion has is to penetrate those practices and to analyse those experiences, introducing a range of reflection that was not available to the original actor. We do not merely judge an actor on what he says that he thinks or feels, but also on what he does and does not do because of those thoughts and feelings. We can see his expressions, his gestures, his actions, his procedures in the context of his peers, his forebears and his successors, exposing his assumptions and his beliefs, which he may not himself have recognised as such.[5]

This kind of analysis is important not only to enable us to reach further into the particulars of the history of experience, but also to study the way in which power dynamics function with the tacit compliance of those who exercise power. Objectivity is a perfect example of this. Science receives its social status from its knowledge claims. Not only have scientists possessed uncommon knowledge, but they have claimed this knowledge is untainted by ideology or political bias. The practice of science has therefore been supposed by many of its practitioners to be non-doctrinaire, undogmatic, merely procedural, banal. If its postulations, theories and results

---

Revolutions (Chicago: University of Chicago Press, 1962); B. Strasser, 'The experimenter's museum: GenBank, natural history, and the moral economies of biomedicine', *Isis*, 102 (2011): 60–96.

[4] See Boddice, *Science of Sympathy*, 137–43.

[5] See the editors' introduction: O. Dror, B. Hitzer, A. Laukötter and P. León-Sanz [eds], 'History of science and the emotions', *Osiris*, 31 (2016): 1–18.

are not to everyone's taste, then it is up to those people to reconcile themselves with what simply *is*. Put another way, science in these terms cannot be reasonably opposed to something like religion, because they are not commensurate objects. Science is a matter of fact; religion is a matter of belief. That kind of opposition has proven enormously problematic, and indeed many scientists are increasingly aware of the contextual and temporal nature of their knowledge claims.[6] This is not to say that science, after all, really is a form of belief (though there are historical examples of this kind of scient*ism*), but that its practices, procedures and operating logic are mutable. It is as much subject to affective and constructionist analysis as belief, or anything else. Such an analysis aims to get to the heart of how science's knowledge claims (or religion's, for that matter) give it the power to influence what society more broadly considers – *feels* – to be true. It looks at the structure of authority, not only in ideas, but also in the way those ideas are presented to, or packaged for, the public.[7] It aims to understand how emotional norms, emotional styles, emotional regimes, etc. are prescribed and, in implicit and explicit ways, enforced.

The importance of this kind of analysis goes beyond systems of knowledge and systems of belief, to the core of political power at every level. It was the impetus behind Norbert Elias' work on the changing codes of etiquette in European courtly culture. Even if we choose to discard Elias' theories about the ways in which such codes were appropriated, internalised and practised, the relationship between 'psychogenesis' and 'sociogenesis' – the central truth of his narrative – must stand: the way people feel is inherently tied to the way people practise (bodily and socially), and the way people practise is inherently tied to the prescriptions of the powerful. That power may or may not come with the threat of real or symbolic violence.[8] It might be positively construed, such as that power that elicited 'ennobling love' among aristocracies.[9] In whatever

---

[6] For a general introduction to debates in this field, see T. Dixon, *Science and Religion: A Very Short Introduction* (Oxford: Oxford University Press, 2008).
[7] See Gross, *Secret History*, for a critical appraisal of science's knowledge claims about emotion. For a general introduction to what is at stake in the history of knowledge, see P. Burke, *What is the History of Knowledge?* (Cambridge: Polity, 2016).
[8] Elias, *Civilizing Process*, 402.
[9] Jaeger, *Ennobling Love*.

way emotions are expressed and intended, there is no getting away from their intrinsic sociality. In Joanna Bourke's terms, 'emotions ... mediate between the individual and the social. They are about power relations. Emotions lead to a negotiation of the boundaries between self and other or one community and another.'[10] Lest the objection be raised that emotional experiences often happen alone, in private, it should be remembered that there is no such thing as a neutral context, no place outside social relations. Being alone does not remove a person from the processes Bourke describes. It may provide opportunities for the expression of subversive or transgressive emotions, thoughts, gestures and so on, but the simple fact that an individual by herself still *knows* what constitutes subversion and transgression speaks to the fact that the dynamics of the emotive process are always there.

Lost emotions

Understanding the power structures that make emotional prescriptions also allows us to understand one of the ways that those prescriptions change. While it could be argued that a swelling tide of emotional suffering could precipitate political or regime change – this is the basis of William Reddy's argument in *The Navigation of Feeling*, for example – it is also likely, and perhaps more frequent, that changes in the structure of power have the effect of ushering in new economies of feeling.

By and large, historians have tended to be interested in how new things came about. They chart reform and revolution, discovery and innovation. Occasionally, they wonder how something came to disappear.[11] On the whole, however, they dwell on replacements rather than the thing replaced. The history of emotions differs fundamentally in this respect, for while it does ask about the emergence of new emotions or emotional regimes, as well as charting shifting trends in emotional styles, it is also motivated to reconstruct what was lost. In part, this motive is political. If historians can provide evidence for emotional experiences that no longer

---

[10] J. Bourke, 'Fear and anxiety: Writing about emotion in modern history', *History Workshop Journal*, 55 (2003): 124.

[11] A salient example might be G. Dangerfield, *The Strange Death of Liberal England* (1935; Palo Alto: Stanford University Press, 1997).

exist, then this goes some way to providing an empirical argument against biological determinists as well as shoring up a role for historians in emotions research in general. But the broader motive is intellectual. It does not ask, as with Whiggish narratives, how have we come to be. Rather, it asks what has been left behind, excluded, overwritten and written out of the story, so that what came to pass could happen. In contradistinction to much of the history of historiography, histories of emotions do not tend to begin with an assumption about what human nature is. They do not apply coolly rational and abstract narratives of political change to their timelines, and nor do they assume an irrational emotionality where 'reason' seems to be absent. In short, these histories do not assume to know or to understand their actors on *our* terms. Their driving assumption is that an understanding of the past is derived from a reconstruction of the ways in which past actors experienced and understood their own times. Historians of emotion prefer the risk of partial misunderstanding, or the inability to fully enter into the reality of the past, to an assumption of objectivity and the risk of anachronism.

Finding 'lost' emotions helps us work out *why* people did what they did. This is the holy grail of historical enquiry. We all know that, in our own worlds, actions are often justified on the basis that they 'felt' right at the time, which is a shorthand way of saying that all kinds of factors were weighed in the balance until a general impression was reached that this, and not that, should happen. We call it a gut feeling, or intuition, or something similar. It is, ultimately, a *feeling* comprised of cognition, sensation, experience and emotion. It is so common that one scans the historiographical field with some surprise that such things have not played a major part in historical reasoning until recently. Moreover, if we can find emotions that have become lost, we can perhaps say something new about the power dynamic that caused them to disappear. Lost emotions, therefore, have a double explanatory power. They tell us about the affective backdrop of historical practices, and they help illuminate how emotional prescription works.

Two prominent historians of emotion independently arrived at the notion of recovering lost emotions. In 1999 C. Stephen Jaeger wrote a long history of the lost emotion of 'ennobling love', as mentioned above, and in 2011 Ute Frevert's Natalie Zemon Davis lectures were published as *Emotions in History – Lost and*

Found.[12] For Frevert, the principal lost emotion in question was honour. In both cases, it is abundantly clear that these emotions were bound up intimately and intrinsically with dynamics of power and social practice, where the outward display of the presence of these emotions was an essential component of a social relationship with power and the maintenance of social order. In the case of ennobling love, the effect of majesty (of a king, a religious leader or an aristocrat) was to inspire a series of bodily practices and public statements of awe that took the specific form of love entwined with ambition. The embodied affective response to the person of power was to pour forth tributes of affection, fidelity and subservience. It was distinct from, and in many ways prior to, romantic love, being a dynamic between men primarily and a relation related to virtue rather than to sex. Curiously, Jaeger describes it as being 'primarily a way of behaving, only secondarily a way of feeling'.[13] It is clear, nonetheless, that this highly public experience was not simply a performance, and I think in the years since Jaeger published his book we might have collapsed the distance or the difference between behaving and feeling. This much is evident in his own description or definition of ennobling love:

> It is a form of aristocratic self-representation. Its social function is to show forth virtue in lovers, to raise their inner worth, to increase their honor and enhance their reputation. It is, or is seen as, a response to the virtue, charisma, saintliness of the beloved ...[14]

We must be careful that the reference to social function does not evacuate the meaningfulness of this experience. Showing virtue is an affective display. Raising one's inner worth is a direct engagement in an emotive process. And increasing honour and enhancing reputation might both be thought of as improving the way one feels about oneself according to one's appraisal of how others feel in one's regard. Jaeger is extremely careful to eliminate 'modern conceptions' of sexuality in order to reconstruct this love in its full historical unfamiliarity.[15] It allows him both to see why aristocratic

---

[12] U. Frevert, *Emotions in History: Lost and Found* (Budapest: Central European University Press, 2012).
[13] Jaeger, *Ennobling Love*, 6.
[14] Jaeger, *Ennobling Love*, 6.
[15] Jaeger, *Ennobling Love*, 7.

relations played out the way they did, in sentiments seemingly private but in fact irrevocably public, as well as exploring the ways in which this kind of love was destabilised and (almost entirely) destroyed by the shifting tides of gender relations, the politics of virtue and the vagaries of sex and sexual love.

Without realising she was pursuing the same ends (Jaeger is not referenced in her work), Nicole Eustace nevertheless constructed a similar argument in her monumental book on American colonial passions up to the revolution in 1776. Love and marriage are demonstrated to be public affairs, bound up with social status and ambition, and related to communal conceptions of the self, where what was good for the individual was secondary, if considered at all, to the good of the commonwealth. In a way, however, Eustace confirms the argument of Jaeger, because in all of her eighteenth-century examples, the politics of marriage and the public nature of love are complicated by gender dynamics and, implicitly, by sex. Female status in society in the eighteenth century was absorbed and nullified by marriage, just as a man's status might be enhanced by it, thus highlighting what Jaeger calls the 'romantic dilemma' or reconciling 'virtue with sex'.[16] A socially ambitious woman, cultivating a new and individual sense of self, would find it difficult if not impossible to reconcile that ambition with marriage in this context. Marrying out of a sense of private, romantic love, might also lead to loss of status because of the poor social optics of an 'ill-conceived match'. As conceptions of the self – individual and collective – competed, so too did private and public practices of love. The sweeping away of ennobling love in the context described by Eustace, of the love for the colonial authority of the King, and those men and those institutions that represented the King, allowed the landscape of public love to change. The kind of socially arranged marriages and alliances of that period scarcely exist today, and we struggle to see the declared love of those unions as *real* love. It is precisely at these moments of incredulity, when we tacitly reassert some notion of stable emotional authenticity, that we need to jettison our assumptions and try to build a picture of what that kind of emotion was really like.

A whole host of works on different lost, or at least unfamiliar, emotions has cropped up in recent years, with particular emphasis

---

[16] Eustace, *Passion*, 107–50; Jaeger, *Ennobling Love*, 7.

on the ways in which experience is refracted by power or authority. While Frevert fully developed an argument about the loss of honour as an emotion, Andreas Holger Maehle re-cast the honour question in a different mode and implied its survival as an emotion in a different and more bureaucratically managed form.[17] David Konstan famously charted the fortunes of the Greek and Latin concepts of 'pity' – *eleos, oiktos, misericordia* – noting the ways in which these concepts depended on an asymmetry of power relations between the one who pitied and the one who received pity, observing along the way that 'multiple meanings inhabit' our 'emotional lexicon'. That fact that we call these things 'pity', among other things depending on the context, and that the original words have not been carried into modern English (unlike many other Greek and Latin terms, preserved almost unchanged) suggests both something preserved and something likewise lost.[18]

Gender, class, politics

The history of gender is the history of power. This is not the place to survey the historiography concerning gender throughout history, save to point to some places where gender history usefully intersects with the history of emotions. The question, for historians of emotion, is to what extent emotions or things like emotions were employed as conceptual and experiential markers of difference between men and women. In other words, to what extent did a biologically determined concept of emotions underwrite narratives of sex differentiation and the kinds of social and political exclusions that were based on such differentiations? It has now become commonly understood that biological particularities have commonly been employed to emphasise identity categories, conflating sex with gender. The body as a biological constant has consistently been used to the social and political advantage of those who would try to frame metrics of strength and weakness, resoluteness and instability, abstract intelligence and intellectual limits. Bodily differences have not only been limited to sex organs, but to brain sizes and differences in its quality, as well as bodily organisation and stat-

---

[17] Frevert, *Men of Honour*; A.-H. Maehle, *Doctors, Honour and the Law: Medical Ethics in Imperial Germany* (Houndmills: Palgrave, 2009).
[18] D. Konstan, *Pity Transformed* (London: Duckworth, 2001), 19.

ure.[19] What a woman is, has, throughout history, been reducible to the (imagined) qualities of a woman's body.

Hence we see the political significance of those who claim that the emotions too are embodied, biological constants, especially if those constants are construed differently in differently sexed bodies. For much of modernity, well into the twentieth century, biological science saw the embodied emotions of women as of a different order of being to the emotions of men. They were differently seated, differently experienced and differently expressed. As a rule, women were thought to be more subject to emotional upheaval, more likely to be overcome by irrational outbursts, and less likely to be able to manage emotional stress. To that end, women were thought to be incapable of enduring higher education because their emotional dispositions would be overwhelmed by it.[20] Their physical, bodily limitations could be damaged by such masculine pursuits, leading to madness or infertility, or dangerous radicalism. While those views were perhaps peculiar to Europe and America in the nineteenth and early twentieth centuries, they express a much longer story of gendered dynamics of power wherein female inferiority was connected to her emotional state.

Evidence for this can be seen in the so-called age of sensibility in eighteenth-century Europe, coupled with the rise of the sentimental novel that could, reputedly, reduce women to passionate wreckage.[21] Evidence can also be found in classical antiquity, where women were removed from public life, subjected to an overt and explicit rule of the phallus, and reminded of their own passionate deficiencies by reference to the troubling tendency of wombs to wander.[22] That remarkable theory, traceable to Hippocrates in the fifth century BCE, was renewed and re-invigorated by Galen in the second century CE, and remained a central tenet of Galenic medicine even until the nineteenth century.[23] While many cases of hysteria (the label

---

[19] A review of the literature is in Boddice, 'Manly mind'; see also, Bourke, *What It Means*; S. Arnaud, *On Hysteria: The Invention of a Medical Category Between 1670 and 1820* (Chicago: University of Chicago Press, 2015).
[20] See Boddice, 'Manly mind'.
[21] The classic text is G.J. Barker-Benfield, *The Culture of Sensibility: Sex and Society in Eighteenth-century Britain* (Chicago: University of Chicago Press, 1992).
[22] See E.C. Keuls, *The Reign of Phallus: Sexual Politics in Ancient Athens* (Berkeley: University of California Press, 1993).
[23] For general approaches, see M.S. Micale, *Approaching Hysteria: Disease and Its*

that we now associate with an emotional breakdown literally refers to the wandering womb) in the post-Enlightenment period were not ascribed to the physical movement of the uterus, such typically female outbursts of uncontrolled emotions were often ascribed to that organ, or else to something to do with female sexuality inherent to the female body.[24] The history of madness, on the one hand, and the history of those people and institutions that would cure madness, on the other, are, in part at least, implicitly about the emotional capacities (or the intellectual capacity to control emotions) of gendered bodies and the extent to which they can be trained, explained, managed, manipulated and medicated.

The possibilities for the opening up of histories of, for example, psychoanalysis and psychiatry, to a history-of-emotions perspective are already being extensively explored.[25] The asymmetry of power between therapist and patient is well known, as are the complex gender dynamics of the asylum, the clinic and the couch. The history of emotions' focus on the ways in which prescriptions are formed by powerful agents and projected onto other bodies who are bound to conform adds an extra facet to this kind of approach. Where analysis worked on the assumption of a universal body and a universal embodiment of emotions and emotional pathology, the history of analysis can deconstruct this narrative to show how gendered dynamics of power were in part built around imposed emotional frameworks.

Analytical authority is revealed to be based upon a conception of a normative emotional style, which it embodied in itself and measured in others in comparison to itself. We can, therefore, see a theory of universal emotions in one of its historical attitudes and chart its change over time. Moreover, we can re-read patient

---

Interpretations (New Jersey: Princeton University Press, 1995); A. Scull, *Hysteria: The Biography* (Oxford: Oxford University Press, 2009); Arnaud, *On Hysteria*; S.L. Gilman, H. King, R. Porter, G.S. Rousseau and E. Showalter [eds], *Hysteria Beyond Freud* (Berkeley: University of California Press, 1993).

[24] See R. Boddice, 'Hysteria or tetanus? Ambivalent embodiments and the authenticity of pain', in Martín Moruno and Pichel [eds], *Emotional Bodies*.

[25] U. Jensen, 'Freuds unheimliche Gefühle. Zur Rolle von Emotionen in Freudschen Psychoanalyse', in U. Jensen and D. Morat [eds], *Rationalisierungen des Gefühls: Zum Verhältnis von Wissenschaft und Emotionen 1880–1930* (Paderborn: Wilhelm Fink, 2008), 135–52; R. Hayward, 'Enduring emotions: James L. Halliday and the invention of the psychosocial', *Isis*, 100 (2009): 827–38.

testimony and experience to demonstrate the effect of emotive effort in the clinical setting, as well as its broader social implications.[26] Nowhere is the expression of an emotional orthodoxy more precisely stated and located than in the works of those who claimed to treat emotional disorders. As a temperature test for emotional style in different periods and different places, as well as for a clear impression of the way in which emotional prescriptions are deployed and enforced, we could do worse than to look at the records of different types of alienist, asylum, psychiatrist and psychoanalyst. In such places we find clear expressions of what it looks like when emotions have gone 'wrong', and their tendency to be gender-associated with femininity, which is also a perfect indicator for what historical actors believed to be emotionally 'correct', and its association with masculinity.[27]

The history of emotions also complicates and augments masculinity studies more generally, especially in its disruption of a vast body of historiographical work that implicitly or explicitly associated masculinity with power, and power with reason. Whether one looks at the historical record itself, or at the works that historians have made out of it, it is striking the extent to which reason is opposed to emotion, where the former is linked to masculine powers of abstract thought, governance and leadership, and the latter is connected to feminine irrationality, weakness, the suitability of women for domestic roles and their lack of capacity for a more masculine public sphere. While gender historians have, for several generations now, unpicked and laid bare the injustices of such a view, along with the structures of patriarchal power that allow such a view to prevail, it is only recently that historians have been able to borrow from emotion sciences a new understanding of cognition that destroys the reason/emotion duality.[28] The result promises further revisions to the history of masculinity that will re-appraise masculine reason as an affective gendered practice.[29]

---

[26] See, in particular, S.L. Gilman, 'The image of the hysteric', in Gilman *et al.* [eds], *Hysteria*, 345–452.

[27] M.S. Micale, *Hysterical Men: The Hidden History of Male Nervous Illness* (Cambridge, MA: Harvard University Press, 2008).

[28] Stearns was probably the first historian to make this claim. See Stearns, *American Cool*, 14.

[29] See, for example, E.L. Milam and R.A. Nye [eds], 'Scientific masculinities', *Osiris*, 30 (2015).

We can say with some certainty that the process of cognition always involves affective behaviour. There is general agreement on this across the disciplines, even if the precise configuration is disputed.[30] The separation of reason from emotion, as if reason were somehow intellectually pure, is no longer supportable. Indeed, the expression of level-headedness, equanimity or coolness in cognitive processes – essentially the old cliché about making decisions with the head and not the heart – is in fact as affectively involved as any other expression. Peter Stearns argued precisely this as long ago as 1994 in *American Cool*, noting that emotions 'relate to the cognitive processes in that they involve thinking about one's own impulses and evaluating them as an intrinsic part of the emotional experience itself'.[31] And it is not as if affect and reason, combined with the recall of experience, the processing of symbols and the body's own states of arousal, are separate and distinguishable processes in the brain and body. Rather, they each are formed of and through the others, so that in reason there is always already affect and experience.[32] Psychologists coined the word 'cogmotion', a portmanteau label combining cognition and emotion, to reflect new understandings of the role of affect in cognition.[33] The concept of reason thereby becomes decodable as an emotional prescription, expressed in a variety of ways over time, which tends to demarcate those who are powerful from those who are not, and often along gendered lines.

Emotions history has the potential, therefore, to shed light on the structural dynamics of gender relations as they were imposed by masculine agents of power. This also provides new insight into the extent to which women were co-opted into the emotive processes of a gendered emotional regime, where emotive success was, in fact, only an affirmation of their subjugation. Resistance to patriarchy is similarly within the scope of emotions research, for any attempt to subvert masculine categories of power can be read as an attempt to subvert gendered emotional regimes. When, for example, Aristophanes explores, albeit satirically, the surreptitious takeover

[30] T. Dalgleish and M. Power [eds], *The Handbook of Cognition and Emotion* (Chichester: Wiley, 1999); Brady, *Emotional Insight*.
[31] Stearns, *American Cool*, 14.
[32] Reddy, *Navigation*, 31.
[33] Barnett and Ratner, 'Cognition and emotion'.

of power in the Athens assembly by women who have allowed their body hair to grow and who wear false beards, he is demonstrating the tenuousness of affective values associated with bodily prowess. Such symbols of masculine authority are the signs of reasoned rule of law, which is shown, in the final analysis, to be driven on both sides by perverse sexual appetites.[34]

The breakdown of the reason/emotion dyad also alters our study of the dynamics between public and private life, and among class relations. When Peter and Carol Stearns attempted, almost by themselves, to get emotions history off the ground in the mid-1980s, they reviewed what they saw as the limited analysis of the emotions up to that point. What they found was a tendency to divide rational and emotional existence along lines that matched perceived divisions between public and private life. Research into the notion of separate spheres had revealed a highly masculine construction of public life and a highly feminine construction of domesticity and family life. It was here that emotional relations had been considered fair game, after a limited fashion. Emotions, according to the reasoning of the time, were not a part of public life. Where emotions did emerge in public life, this was considered to be the breakdown of reason and not befitting of the politics of human affairs.

While the prevailing trends in political history had, for decades, focused on elite machinations of power, newer trends in history from below mirrored this kind of analysis. Mass movements that led to political demonstrations, crowds, riots and so on, were forced into the public political character of strategic reasoning because an association between them and emotional behaviour seemed to risk denigrating those movements. If actions were led by emotions, according to the Marxist analysis of the 1960s and 1970s, then they were not the actions of political equals, not intentional and not worthy of serious analysis. In order to make working-class politics a subject worthy of serious study, there was a perceived need to strip it of its apparent emotionality, of that 'wild' experience of emotional contagion, parsing collective behaviour as predetermined political strategy. The Stearns started, early on, to unravel this kind of reasoning and they have been aided since then by these changes in the way we approach cognition. Emotional behaviour is not, *ipso facto*, irrational behaviour, just as 'reasonable' behaviour is not, *ipso facto*,

---

[34] Aristophanes, *Ecclesiazusae* (Assemblywomen) (391 BCE).

devoid of emotion. That so much of the historical record suggests the opposite, and that historians have tacitly confirmed as much, opens up enormous revisionist possibilities. The questions we ask shift ground: no longer, 'what did the reasonable people do?' or 'what was the emotional reaction?'; rather, 'what did the people do on the basis of their assertion that their reason was uncoloured by emotion?' or 'what was the *cogmotional* reaction?'

Being human

The history of emotions opens up, as it does with class and gender, new vistas in the history of race and ethnicity. Massive strides have been taken in recent decades in deconstructing the power vectors that draw lines of exclusion in society. We know about concepts of whiteness, and about the political definition of being human, both of which have variously defined the limits of social and political inclusion.[35] We have also learnt about the experience of such exclusion, as subaltern and post-colonial studies have given voice to the oppressed, the enslaved, the colonised and the victims of prejudice.

The potential offered by the history of emotions is to add experiential colour to both sides of the inclusion/exclusion divide, to look at the effects of emotional prescription in the worlds of oppressors and the ways in which structures of racism were enforced through feelings of difference.[36] Conceptual notions of emotional superiority are implicit in the casting of racial others as emotionally animalistic. This might have been interpreted as an intellectual gloss on racist world views until recently, but now we are beginning to see how concepts of emotional difference fed into emotional experience and emotional perception of racial others. Conversely, though to a lesser extent, we are beginning to see evidence of the effect of power dynamics that emphasised emotional animality on racial others on the other side of the exclusion boundary. Conformity to oppressor prescriptions included emotional conformity, making for extremely strict emotional regimes that challenged those

---

[35] See chapter 1, note 12.
[36] On this, Eustace, *Passion*, is exemplary. For a general appraisal of where we have been, and where we might go, see B. McElhinny, 'The audacity of affect: Gender, race, and history in linguistic accounts of legitimacy and belonging', *Annual Review of Anthropology*, 39 (2010): 309–28.

deemed racially inferior to meet almost impossible standards of emotional expression, given the often harsh or torturous conditions in which emotives took place.[37] Perhaps most interesting of all are studies that explore the structures of emotional othering and the effective ways in which emotional prescription can transform enslaved experiences of colonial oppression into colonial visions of benevolence, pity and humanitarianism. When others are excluded from the realm of being human according to imposed constructions of emotional or sentimental inferiority, the logical inference is that colonial order is brought to bear over the colonised for their own good.[38]

Taken together, these configurations of power dynamics along gender, class and race lines all add up to a history of humanness to which the history of emotions can materially contribute. Various scholars have pointed out that those who are relegated by the powerful to a category outside of the human, a category that has included at different times women, children, African slaves, Irish people, native populations from across the world, and many others, have their non-human or sub-human status marked out by an inferiority of emotions. This might mean an overburden of unregulated and uncivilised emotions that run amok over any semblance of reason, or it might mean a dulled disposition that is incapable of tender emotions that have tended to be the self-definition of civilised beings. In many cases, according the shifting grounds of exclusion, it could be both these things at the same time, without much depth of reasoning about the apparent paradox.[39]

Considered in this way, emotions take us to what Dominick LaCapra has called 'the limits of history', and beyond. History,

---

[37] Eustace, *Passion*, 41–3, 72–3, 299. For a curious account of the way in which the laughter of the vanquished challenged the emotional style of the colonial victors, see S. Swart, '"The terrible laughter of the Afrikaner" – Towards a social history of humor', *Journal of Social History*, 42 (2009): 889–917.

[38] L. Festa, *Sentimental Figures of Empire in Eighteenth-century Britain and France* (Baltimore: Johns Hopkins University Press, 2006); Bourke, *What It Means*, 133–63.

[39] Bourke, *What It Means*, provides excellent coverage on this. See also, Boddice, 'Manly mind'; for one example (candidates are legion) of the ease with which othering distinctions are attached to phenomenological differences in experience, especially through the rhetoric of scientific or medical objectivity, see K. Woodrow, G. Friedman, A.B. Siegelaub, M.F. Collen, 'Pain tolerance: Differences according to age, sex and race', *Psychosomatic Medicine*, 34 (1972): 548–56.

or rather, its practice in historiography, has explicitly always been about the human, its nature, its affairs, its politics, its social and personal relations, its culture. Fundamentally, there are major question marks over the extent to which historicism can apply to non-human beings, though a burgeoning literature would suggest that a good number of scholars at least recognise the possibility. The standard barrier to such studies is the question of how to record the history of an animal without recourse to anthropomorphism, that is, without putting accounts of non-humans in the specific reference point of humans who, after all, are the ones who leave a historical trace. Most histories of animals, as with most politics about animals, are actually about human–animal relations, with a strong emphasis on human morals, duties and concepts, such as rights, citizenship, personhood, etc. Beyond this, we can record natural histories and evolutionary histories, but then we are beyond the realm of historiography.[40]

Hope is in part kindled by the fact that there are histories of those designated non-human who are, nonetheless, biologically human – the aforementioned list of women, children, racial 'inferiors', slaves and so on – even though they suffer from the same epistemological barrier. Those marked as outside of humanity tend not to leave traces, tend not to speak for themselves and tend not to be considered in and of themselves, but only as part of a relation to those marked 'human'. Yet a range of different scholars, in post-colonial and subaltern studies, in philosophy and in cultural studies, have risen to the challenge. One of their primary strategies is to outline how the processes of exclusion work, how the other's presence is constructed as disappearance, how the very boundaries of humanness are drawn.[41] Here it seems the emotions could play a vital role, for the way in which human emotions are marked out from non-human emotions does not make for a merely intellectual boundary. Rather, the construction of species-specific emotional

---

[40] For representative examples, see R. Boddice, *A History of Attitudes and Behaviours toward Animals in Eighteenth- and Nineteenth-century Britain: Anthropocentrism and the Emergence of Animals* (Lewiston, NY: Mellen, 2009); B. Sax, *Animals in the Third Reich: Pets, Scapegoats and the Holocaust* (New York: Continuum, 2000); E. Fudge, *Perceiving Animals: Humans and Beasts in Early Modern English Culture* (Houndmills: MacMillan, 2000).

[41] Boddice [ed.], *Anthropocentrism*; LaCapra, *History and Its Limits*; G. Agamben, *The Open: Man and Animal* (Palo Alto: Stanford University Press, 2003).

repertoires and possibilities directly informs practices and experiences of excluding. From these we can begin to piece together the practices and experiences of being excluded. We find in these accounts of the human other, or of the human made non-human, the potential limits of the concept of the emotional regime, according to Reddy's own standard. For a being rendered non-human, a being not merely oppressed but completely othered, is excluded to an extreme in which no emotive process applies. There is no standard, no emotional style, to which to conform because these beings are beyond the scope of emotional prescription. Their worldly suffering may be great, but they might also be said to be at great emotional liberty to feel and express what they may. The brutality of social exclusion means that punishment will define experience irrespective of emotional demeanour. There is no standard that can be reached, either from the point of view of the excluded or the excluder, where an emotive process ends in satisfaction. For the excluder, all the emotions of the excluded are irrelevant. And for the excluded, no emotive process ends up with the feeling or recognition of conformity or belonging. Those outside of the political regime are also outside of the emotional regime. And those outside *in extremis* are also outside of the human realm.[42]

If we acknowledge that those marked as 'not-people' are essential to historiographical practice, then the question of the non-human opens up more generally. I do not want to dwell here for long on the question of the animal, save to point out the methodological problems inherent in attempting to historicise animal emotions. Most comparative psychologists now agree, against centuries of intellectual tradition that maintained the opposite, that animals, especially mammals, but also birds, have the capacity for emotion and do indeed experience emotions. Some, it is argued, are capable of empathy, narrowly defined, and enter into emotional relationships with humans. We must be careful about what is meant here, and about what we do with this information.

To begin, when psychologists confirm the capacity for animals to experience emotion, they are referring to specific cognitive and physiological indicators, as well as observations of behavioural patterns, in order to ascribe affective states and moods to animals. This

[42] Agamben, *Homo Sacer*.

is work by analogy, comparing human brain patterns to animal brain patterns.[43] Animal emotions can then, somewhat irresistibly, be labelled: anger, love, fear, depression and so on. A whole raft of political arguments can follow such biological observations, but historians must be cautious. Given the emphasis in the history of emotions on what emotions mean, and the importance of interpreting emotional experience in cultural context, we are inevitably limited in applying our methods.

Non-human emotions, though they doubtless exist, cannot be understood experientially from the animal's point of view. To enter the animal's point of view is an imaginative leap (some have indeed tried to make it), but it depends on a degree of inference far beyond what it takes to enter the historical human's point of view.[44] This is not because of a species affinity per se, but rather more prosaically because of the traces that humans leave of their experiences that other animals do not. And, in the end, what humans say about the experiences of animals – that is to say, what it feels like to be them, beyond what we can observe as anatomical fact or physiological function – always ends up being a statement about the experience of humans. We are, as a species, ontologically bound.[45]

The empathic connection that is mythologised as a genuine entering into the experiences of another is, in the case of communion with animals, here exposed for what it really is: a projection of one's own experiences (past and current) in an attempt to match what we see, or think we see in something else. In the case of other humans (living and dead), we can at least look for corroboration of the projections we make about their emotional states. In our own culture in our own time we might find ourselves right a lot of the time. When projecting into the dead, we might find ourselves

---

[43] For interdisciplinary coverage and a good introduction to the various ways to enter into the animal mind, and the ever-present risk of anthropomorphism, see J.A. Smith and R.W. Mitchell [eds], *Experiencing Animal Minds: An Anthology of Human-Animal Encounters* (New York: Columbia University Press, 2012).

[44] See, for example, T. Nagel, 'What is it like to be a bat?', *Philosophical Review*, 83 (1974): 435–50; J. von Uexküll, *A Foray Into the Worlds of Animals and Humans: With a Theory of Meaning* (1934; Minneapolis: University of Minnesota Press, 2010); J. Derrida, *The Animal That Therefore I Am* (New York: Fordham University Press, 2008).

[45] See Boddice, 'End of anthropocentrism', in Boddice [ed.], *Anthropocentrism*, 1–18.

wrong more often. But animals, with few exceptions, do not and cannot corroborate what we project unto them.[46] We anthropomorphise all the time, even when we determine not to.[47] Some have tried to make a virtue of anthropomorphism, to make a case that it is reasonable to extrapolate kindred experiences in animals to those in humans, since in so many functional ways we are evidentially kindred.[48] For psychologists and ethologists, this remains controversial. For historians, perhaps, this is less so, and may in fact be illuminating. Though the post-human turn has had a dramatic effect on some disciplines, especially in anthropology and sociology, it has yet to reach historiography to any great extent.[49] Historians remain focused on human pasts, even when they entertain the idea of network theories and intersubjectivities that promise to transcend the human. In effect, such approaches complicate the human past, altering the stories we tell by focusing on things beyond the social, as it were, to include the influence of ecosystems and objects on the human past. Agency can be ascribed to non-human actors, but historians tend to be interested in those agencies only insofar as they change the stories we tell about people. What people say about animal (or non-human) emotions, therefore, not only tells us about the presence of these non-human agents but also about the assumptions and projections that people make about them. It tells us what people do to, with and for them. Anthropomorphism is a shifting register of the projection of human emotions onto animals. By charting the emotions ascribed

---

[46] P. Eitler, 'Doctor Dolittle's empathy', in Frevert *et al.*, *Learning How to Feel*, 94–114; R. Boddice, 'Species of compassion: Aesthetics, anaesthetics, and pain in the physiological laboratory', *19: Interdisciplinary Studies in the Long Nineteenth Century*, 15 (2012).

[47] See L. Daston and G. Mitman [eds], *Thinking with Animals: New Perspectives on Anthropomorphism* (New York: Columbia University Press, 2005); R.W. Mitchell, H.L. Miles and N. Thompson [eds], *Anthropomorphism, Anecdotes and Animals* (New York: SUNY Press, 1997).

[48] See B. Rollin, *The Unheeded Cry: Animal Consciousness, Animal Pain, and Science* (Oxford: Oxford University Press, 1989). Rollin, in turn, was inspired by George John Romanes' comparative psychology that was forgotten in the wake of behaviourism. See G.J. Romanes, *Animal Intelligence*, 3rd edn (1882; London: Kegan Paul, Trench, Co., 1883).

[49] For example, D. Haraway, *When Species Meet* (Minnesota: University of Minnesota Press, 2008); N. Taylor and T. Signal [eds], *Theorizing Animals: Rethinking Humanimal Relations* (Leiden: Brill, 2011).

to animals, we are actually charting the emotional repertoire of humans. It is a clear indicator of how emotions change over time.[50] There is, therefore, much promise in the pursuit of the history of human–animal relations, or interspecies interactions, for records of the beast throughout history tend to reveal the limits of the human emotional imagination.[51] Animals are, in many periods, constructed as the dark reflection of people, representing perhaps the beast within us that is covered with the veneer of civility or humanity.[52] We can find such testimony in antiquity, in the medieval period, in the Renaissance and in modernity.[53] It is expressed differently, but in structurally similar ways. To study the imagination of the bare emotional being, the animal devoid of obligations to fulfil emotional prescriptions or social expectations (in short, to see the possibility of the being without the dynamic emotive process), is to reveal the emotive process itself in those marked human. Accounts of the beast within, imagined through accounts of experience with animals in the world, are expressions of understanding about the effort it takes to control human emotions. Civil behaviour from Plato to the present is manifested as emotional control, and specific constructions of the wild animal illuminate the nature (culture) of that control.

I have argued elsewhere that the history of the animal, construed in this way, unlocks the structure of intrahuman power dynamics and the rationale of exclusionary violence.[54] Where those considered less human, sub-human or non-human are excluded on the basis of their closeness to or kinship with animality, so the concept of animality becomes central to the analysis of the day-to-day functioning of power. For the most part, the question of what makes humans distinct from animals has, throughout history, been thought of as an intellectual or philosophical question.[55]

[50] See Boddice, *History of Attitudes*; Bourke, *What It Means*.
[51] See E. Fudge, *Brutal Reasoning: Animals, Rationality, and Humanity in Early Modern England* (Ithaca: Cornell University Press, 2006).
[52] The exception is Descartes, who saw in animals the machine within us that was, in humans alone, endowed with an immortal soul.
[53] See Boddice, *History of Attitudes*, 25–80.
[54] Boddice, 'Manly mind': 339–40.
[55] See R. Sorabji, *Animal Minds and Human Morals: The Origins of the Western Debate* (Ithaca: Cornell University Press, 1995); G. Steiner, *Anthropocentrism and Its Discontents: The Moral Status of Animals in the History of Western Philosophy* (Pittsburgh: University of Pittsburgh Press, 2005).

The emergence in recent times, however, of an awareness of the everyday practices associated with such boundary drawing has made the question of the animal a socially and culturally significant pursuit. The history of emotions has a massive contribution to make in this respect, for the historical understanding of the animal as 'wild' or as 'natural' is bound up with an appreciation of its emotional capacities (or its lack thereof). In effect, the construction of the non-human – be it an oppressed human being or an animal – establishes the cultural or civilisational parameters of what it means and what it takes to be human, a figure of emotional control.

5

PRACTICE AND EXPRESSION

Evolutionary politics of expression

What is in a face? Are the eyes the window to the soul? Does happiness equate to a smile? How do we even know when a smile is a smile? Has it always been the same? What about the rest of the body? To what extent do we depend on all of the body's gestures to make sense of what we see? And what else does that sense depend on?

These are the kinds of questions that have driven the politics of expression for at least the last two centuries. They are high-stakes questions because, depending on how one answers them, the essence of what it is to be human changes. If a smile is a universal indicator of human happiness, and the smile is the same everywhere, then we can claim to know something fundamental about being human and human *being*, everywhere and for all time. Not only would such an observation be fundamental to the ways in which the biological sciences operate, but history and anthropology would be forever grounded and bounded by such an unbendable observation.

It will be clear from most of this book that such an observation does not hold sway with (most) historians or anthropologists, and that it is questioned by many biologists, neuroscientists and psychologists. But there is a strain of psychology that purports a universalism of expression, with profound implications for the epistemology of the emotions and a whole host of social and political ramifications. As we saw with the linguist Wierzbicka, the assertion that the corners of the mouth being raised (a smile) *always* means 'I feel something good now', permits a sweeping analysis of human nature – psychology, anatomy, physiology and the limits of culture – as well as potentially providing a socio-political agenda for making happiness. If people could only be induced to smile more, then they would more often be given to feel 'something good'. It is a logic Arlie Russel Hochschild pursued in her research into emotional labour, where an employer's dictum that employees *must* smile in their interactions with customers did in fact lead to a greater sense of happiness or job satisfaction. But here we must be very cautious, for not only must we question what a smile is, and what it means, but we must also query whether we can say with any confidence that a smile *causes* happiness. That was not Hochschild's argument, for at its core was an emphasis on effort, which we also see in Reddy's understanding of the way in which people strive to feel the correct (that is to say, the prescribed) feelings in a given context.[1] It might, therefore, be more accurate to say that, quite often, a smile precedes happiness. It is a bodily practice, in certain cultures at least, employed precisely to try to generate the feeling supposed to match it. In that case, a smile might mean, 'I *strive* to feel as if something good is happening now'. It might mean a host of other things too, but we are already far from universal human concepts and the capacity to read emotions as 'face value'.

The reason this topic even needs to be broached at all is its prevailing influence, some of which is already detailed in chapter 2. At the forefront of research into the expression of emotions and the chief advocate of emotional universals, or common 'basic' emotions, is Paul Ekman. In his 1971 article, with Wallace Friesen, Ekman explicitly argued for 'constants across cultures in the face and emotion', pointing to clear evidence that 'the association between particular facial muscular patterns and discrete emotions is universal'. There were, at the beginning, some caveats. Their argument did not 'imply the absence of cultural differences in the face and emotion', since 'cultural differences will be manifest in the circumstances which elicit an emotion, in the action consequences of an emotion, and in the display rules which govern the management of facial behavior in particular social settings'. They concluded the article with reference to the 'cultural differences in the antecedent and consequent events' of emotions and to cultural 'differences in attitudes about particular emotions'.[2] In short, they left a lot of room for culture in an argument about biological

---

[1] Hochschild, 'Emotion work'.
[2] Ekman and Friesen, 'Constants': 129.

universals. Over time, however, culture was slowly shunted out of the picture as Ekman sought ways to capitalise on the fundamental observation concerning emotional expression and basic emotions.

We will return to basic emotions presently, but it seems germane here to make mention of the scholarly tradition into which Ekman entered, and the scientific justifications he could allude to in order to add weight to his argument. Ekman is the end point of a very long debate about human facial anatomy, what it does and, importantly, why it does it. The reputed anatomist Charles Bell (1774–1842), for example, wanted, at the beginning of the nineteenth century, to offer a corrective to artists whose representations of facial expressions and emotions were, in his opinion, impossible. The human facial structure was such that however plastic it was in practice, it was nonetheless limited in what it could do. Anatomical research unfolded the mechanics of expression, and the logical limit to the ways in which emotions could be worn on the face. Importantly for Bell, at the beginning of the nineteenth century, anatomy was there by *design*, as evidence of the Creator. This was, in the end, God's image, and its essence was universal. The expressions were designed to enable communication of emotions, translating the 'internal emotion' to the face in predictable, reliable ways. God had made 'systematic provision for that mode of communication and that natural language, which is to be read in the changes of the countenance'. There was, for Bell, 'no emotion in the mind of man which has not its appropriate signs; and that there are even muscles in the human face, to which no other use can be assigned, than to serve as the organs of this language'. Bell asserted that 'experience or arbitrary custom' did not change this 'universal language', for the face was an 'index of the mind, having expression corresponding with emotion of the soul'.[3]

It is not my intention here to dwell in particular on the historical epistemology of the nineteenth century.[4] Nevertheless, I dwell in particular on Bell because of Charles Darwin's reaction against his work, and because of Darwin's subsequently enormous influence on contemporary psychological understandings of the emotions. Bell's influence also cast a shadow over the ways in which non-

---

[3] C. Bell, *Essays on the Anatomy of Expression in Painting* (London: Longman, Hurst, Rees, and Orme, 1806), 88.
[4] I have explored this at length in *Science of Sympathy*.

human animal emotions have been considered, since the 'range of expression' in 'lower animals' was a 'mere accessory to the voluntary or needful actions of the animal'. This 'accessory expression' was not to 'any degree commensurate to the variety and extent of the animal's passions'.[5] While Bell's intent was to say that animal passions were more varied than they appeared, the inspiration taken from this observation was that animal expressions of emotion or pain ought not to be taken as signs of real emotion. Here we find some of the roots of the behaviourist line that stated that, far from a facial limitation that belied hidden passionate depths, animals were essentially emotionless.[6]

Bell's influence on Darwin was great, but construed negatively. Darwin felt that he had to reject the intelligent design thesis. Instead of correcting this part of Bell's work, however, he felt it necessary to correct all of it. If expression was not *designed* to communicate emotions to others, then the purpose of expression was not to communicate at all. Instead of finding a natural-selection explanation for the role of expressions in emotional sociability, Darwin came up with something entirely different. Expressions were therefore ruled functionally useful for some other purpose, which in turn became associated with, but not intrinsically connected to, certain emotional states. Once acquired and used to fulfil these functions, the particular muscular movements were passed down by inheritance. Darwin's great work on emotional expression thus depended not on that theory for which he became most famous – natural selection – but rather on a Lamarckian mechanism of inherited habit. Moreover, the focus on explaining expression in this way made the work less about emotion itself than about the misleading association of expression with emotion. To explain expression, as an evolutionary universal, it turns out Darwin did not really need the emotions at all.[7]

Darwin had explained the evolution of the emotions elsewhere, namely in *Descent of Man* (about which I have written elsewhere), but the important legacy of *Expression* is that, in departing from

---

[5] Bell, *Essays*, 85.
[6] Famously first stated by C. Lloyd Morgan and known as 'Morgan's Canon': C.L. Morgan, *An Introduction to Comparative Psychology* (London: W. Scott, 1894), 59.
[7] Darwin, *Expression*; Gross, 'Defending the humanities'; Boddice, *Science of Sympathy*, 35–7; Dixon, *From Passions*, 159f.

Bell's reasoning, Darwin had nevertheless concurred that emotional expressions in humans were universal. He had also confirmed Bell's anatomical observations about the configuration of the human face and its capacity to make a very large but ultimately limited range of movements. To aid his argument, Darwin had employed a set of photographs that had been crafted by Guillaume-Benjamin-Amand Duchenne de Boulogne, a French neurologist who had used galvanic apparatus to great effect in artificially producing vivid 'emotional' expressions on the faces of test subjects. For his part, Duchenne too had been influenced by Bell, and followed his artistic bent in attempting to re-create nature precisely.[8] With much trial and error, Duchenne worked out where to place the electrical current so as to stimulate muscles that made emotions appear. One subject in particular, who had no sense of feeling in his face, was able to undergo the galvanic tests without discomfort, and therefore became the face of universal emotions. However, Duchenne was never under any illusion that the expressions he produced were anything other than replicas of the emotions they represented. To emphasise this point, Duchenne produced emotional expressions on one side of the face only, leaving the other side 'neutral', or else produced compound emotional expressions by inducing seemingly opposite representations at the same time (such as joy and grief). Duchenne wanted, like Bell, to demonstrate the inaccuracies in depictions of classical beauty. The anatomy did not lie.

But the anatomy did not, in and of itself, contain emotions. When Darwin appropriated Duchenne's images, he often had the galvanic apparatus removed from the scene, so as to depict the experimental subject *as if* he were truly undergoing the emotion. In other images in Darwin's *Expression*, actors are employed to simulate facial expressions, which Darwin then circulated among friends and colleagues in his bid to confirm that expressions were universal. One of these images was of grief, or rather, the upper part of the face feigning grief. As Darwin pointed out, the lower portion of the woman's face showed a different emotion altogether, as a result

---

[8] For Duchenne, see A.M. Drouin Hans, 'Des électrodes pour une âme fantôme: l'anatomie de Duchenne de Boulogne', *Ludus Vitalis*, 18 (2010): 89–122; S. Dupouy, 'Les visages électriques de Duchenne de Boulogne', *Annales historique de l'électricité*, 8 (2010): 21–36.

of 'being absorbed in the attempt'.[9] After Bell, these experiments in the limits of expression, the evolution of the human anatomy and the extent to which emotional representations could be reproduced by artifice had little to do with emotions per se. Though these works have been used extensively to talk about the emotions in humans, the original intent was to talk about expression only, and with a full knowledge that what was being depicted was nothing at all to do with the emotions.

Faces, bodies and basics

Ekman was inspired by the work of Silvan Tomkins, the pioneer of 'Affect Theory'. Affect Theory posits a transhistorical biology in which certain 'affects' – a word deployed explicitly to refer to that part of emotional behaviour which is innate, built in, hardwired and automatic – are connected to certain expressions of the face. By biologising the fundamental ingredients of emotional behaviour, it was also logical to situate that biology in the part of the body that literally faces outwards. The face becomes a transmitter of that which is timelessly human. We are, so the theory goes, born with this affective repertoire, which includes nine affects: joy, interest, startle, anger, disgust, dissmell (a reaction to a bad smell), distress, fear and shame. While there is acknowledgement that culture gets added into and modulates these affects and their facial signs, the basic elements of affective behaviour are nevertheless considered to be innate.

Affect Theory is popular, for good reason. In certain respects, it posits an egalitarian view of what a human being fundamentally is. It permits researchers to look for the source of affects in the brain, as if they exist there objectively. And it allows researchers to analyse experience with the face as a foundation. As per Tomkins' original idea, affects happened automatically, but they were only experienced as affects because of the way the face responded to the automatic stimulus. It is a subtle re-expression of the theory of William James: that we do not see a snake, feel afraid, then run, but see a snake, run, then feel afraid *because* of the running. In Tomkins view, however, the face was the primary location of affective cues that tells the brain what the experience is. Whatever particularities

[9] Darwin, *Expression*, 182.

a historian might come up with, affect theorists would posit that the basic human biology and automated innate systems of affect remain the same.

Tomkins' research in this area, which was first published in 1964, pre-dates what we now know about brain plasticity, about micro-evolution and epigenetics, and about the historical changes in responses to sensory stimuli.[10] Much of this will be covered in the next chapter. The work, however, was enormously influential. The central idea of an essentially fixed biological body can be found in the popularising work of Antonio Damasio, for example, though his focus is not the face so much as the body's internal physiology.[11] In 2015 I witnessed a talk by a Shakespeare scholar who argued that direct lines could be drawn between the reception of contemporary news media about the extremist group Isis (*Daesh*) and audience reception of Hamlet in Elizabethan England, the reasoning being that the human endocrine system has not changed in thousands of years and that affects are automatic. This kind of reasoning has made it into published works, threatening the very essence of what it is that the humanities, and the history of emotions in particular, do. When scholars in the humanities bow down before certain influences from neurobiology but do not have the requisite experience or knowledge to challenge them, we end up with throwaway analyses that beg more questions than they provide answers.[12]

---

[10] S.S. Tomkins and R. McCarter, 'What and where are the primary affects? Some evidence for a theory', *Perceptual and Motor Skills*, 18 (1964): 119–58. The full expression of Affect Theory can be found in S.S. Tomkins, *Affect Imagery Consciousness*, 4 vols (New York: Springer, 1962–3, 1991–2).

[11] Damasio's influence is also huge, but his work is of questionable relevance for historians, precisely because of its implicit but nonetheless fundamental resistance to an historical body/mind. Moreover, the neurobiological focus of his work tends towards an explanation of the mechanics of feeling/emotion in order to understand what emotions are/how emotions are situated. History tends in the opposite direction: to what things mean and to what things do. Damasio's key works are *Descartes' Error: Emotion, Reason, and the Human Brain* (New York: Putnam, 1994); *The Feeling of What Happens: Body and Emotion in the Making of Consciousness* (San Diego: Harcourt, 1999); *Looking for Spinoza: Joy, Sorrow, and the Feeling Brain* (San Diego: Harcourt, 2003); *Self Comes to Mind: Constructing the Conscious Brain* (New York: Pantheon, 2010). For extended criticism see Gross, *Secret History*, 29–39.

[12] See, for example, Ros King's assertion that, 'Recent advances in neuroscience, which show that emotions are the result of involuntary chemical responses to an environmental change ... suggest universality, because they belong to pre-

More profound, however, is the connection between Affect Theory and Paul Ekman. Ekman himself has written of the influence of Tomkins' insights on his own research, which really opened the door towards basic emotions and universal expressions.[13] Despite the advances made in diverse fields, from anthropology to the neurosciences, which are steadily bringing together a rich understanding of the biosociality or bioculturality of the emotions, Affect Theory essentially lives on through Paul Ekman.

When Ekman edited and introduced a new 2003 edition of Charles Darwin's *Expression*, it was clear that there was an attempt at once to make an intellectual and epistemological connection. Ekman is the heir to a certain interpretation of Darwinian emotions. The heavy-handed editorialising was done with a mind to correcting Darwin, bringing him up to date, as it were, with the state of the art as Ekman saw it. It was a stunning move that emphasised the most reputable of all intellectual foundations for Ekman's own work, while at the same time denying the possibility of a history of the emotions as we have come to know it. Certainly, the evolutionary science would permit a historical view, but only over the extremely long term; a term so long, in fact, as to go beyond the remit of historians entirely.

Strikingly, just two years after William Reddy's *Navigation of*

---

conscious changes in the body. It seems that muscle movements can even *cause* the endocrinal excretions that in turn cause certain emotions ... Some modern "humanists," such as Daniel Gross in his polemical (and therefore popular) *The Secret History of Emotion*, have felt the cause of the humanities to be threatened by this. But they need not worry, provided we notice Antonio Damasio's important distinction between "emotions" (nonconscious adjustments in the body at the muscular-visceral-endocrine level) and "feelings" (conscious experience or awareness of those emotions). Little can be done about emotions; they are how the body has evolved to work. But once in the realm of consciousness, feelings can be mediated ...'. Such a statement blithely disregards the substantial criticism of Damasio's approach in the work of Gross and others. It is to be hoped that works such as this book will help scholars avoid such neo-Jamesian reductionism and uncritical reception of pop-science and the analytically out-of-step insistence on a conscious/unconscious dyad. See R. King, 'Plays, playing, and make-believe: Thinking and feeling in Shakespearean drama', in L. Johnson, J. Sutton and E. Tribble [eds], *Embodied Cognition and Shakespeare's Theatre: The Early Modern Body-Mind* (New York: Routledge, 2014), 27–45, at 34.

[13] P. Ekman, 'Silvan Tomkins and facial expression', in E.V. Demos [ed.], *Exploring Affect: The Selected Writings of Silvan S. Tomkins* (Cambridge: Cambridge University Press, 1995), 209–11.

Feeling was published, Ekman declared in the introduction to his edition of Darwin that 'the intellectual climate had changed', putting science more closely in alignment with Darwin's universalism, against what Ekman saw as the vivid imaginations of 'cultural relativists or social constructionists'. Certainly, culture played a part in 'our attempts to manage our emotions, our attitudes about our emotions and our representations of them verbally', but this did not so much as dent the more important point that 'expressions do show universality'.[14] All notions of a dynamic relationship between body and world, expression and emotional ambiguity, feeling rules and feelings, passed Ekman by as he stuck to the usage of 'social constructionists' as a pejorative. That Reddy's entry into the field had itself come under the heading of 'Against constructionism' did not give him pause.

Ekman's contribution does not end with universal expressions, however. Those expressions are, logically, connected to a series of universal emotional conditions, which Ekman labelled 'basic emotions'. Here lies the grand departure from Duchenne and Darwin and a rapprochement with Bell's original argument about the ways in which human emotions are naturally communicated by the face. Ekman no longer needed Bell's intelligent design. He could make the argument that, in his opinion, Darwin should have made in *Expression*. Yes, emotional expression is connected to emotional communication. It has evolved in humans by natural selection, and is everywhere the same. Ekman's *Expression* is, therefore, the Darwinian work that Darwin did not write.

Exactly how many basic emotions there are has changed over time in Ekman's work, but the primary list of six contained anger, disgust, fear, happiness, sadness and surprise. Where culture seemed to belie their universality, it was, in Ekman's opinion, something like a veil, difficult to penetrate, that only covered those emotions that all humans shared. There are many criticisms about the concept of basic emotions, but the position is widely supported and has made Ekman's reputation, not only as a scientist but also as a government contractor and something of a media celebrity.

The conviction that the face betrays the heart, combined with sophisticated computer technology that can measure even the

---

[14] P. Ekman, 'Introduction to the third edition', in C. Darwin, *The Expression of the Emotions in Man and Animals* (London: HarperCollins, 1998), xxxv.

smallest observable motion of the face, put Ekman in the lie-detecting business, notably conducting visual screenings as part of airport security, and into Hollywood. His theories of microexpression and apparent ability to detect liars were the basis for the character Cal Lightman in the Fox drama *Lie to Me*, putting Ekman in *Time* magazine's list of the 100 most influential people in the world for 2009.[15]

Historians of emotion have to know Ekman's work, and Affect Theory in general, and be able to challenge it effectively; otherwise, the history of emotions will be haunted by a popular science that refutes its possibility, or else severely limits its scope. In the early days of the history of emotions Peter Stearns was prepared to accept that there might be some universal emotional or affective backdrop to being human, but found so much cultural variation in expression that this universalism was deemed hardly relevant, let alone substantially worthwhile. Yet Ekman would doubtless counter that even Stearns was wrong, and that the variety he had discovered was simply imagined. It is not sufficient, in my opinion, that our own empirical data as historians shows a great wealth of emotional experience that does not fit into either the universal expressions schema or the basic emotions schema. We are also behoved to know how to challenge Ekman's and his followers' own data and their methodology.[16] In a curious twist, the methods used to challenge Ekman are transferable skills: they are a good model for how to do the history of emotions more broadly. Effectively, Ekman's work has already become a historical source. We can read it for its emotional epistemology, examine its affective gaze and analyse what emotional, social and political practices rose up in its name.

Central to Ekman's work is the face and people's ability to recognise the facial expressions of others as indicators of their emotional state. In this he shared Darwin's excitement that photography (and later video) could capture expressions that were otherwise fleeting,

---

[15] Paul Ekman International PLC claims that 'Ekman trained staff are 50 times more effective at spotting high risk passenger', www.ekmaninternational.com/paul-ekman-international-plc-home/news/ekman-trained-staff-are-50-times-more-effective-at-spotting-high-risk-passengers.aspx, accessed 14 December 2016; 'The 2009 Time 100', http://content.time.com/time/specials/packages/completelist/0,29569,1894410,00.html, accessed 14 December 2016.

[16] For influential challenges to Ekman, that undermine the entire basis for basic emotions, see Feldman Barrett, 'Natural kinds' and 'Emotion paradox'.

and that whatever was captured would be recognisable by anybody. The same methodological flaws that dogged Darwin also dog Ekman. In 1976 Ekman published the 'Pictures of Facial Affect' series of photographs: a set of 110 images of the expression of the six basic emotions.[17] The images are of Caucasian actors *acting* the expressions of the emotions Ekman believed to be universal. To be clear, the images did not depict any emotions at all, per se; they depicted simulated emotional expressions, held long enough to be photographed. This fact alone ought to give us significant pause. If these expressions are recognisable across cultures as the equivalents of anger, disgust, fear, happiness, sadness and surprise, even though, in these instances, they represent only dissimulation, then a major flaw emerges in the theory that what can be seen on the face has something to do with the emotion it is supposed to represent.

As Clifford Geertz pointed out in 1973, to know the difference between a twitch, a wink and a burlesqued wink involves a deep knowledge of cultural and situational context.[18] As with actors, whether used by Ekman to make a scheme of universal expressions, or by Darwin to try to simulate grief, any facial expression that is rehearsed in order to give the appearance of something that is not there speaks to the effectiveness of human facial expressions to deceive, to mask, to conspire. In the case of the burlesque wink, the message it conveys depends on who knows what beforehand. Those in on the conspiracy recognise the gesture as saying something other than what is represented, whereas those out of the loop are supposed to receive the wrong impression. Much was the same with Darwin's half picture of a grieving frown. One could hypothesise in advance that those shown the picture without any contextual knowledge might recognise grief, but the obvious conclusion is not, therefore, that grief has a universal sign, but that people are not adept at discriminating between authentic experience and feigned experience. That picture is particularly telling, because only half of the actor's face is included. As Darwin told his co-conspirators, the actor had difficulty mastering the whole facial expression of grief, and therefore had to do it by parts.

---

[17] P. Ekman and W. Friesen, *Pictures of Facial Affect* (Palo Alto: Consulting Psychologists Press, 1976).
[18] Geertz, 'Thick description', 6–12.

The editorialising involved in presenting a partial face is revealing of the extent to which humans rely on visual clues from the whole face and the rest of the body in their efforts to work out what is going on. Seldom are we confronted in life with bits of faces, foreheads, chins and isolated eyes, and have to decipher their visual clues in isolation. Moreover, the fact that Darwin instructed the actor to act as if he were in grief highlights the tautology inherent in any such methodology. The image of grief, or any other emotion, is assumed to exist prior to its enactment.

Tautology also defined the photographic experiments of Duchenne. While the grimaces produced by the galvanic apparatus were not exactly predictable, Duchenne's conceptualisation of emotion categories was. He produced expressions that fitted into preconceived emotion words, such as 'terror'. Again, the absurdity lay in the fact that the experimental subject was undergoing none of the emotions he expressed in such iconic fashion. But this was compounded by the fact that any expressions produced by Duchenne that did not fit into ready-made categories of emotion were discounted. There was no room to say, 'I don't know what this expression signifies'. Experimentation continued until the face matched the expectation that had been formed a priori.[19]

Ekman's sets of photographs suffer from the same flaw. They neither represent emotion – the expressions are acted – nor do they leave any room for modification of the emotion set, which is decided beforehand. Ekman's photographs were also criticised for being entirely of Caucasian faces, which led to a new set that also included Japanese faces. Even then, the emotion categories were decided a priori. Ekman's model does not leave room for uncertain expressions;[20] participants in emotion recognition experiments are led to the desired response.

All of this is to say nothing of the fact that humans do not, in the course of ordinary interaction, study faces frozen at what we might call 'peak expression'. Expressions and gestures are fluid, fleeting and involve movement of parts from one place to another. Expressing is not defined by attempting to reach a fixed expression

---

[19] I thank Otniel Dror for making this observation at the 'Emotional Bodies' conference in Geneva, October 2014.
[20] P. Ekman and D. Matsumoto, 'Japanese and Caucasian facial expressions of emotion and neutral faces' (San Francisco: San Francisco State University, 1988).

point, but a process of facial and bodily change, coupled with words and noises, and taking place in a context. All of these things allow us a chance to understand, or misunderstand, the emotional state of another person, or to be misled or confused. Cameras lie. Cameras have always lied. If the photographs of emotional expressions that have formed the key repository of sources in the politics of an evolutionary science of human expressions have taught us anything, it is that humans lie too, and lie well.

In sum, no gesture by itself necessarily says anything about anything. It might be useful for historians and psychologists alike to be reminded of Sartre's approach to the emotions, which emphasised the essential importance of signification in all emotions. Emotion, he told psychologists, '*does not exist*, considered as a physical phenomenon, for a body cannot be emotional, not being able to attribute a meaning to its own manifestations'. Only through *signification*, that is, an appraisal of what an expression means and how it is evaluated, can we really study the emotions.[21]

What we are left with after all of this is the knowledge that at a certain point in the second half of the twentieth century certain psychologists reacted negatively to the lengths certain anthropologists were running to in their social constructionist worldviews. They pursued a research agenda based on an opposite hypothesis: that all humans shared a set of basic emotions and that human emotional expressions for those basic emotions also obeyed universal laws. Nature was strongly asserted as a deterministic cause, and whatever masks, costumes and customs culture wove over the top of this nature, it did not alter or substantially affect that nature. In the name of this theory, certain scientific practices were called into question, while others, with high levels of funding, were used to alter security screening methods to include facial profiling. Battle lines were drawn according to nature/nurture, universalist/ constructionist points of view, with researchers in different fields working with diametrically opposed notions of what the object of their research – emotions – was.

Only with the theoretical insights from anthropology and cultural studies about bioculture on the one hand, and with the sophisticated brain research of social neuroscientists on the other,

[21] J.-P. Sartre, *Sketch for a Theory of the Emotions*, trans. Philip Mairet (London: Routledge, 2002), 11–14, esp. 10.

did the universalist/constructionist dyad begin to crack. Its primary assertion is that there is no nature *or* nurture, but always both, always mutually and dynamically involved, affecting both body and world, to a point where both the words 'nature' and 'nurture' have become unhelpful. This story is not yet complete. Adherents remain in the old camps. But this is one potential – if schematic – narrative line for a history of the emotions in the late twentieth century. It matters – at the level of the body, at the level of practice – what people think emotions are. The shifting epistemological ground *about* emotions, in combination with the shifting social ground *of* emotions, affects us experientially.

Daniel Gross appeals to both of these categories in his extremely useful demolition job of popular neurobiology, *The Secret History of Emotion*. We must make a distinction here, and clearly mark that Gross takes aim substantially at the crude biologising expressed by the likes of Antonio Damasio, with links to Tomkins, Ekman *et al*. Essentially, he challenges this kind of work for its lack of a social theory, or of any kind of experience with the humanities. Damasio's work in particular is singled out as an example of 'how brain science of emotion goes awry when it blunders into social fact'.[22] Despite a gloss of interdisciplinary value, Gross accuses Damasio's work of 'stripping' the 'social quality' of emotional appearances and representations.[23] Meaning is denuded of context. Social development is reduced to evolutionary forces.[24] Over the course of *Secret History*, Gross re-builds a model of the social basis and political economy of emotion, based principally on the rhetorical management of emotional distribution:

> Instead of wondering perennially why it has taken so long to extend the range of human compassion to women, to slaves, to non-Europeans, to the poor, to the disabled, and so on, we would do better to track the history of terms such as *pride, humility, pity,* and *compassion* and see how they have been mobilized for strategic purposes; how, for instance, particular communities are composed by the notion that they have a monopoly on that compassion that would be extended to others.[25]

---

[22] Gross, *Secret History*, 29.
[23] Gross, *Secret History*, 32.
[24] Gross, *Secret History*, 32–6.
[25] Gross, *Secret History*, 178–9.

This is the baton picked up by Thomas Dixon, by Paul White, and by me; but the first lap was run by Thomas Haskell in the 1980s, even if at that point he did not consciously plot a history-of-emotions course (see chapter 7).[26] In the running, and in the passing of the baton, the approach has been developed, though the advancement is implicit in the last quote from Gross' work. It is not merely the history of words and concepts that animates a history of emotions, or that makes emotions social; rather, it is in the way in which those words are 'mobilised'. What do words *do*? What do people do with, through and because of those words? The drawing and re-drawing of rhetorical boundaries is intertwined with the possibilities for practice. Emotions are defined, yes, but only insofar as emotions are *done*.

Practice theory

In a 2013 work on senses in religious communities in the seventeenth and eighteenth centuries, one of Nicky Hallett's principal aims was to examine 'how the practice of writing itself shaped the … sensitivities' of nuns. She explored the extent to which 'their experience and in turn their understanding' was re-worked 'under pressure of textualisation'.[27] It is a question at the heart of emotive analysis, if we take the broad view that emotional utterances include all forms of expression, beyond speech, such as gesture and writing. Hallett finds an 'interactive', we might say dynamic, relationship between 'expressiveness and experience', which echoes other research that resists any notion of a transhistorical biological substance in which sensation, affect and emotion lie, as it were, prior to cultural influence.[28] The reasoning here is straightforward enough: since it is impossible to sense or to emote outside of a cultural framework, it is therefore impossible to sense or emote without a framework of evaluation that is also culturally embedded. While the biological mechanisms that permit the construction of

---

[26] T. Haskell, 'Capitalism and the origins of the humanitarian sensibility', part 1, *American Historical Review*, 90 (1985): 339–61.

[27] N. Hallett, *The Senses in Religious Communities, 1600–1800: Early Modern 'Convents of Pleasure'* (New York: Routledge, 2013), 21.

[28] Hallett, *Senses*, 22. See, for example, F. Bound Alberti, 'Medical history and emotion theory', in F. Bound Alberti [ed.], *Medicine, Emotion and Disease*, xiii–xxix.

experience doubtless exist, their functioning is literally meaningless without context. And, as I document in various parts of this book, some of that machinery is also forged in the crucible of culture. Emotion (or affect) and expression are not two things, but one process. Practices, including bodily practices such as gesture, are the sign of that process.

The clearest statement of a research agenda along these lines came from Monique Scheer in 2012, in what has proven to be an influential article.[29] At its core is an approach loosely following the theories of Pierre Bourdieu, expressed as an attempt to collapse both the psychologism that makes all emotions a product of the mind and the biologism that would have them all be a product of the body. As a corollary, Scheer also collapses the distinction between conscious and unconscious by emphasising the historicity and worldliness of the body. By focusing on emotional practices, mind, body and world are all implicated, all the time. Distinctions made in other disciplines between expressions, representations and norms on the one hand, and so-called 'real' emotions on the other, are also collapsed. As we have seen with many other historians of emotion, it is essential to our work that the existence of emotions in either the body or the mind as objective things, separate from and isolatable from the dynamics of cultural presence, is dismissed. Just as I have argued about pain being a value applied to certain configurations of stimuli and response, so it is also essential to see emotion as an *output* of the brain.[30]

Practice theory, as detailed by Scheer, understands the things we physically do in the world – practices – to be part of the experience-making work of being human. Borrowing from Extended Mind Theory, a sub-field of the philosophy of mind, Scheer subscribes to a view that 'experience and activity' are not 'separate phenomena'. Experience is 'something we *do* – and that we do with our entire bodies, not just the brain'.[31] As with cultural theorists like Sara Ahmed, Scheer postulates that the notion of an inner feeling and an outer expression only emerges as an effect of emotional practices. Practices create emotion knowledge of this kind and

---

[29] Scheer, 'Emotions'.
[30] Boddice, *Pain: A Very Short Introduction*; this is derived from R. Melzack, 'Evolution of the neuromatrix theory of pain', *Pain Practice*, 5 (2005): 85–94.
[31] Scheer, 'Emotions': 196.

make us aware of it. Such a process of inward to outward movement is meaningless if thought of as universal, automatic or unsituated. Moreover, 'practice may also create bodily manifestations seemingly independent from the mind, ego, or subject, depending on historically and culturally specific habits and context.'[32] Emotional experience, in part, *follows* the processing and translation of movement or action. But not only, and emotion cannot be reduced to the movement or action itself. Practice theory is not simply a throwback to the formulation of William James, but an intermixing of cognitive, bodily and social understandings, not of what emotions are, but of what emotions *do*.

Importantly, Scheer's theory of practice applied to emotions moves us on both from Reddy's understanding of conscious self-management and neurohistory's adherence to a notion of the automatic affect as universal biological background, to an overlay of human neuroplasticity. In many ways, the neurohistorical approach takes the history of emotions much further ahead (hence the discussion of it in the chapter that follows this one), but it only works in a coherent way with other work in the history of emotions if Scheer's approach is first adopted. The essential component here is the substantial theoretical rejection of the conscious/unconscious duality, for while practice theory does 'encompass intentional, deliberate action, it also includes, and indeed stresses, habituated behavior executed without much cognitive attention paid. ... [S]ubjects (or agents) are not viewed as prior to practices, but rather as the product of them'.[33] Such a view re-casts automatic behaviour as no less a product of being in the world than Reddy and others classify conscious behaviour. This position is justified by empirical histories of the self, which show that 'automatic' practices encompass the ways in which people distribute 'attention to "inner" processes of thought, feeling, and perception'. Scheer documents the ways in which 'interiority, self-reflexivity, distinct faculties of feeling and thinking', markers of the qualities of modern Western concepts of the self, 'have been intensely cultivated at certain times in specific social and cultural constellations'.[34] The site of this culti-

---

[32] Scheer, 'Emotions': 198.
[33] Scheer, 'Emotions': 200.
[34] Scheer ('Emotions': 200) here references C. Taylor, *Sources of the Self: The Making of the Modern Identity* (Cambridge: Cambridge University Press, 1989)

vation is the body (including the mind as neurological stuff): 'The materiality of the body provides not only the locus of the competence, dispositions, and behavioural routines of practice, it is also the "stuff" with and on which practices work.'[35]

Scholars working in the history of the senses, who saw themselves as connected to the history of emotions, even if historians of emotions had not really recognised the scholarship to any great extent, had already asserted as much. The year before Scheer's seminal article, Matthew Milner had made substantially the same argument in a monumental book on the senses in the English Reformation. The argument does not require any particular reaching out to Bourdieu or other theorists, and may in fact be more appealing without it. The interpretation of empirical evidence by itself is sufficiently compelling:

> Constant in sixteenth-century reform was the monitoring and prescription of behaviours and religious practices, estimably in the hope belief would be altered. Nonetheless new doctrines were interpreted from within the matrix of old ones and their practices. Analogous behaviours offered varying shades of grey that tended, as in the laying of hands at ordination, to obscure clear assertion something different occurred when traditional gestures were only re-contextualized rather than dramaturgically altered. This was the heart of non-conformists' objections to the Elizabethan settlement; not doctrine per se, but practice. The power of practice to impede or foster the creation and alteration of beliefs becomes evident when we realize that liturgical texts, as much as doctrinal treatises and catechisms, were propositions for belief which were only realized when they were endorsed and ow[n]ed by believers in actual religious practice.[36]

Internalisation by doing is a process that produces automaticity. That feeling of naturalness, of posture, of expression, of feeling and belief, comes through doing. This goes a long way to explaining why changes made in the abstract, at the level of intellectual reasoning, or prescription for new behaviour made formally or informally can

---

and R. Porter [ed.], *Rewriting the Self: Histories from the Renaissance to the Present* (London: Routledge, 1997). More recent works have explored changing practices of the self in greater depth, adding compelling substance to the theory. See Eustace, *Passion*; Sullivan, *Beyond Melancholy*.

[35] Scheer, 'Emotions': 200.
[36] M. Milner, *The Senses and the English Reformation* (Farnham: Ashgate, 2011), 346.

be so disruptive. Liturgical change, just to take this example, did not simply mark theological shifts, but helped in the unmaking and remaking of the self, at the level of the senses and the emotions – at the level of *feeling*, realised through practice. Implicated at all times is the 'knowing body', or the mindful body.[37] Again, this concept will re-emerge with even greater potency in the next chapter. For now, suffice it to say that any insistence on automatic processes that are biological, which is a shorthand way of saying 'culture free', must be challenged. People are 'supremely practiced at the subtleties of movement, posture, gesture, and expression that connect them with others', skills that also 'communicate to themselves who they are'. Scheer insists that such practices are 'neither "natural" nor random', but rather 'adhere to a learned repertoire that positions a person in a social field'.[38] I would qualify this somewhat, for by saying something is not natural, it presupposes something else that could be. In fact, the theory demolishes even an implied opposition between nature and culture. The logical conclusion, in contrast, should be that since the emergence of humanity as we recognise it as such, humans have been natural–cultural beings. We are, from an evolutionary point of view, biocultural. When we interact, emotionally communicate or emote in our cultural context, we are practising emotional behaviour that is learnt, situated, shared and, when emotive processes work well, feels *as if* it is natural.

Other people's expressions

If Ekman *et al.* are wrong when they argue that other people's emotions are literally written on their faces, then what are we doing when we see emotions in others? Answering this is essential for the historian of emotions, because very often we do not have more than a picture, a photograph or a description of an emotion. How do we read them? What are we doing when we empathise? What is involved, and is empathy historical? When other people express emotions, whether verbally or gesturally, we might, in the course of everyday interactions, *know* how they feel. In shared experiences, such as a musical performance, a football match, a protest march, a religious service, we might feel that we are all feeling the

---

[37] Scheer, 'Emotions': 201.
[38] Scheer, 'Emotions': 202.

same kind of feeling. We are living, it would seem, each other's emotions.[39]

Neuroscientific research into empathy has claimed to have found the mechanisms by which empathy works, and it finds that this mechanism is held in common by all of us. The so-called 'mirror neuron' was found in monkeys to activate in response to another's motor activity. The brain's response to the sight of certain movements was to mirror the experience of those movements, *as if* the monkey had itself made them. From this it has been extrapolated that we enter into the emotions of others via their gestural clues. Facial expressions become the window to the inner emotional experience of somebody else. A relationship between motor neurons and affect is assumed, whereby our reception of the movement of others is connected to its associated feeling. Thus, we feel what others feel. The explanatory power of the mirror neuron has been massively inflated: 'The instantaneous understanding of the emotions of others, rendered possible by the emotional mirror neuron system, is a necessary condition for the empathy which lies at the root of most of our more complex inter-individual relationships.'[40]

So does that mean that empathy is a hardwired universal? Such a conclusion would be convenient for sure, but it would make a serious dent in the history-of-emotions project, and there are strong reasons to doubt it. Neuroscientific research that has located the neural 'mirrors' in the brain that make empathy possible also demonstrate that the reading of emotions outside of the self are nevertheless mediated through the self. In a 2004 article, Decety and Jackson laid out the 'functional architecture of human empathy'.[41] Larry McGrath summarises the systems upon which

---

[39] Empathy has become a multi-disciplinary research object. For an overview (which excludes history) see E.-M. Engelen and B. Röttger-Rössler, 'Current disciplinary and interdisciplinary debates on empathy', *Emotion Review*, 4 (2012): 3–8. For an interdisciplinary attempt that includes history, see U. Frevert and T. Singer, 'Empathie unde ihre Blockaden: Über soziale Emotionen', in T. Bonhoeffer and P. Gruss [eds], *Zukunft Gehirn: Neue Erkenntnisse, neue Herausforderungen* (Munich: Beck, 2011), 121–46.

[40] G. Rizzolatti and C. Sinigaglia, *Mirrors in the Brain: How Our Minds Share Actions and Emotions*, trans. Frances Anderson (Oxford: Oxford University Press, 2006), 190–1.

[41] J. Decetey and P.L. Jackson, 'The functional architecture of human empathy', *Behavioral and Cognitive Neuroscience Reviews*, 3 (2004): 71–100.

empathy depends in this study as follows: 'shared representations of self and other', 'the cognitive capacity to take the perspective of another' (imagination), and 'the regulatory mechanisms that "tone down the self-perspective to allow the evaluation of the other-perspective"'.[42]

To translate, what happens in empathic situations is dynamic, depending not only on the emotional expression of the other, but also on the cognitive processing of the receiver. Here the question of emotional style and the emotive process re-enter the scene, for empathy is contingent on knowing what is being encountered, or at least being able to assemble a knowledge of what is being encountered, extrapolated from past experience.[43] Empathy functions in circumscribed emotional latitudes or bandwidths and its functionality depends on membership of a system of emotional knowledge.[44] To be out of time and out of place is to risk either a failure of empathy activation or else a complete misreading of the other's mind. Not only does this present social barriers to universal empathy in our lives, but more specifically it throws up a barricade to historical analysis that we must traverse with care.

Historians frequently empathise with historical actors. They should be forgiven. I remember coming to the end of a long series of letters written by George John Romanes, the Darwinian disciple. As the brain tumour that would ultimately kill him progressed, so his correspondence became tinged with a sense of his own mortality. As his handwriting faltered, he apologised to his correspondents, explaining the frustration of his failing eyesight and motor skills. One comes to know a subject. To read of his decline in his own hand was moving, deeply affecting and not a little difficult. Nonetheless, my emotional response to these letters had to be packed away in the course of analysis, because I could not assume that my response was, for all its empathy, hitting the right notes. To understand what a contextual empathy might have been like, I had

---

[42] L.S. McGrath, 'Historiography, affect, and the neurosciences', *History of Psychology*, 20 (2017): 129–47.

[43] See Scheer, 'Emotions': 214, and *n* 101, 102, 103.

[44] See, for example, B.M. Hood, *The Self Illusion: How the Social Brain Creates Identity* (Oxford: Oxford University Press, 2012), 63–70; A. Young, 'Mirror neurons and the rationality problem', in S. Watanabe, L. Huber, A. Young and A. Blaidsel [eds], *Rational Animals, Irrational Humans* (Tokyo: Science University Press, 2009): 55–69.

to add back in the context of religious doubt that nagged Romanes' life, as well as the polarising convictions of his correspondents in the worlds of science and religion, respectively. I had to understand the context, meaning and reception of death and its correlation with age, as well as Romanes' own appreciation of these things. In sum, whatever I may have felt at Romanes' first-hand account of his own demise, my feelings were of a different order of magnitude, if not of a different order altogether, to Romanes' own, and of those around him who suffered his loss. To reconstruct that emotional world is possible and necessary. We do not have the luxury of an a priori fundamental understanding of the experience of disease, illness, death and grief. Just as we have to learn empathy for ourselves in the present, so we have to learn it differently for the past.

Moreover, our capacity for empathy seems to be unevenly applied. A 2012 study found that being cognitively preoccupied negatively affected the extent to which test subjects empathised with sadness. Meanwhile, those test subjects told to focus on being empathetic were found to have a greater stimulus response to the 'sadness' with which they were confronted. A control group given no specific instruction fell between these two poles.[45] Empathy, therefore, depends upon attention, just as the affective response to our own suffering, be it social suffering or physical pain, is also modified by the amount of attention we direct to it. Think of the old dictum that a grieving person should 'keep busy'. It may not ultimately alleviate the source of the suffering, but as practical advice, it has some merit according to the neuroscientific research.

Historians can make use of this kind of observation. Bracketing for a moment the question of empathy per se, the specific conceptual configurations of which, as we have seen, are situated in the twentieth and twenty-first centuries only, we can nevertheless assume that shared suffering and shared emotions did take place in other periods. What we cannot say, without contextual research, is what the effects of this sharing would have been. If empathy requires both experience (one has to know or be able to extrapolate, on some level, what one is looking at) and attention, then historical examples of it are obviously going to look significantly

---

[45] L.T. Rameson, S.A. Morelli and M.D. Lieberman, 'The neural correlates of empathy: Experience, automaticity, and prosocial behavior', *Journal of Cognitive Neuroscience*, 24 (2012): 235–45.

different according to specific circumstances. What empathic responses mean and what they practically imply is also unstable. We cannot, for example, assume that empathy is the key to human goodness. Neither the historical record nor the neuroscientific research bears out such a pretext.

As Allan Young has pointed out, neuroscientific research on empathy has been led by an assumption – a powerful paradigm, in fact – that empathy is normative and leads to the kinds of positive social interaction that makes societies functional. Non-normative individuals, such as psychopaths, are said to be without empathy.[46] Yet functional neuroimaging data suggests that empathic 'mechanisms' often do work in those who take pleasure in the pain of others. There is nothing implicitly moral about empathy, and nor does it equate simply to a 'social glue' formulation of human social evolution. The idea of the evolution of altruism is so powerful, however, that little research has been done on what Young calls 'empathic cruelty', or even on close correlates such as *Schadenfreude*.[47] In sum, even if mirror neurons and the empathic mind are the stuff of biological certainty, what happens as a consequence of their activation is not foretold, and nor is their activation constant. The evolutionary biological account of empathy does not tend to recognise this mutability. This is not to say that surprising contextual histories of empathy might not add to the evolutionary story of social development, but at first blush they must provide a serious challenge to it. Historically speaking, empathy and its loose correlates, sympathy and compassion, have pointed towards social disintegration, exclusion, stratification and chauvinism, as much as they have pointed towards cohesion, reciprocity and community building.[48]

---

[46] S. Baron-Cohen, *Zero Degrees of Empathy: A New Theory of Human Cruelty* (London: Allen Lane, 2011); cf. A. Young, 'Empathy, evolution, and human nature', in J. Decety, D. Zahavi and S. Overgaard [eds], *Empathy: From Bench to Bedside* (Cambridge, MA: MIT Press, 2011), 21–37.

[47] A. Young, 'Empathic cruelty and the origins of the social brain', in S. Choudhury and J. Slaby [eds], *Critical Neuroscience: A Handbook of the Social and Cultural Contexts of Neuroscience* (Oxford: Blackwell, 2012), 159–76; on Schadenfreude, see W.W. van Dijk and J.W. Ouwerkerk [eds], *Schadenfreude: Understanding Pleasure at the Misfortune of Others* (Cambridge: Cambridge University Press, 2014).

[48] See, for example, the sympathy ideology of the early eugenicists, in Boddice, *Science of Sympathy*, ch. 6. See also K. Ibbett, *Compassion's Edge: Fellow Feeling and*

All this begs the specific question of what we see when we look at expressions in the past, captured as they are in paintings and drawings, tapestries, sculpture and photography. Looking at the history of art, which provides a record of facial and bodily gestures stretching back to the dawn of civilisations around the world, one finds a vast array of facial expressions, the presence of which can be interpreted to betray the affective content of a composition. Understanding those expressions takes work. The realist revisionism of Charles Bell and others cast a pall over the whole history of art for making 'mistakes' about expressive possibilities. In showing the limitations of the human face, and of the 'correct' expressions of certain emotions, Bell demonstrated both the technical ineptitudes and the fraudulent endeavours of past masters. With great verve and nerve, Bell reduced the quality of a painting or sculpture to its verisimilitude, according to his own understanding of the relation between emotions and faces. Thus, Bell carved out his own place in the history of emotions, but his art-historical analysis requires further development.

I want to be clear here that in sketching a way to 'read' art for its emotional content I am specifically looking to guide historians of emotion. I recognise that there are many ways to look at art, and that any given work exists in the present and has an effect on a viewer as a present object. I am not interested, per se, in the way in which viewers respond to historical works of art in the here and now, but rather in the way in which historical works of art are valuable evidence about the emotional repertoire of the time and place in which the work was created. My art-historical approach therefore involves reading historically. As with other sources, I suggest we begin with the assumption not of contrivance or error, but that depictions of emotions carry their own 'authenticity': that is, they represent what they were intended to represent. If we do not readily understand this intent; if we cannot readily read the expression; if the expression appears to us false or incorrect – all these things are our problem, not a problem of the work of art. It is our job to overcome them.

A ready example comes from the long history of depictions of Christian martyrs, often shown in the process of being martyred in

Its Limits in Early Modern France (Philadelphia: University of Pennsylvania Press, 2017); Konstan, *Pity Transformed.*

all manner of gruesome ways.[49] What are we to make of the fact that, very often, the faces of the martyrs are somewhat blank, doleful perhaps, but hardly presenting what one might tend to think of – thinking presently – as screaming pain and terrible fear? To read works of art in context we must acquire the 'period eye', so named by Renaissance art historian Michael Baxandall: a way of seeing that takes full account of the cultural and political context of a work of art's production.[50] To understand what is depicted in the face of a Christian martyr, or in the face of Christ as the 'man of sorrows', one needs to know when it was produced, perhaps why it was produced, for whom it was produced and the framework of reception into which it would have been received. It was, among pre-Reformation European Catholics, for example, important that the pain of martyrs was depicted as being virtuously endured. To embrace pain and to suffer willingly were marks of being Christlike. A culture of asceticism in which suffering was actively sought provides a backdrop for such imagery, which served as a stimulus to the emulation of Christ's passion. Since the meanings applied to sensory stimulation are at the heart of emotional experience, we should conclude that this kind of pain endurance was not experienced in the same way as, for example, a banal toothache, or of any of the wealth of pain complaints in contemporary, secular, developed societies.

The apparently blank faces of the Christian martyrs are not mistakes or fanciful propaganda works that are false in their representations. Rather, they are clear indicators of an emotional style, of prescriptive feeling rules. When put into the context of textual accounts of religious discipline and asceticism, we must accord them their time-bound 'authenticity'. The emotive latitude of medieval and early modern religious life will not be accessed via our own contemporary expression maps and assumptions of empathic universality. To enter into the emotional expressions in the history of art requires an empathic education. Our own

---

[49] Moscoso, *Pain*, 12–18; see also M.B. Merback, *The Thief, the Cross and the Wheel: Pain and the Spectacle of Punishment in Medieval and Renaissance Europe* (London: Reaktion, 2001), and E. Cohen, *The Modulated Scream: Pain in Late Medieval Culture* (Chicago: University of Chicago Press, 2010), 227f.

[50] M. Baxandall, *Painting and Experience in Fifteenth-century Italy: A Primer in the Social History of Pictorial Style* (Oxford: Oxford University Press, 1988), 29–108.

experience is not (necessarily) there. There is an 'empathy wall' between us and the past.[51] It is not insurmountable, however. We can learn to 'see' in the ways past actors saw. It is this, ultimately, that Lynn Hunt calls for in her attempt to reach the 'experience of revolution': revolutionary imagery (in the form of prints) 'had direct bodily effects via both the unconscious bodily emotions and conscious embodied feelings'.[52] Scheer would probably object that the dualism here, between a background of unconscious and historically stable body of emotions and a historically contingent set of embodied feelings that are conscious, is a false one. The body too is part of that cultural context. Baxandall did not, it must be remembered, talk of 'period sight', but of the 'period *eye*'. The sense of sight, after all, is nothing without the physical eye, part of a biological body and a sensory system that is historical and mutable. Bodily reactions to depictions of the emotions are dependent on an implicit understanding of what is being depicted. To that end, they cannot be separated away from conscious feelings about what is being seen.

This discussion, which has mutually implicated the emotions and the senses, the body and the mind, and the world in which these are situated, takes us on a step towards the development of a methodology that can fully integrate all of these factors. It is time to take leave of your senses and consider the senses of others.

---

[51] The phrase is borrowed from A.R. Hochschild, *Strangers in their Own Land: Anger and Mourning on the American Right* (New York: The New Press, 2016), 5.
[52] L. Hunt, 'The experience of revolution', *French Historical Studies*, 32 (2009): 671–78, at 677.

6

EXPERIENCE, SENSES AND THE BRAIN

Take five

How do you feel? The question, a commonplace query if ever there was one, is actually enormously complex. That we handle it as a kind of banal enquiry is at once a testament to the ways in which we process our experiences in context, as well as being a pointer to how little reflexivity is generally applied to difficult questions. It is at once a question about our state of health, our emotional disposition in a given moment, our sentiments about a certain subject or event, an enquiry into our judgement (as a synonym for 'what do you think?') and a literal investigation into our senses, on three levels. It might ask us to identify the level of, say, pain in a given moment: during a dental procedure, for example. It might ask us to rate or evaluate another sort of sensory experience: how do you feel about the chocolate cake, about the noise levels, about the view? And it is also literally an enquiry into *how* we feel. What are the mechanisms involved in allowing us to make *sense* of the world? The conceptual confusion of all this, compounded by the semantic overlap, which conflates the sensory and the cognitive in the word 'sense', suggests the rich possibilities in a study of the senses. Moreover, it suggests that the senses ought properly to be a part of the history of emotions.

There have been significant inroads into the history of the senses, most of which connect to a history of the emotions, but seldom have historians of the emotions substantially noticed. In 1989, for example, David Howes made a strong case for the relationship of the senses to 'affective mechanisms' and demonstrated the extent to which certain senses, particularly the sense of smell, became more powerful from the mid-eighteenth century, whereas sight became less perspicacious in being able to discern – to *see* – the dynamics of social hierarchy.[1] Shortly afterward, Alain Corbin explicitly proposed a radical history of the senses, which would be framed in part by entering into the sensual world of historical actors, constructing soundscapes and olfactory maps, but also, importantly, trying to reconstruct the specific historical tuning of the senses to those stimuli. In other words, the 'historicity of the modalities of attention' had to be taken seriously.[2] The functioning of an ear, an eye, a nose, or at least the brain's interpretation of signals from those organs, could not be understood to be ahistorical. Senses were conditioned in the past, much as we condition our own. The presence of odorous particulate matter in the atmosphere or of vibrations within the audible spectrum does not automatically lead to a smell evaluation or a listening evaluation of a certain kind. Our affective response to such things is based on where and when we are, as well as who we are and to what we are accustomed.

As with emotions, passions, sentiments and so on, the feelings and the senses have a history that is at once a history of culture and a history of the body. Just as with the emotions, what people have thought was happening when they sensed something had an effect on what was sensed and the meaning of what was sensed. The evaluation of sensual experience that makes meaning out of sensation hinges on the same dynamics that make meaning of emotions, and their combined histories conceptually overlap in significant ways. At root, of course, both the emotions and the senses are *outputs* of the brain, rather than existing materially somewhere. Sight, for example, is processed by the eye, but is not a quality of the eye. Seeing is what happens after visual stimuli are processed and made into visual experience by the brain. As with the other senses, visual experience is never devoid of or separate from an affective evaluative cognitive process. We do not see, as it were, neutrally. To see a creepy clown and be afraid is not a sequential process in which seeing is unrelated to fear, but a conflated set of processes in which affective evaluation is bound up with optical processing, all of which is also bound up with cultural experience.

---

[1] D. Howes, 'Scent and sensibility', *Culture, Medicine and Psychiatry*, 13 (1989): 81–9.
[2] Corbin, *Time*, 183. Corbin is the father of the field, which has its roots in the *Annales* school, his opening contribution being *Le miasme et la jonquille* (Paris, Aubier-Montaigne, 1982), translated in 1986 as *The Foul and the Fragrant* (Cambridge, MA: Harvard University Press).

What we see, therefore (and by extension, what we smell, taste, hear and touch), is not objectively what is there. Our relation to the objects of perception, much as with our relation to the objects of emotion (our associations), is filled in by the brain. In a broad anthropological survey, Constance Classen concluded that 'the dominant sensory medium of symbolic orientation can vary widely from culture to culture and can only be understood within the context of a particular culture and not through generalized external sensory paradigms'.[3] The interrelation and hierarchy of senses will be different in different places, and will dramatically impact how the world is encountered and evaluated. As Classen goes on to observe, 'sensory models are conceptual models, and sensory values are cultural values. The way a society senses is the way it understands. ... Sensory values not only frame a culture's experience, they express its ideals, its hopes and its fears.'[4] Such an observation underpins the work of Piero Camporesi, who delved into the sensory world of medieval and early modern Italy. Plants, animals and the earth itself were anthropomorphised so as to exist in sympathetic and sensitive relation with humans, who sowed, planted and harvested while taking 'account of plants' sentimental needs, their deep, delirious desire for affection and companionship'. Existential hopes and fears were rooted in a sensory awareness of – and a meaningful emotional relationship with – the inanimate life upon which humanity depended. It was a relationship 'profoundly different from our current aloofness and cold indifference' to the vegetable world.[5] The senses, as with the emotions, are fair game for historians.

There is already a significant body of work in this area, and much of it explicitly makes the connection with the history of emotions. Robert Jütte, for example, begins his survey of the history of senses from antiquity to cyberspace by reference to the common points of departure for the history of emotions, Lucien Febvre and Norbert Elias, where *mentalités* and manners, respectively, were bound with nuances of meaning, changes in the human processing of sensory

---

[3] C. Classen, *Worlds of Sense: Exploring the Senses in History and Across Cultures* (London: Routledge, 1993), 135.
[4] Classen, *Worlds of Sense*, 136.
[5] P. Camporesi, *The Anatomy of the Senses: Natural Symbols in Medieval and Early Modern Italy*, trans. Allan Cameron (Cambridge: Polity, 1994), 20–1, 195–6.

experience, and emotional behaviour.[6] More to the point, he begins his study with the observation that historians must break with 'the aprioristic assumption of the "naturalness" of sense perception', which is to say that we should view bodies themselves as historical.[7] A very long timeline reveals apparent changes in the acuteness of certain senses, formed by changing bodily and cognitive interactions with the kind of world in which humans have lived. The objects around which we orientate ourselves and which give meaning to our lives impact how we experience them. It matters, from an affective and sensory point of view, whether printed texts exist, for example, who has access to them and how readily. The human sensory world among oral traditions was likely in stark contrast to textual traditions, just as the sensory world around us is being changed by the online experience. The medium is not merely the message. The medium is world-making; or, to be more precise, the medium allows the human brain to make the world.

Curiously enough, Jütte also begins with some meaningful passages from Marx that echo the constructionist view.[8] We can abstract these kinds of observations from their original political agenda and see that Marx's comprehension of the human construction of the world for human ends does in fact accord with certain neuroscientific, biocultural understandings of the creation of experience. Marx thought it 'obvious that the *human* eye enjoys things in a way different from the crude, non-human eye; the human *ear* different from the crude ear, etc.', and with his distinct grasp of historicism it was also as obvious that humans at different stages of social development and at different points on the social scale would sense the world differently: 'The care-burdened, poverty-stricken man has no *sense* for the finest play; the dealer in minerals sees only the commercial value but not the beauty and the specific character of the mineral; he has no mineralogical sense.'[9] Each individual

---

[6] R. Jütte, *A History of the Senses: From Antiquity to Cyberspace* (Cambridge: Polity, 2005), 11–12.
[7] Jütte, *History of the Senses*, 8. Such a framework was echoed, in almost the same terms, by David Howes in his 'Introduction: "Make it New!" – Reforming the sensory world', in D. Howes [ed.], *A Cultural History of the Senses in the Modern Age* (London: Bloomsbury, 2014), 1–30, at 28.
[8] Jütte, *History of the Senses*, 9–10.
[9] K. Marx, 'Private property and Communism', *Economic and Philosophic Manuscripts of 1844*, vii, viii.

thinks, senses and feels his way into the world, and this takes Marx – and us – beyond the canonical five senses:

> Only through the objectively unfolded richness of man's essential being is the richness of subjective *human* sensibility (a musical ear, an eye for beauty of form – in short, *senses* capable of human gratification, senses affirming themselves as essential powers of *man*) either cultivated or brought into being. For not only the five senses but also the so-called mental senses, the practical senses (will, love, etc.), in a word, *human* sense, the human nature of the senses, comes to be by virtue of *its* object, by virtue of *humanised* nature. The *forming* of the five senses is a labour of the entire history of the world down to the present.[10]

Marx here supplies us both a collapse of the nature/culture binary and an agenda for the history of emotions and the senses, the sources for which are the very objects and relations – the material world and human intercourse – around which human experience is orientated. The sense that an object is meaningful in a certain way, coupled with the understanding that for another person the same object can be sensed as meaningful in a different way, and that the possibilities are endless, gives us both cause to pursue this topic historically as well as the political motivation so to do. I do not mean 'political' in the crude sense, and nor do we need to share the political agenda of Marx. Rather, it is to say that Marx, like most historians, had the human at the centre of his historiographical practice. He understood, as we strive to understand through the history of emotions, that the affective meaningfulness of life – the perception of experience as a human sense – was bound up with material conditions and the social reality of the world. A person's *objective* reality was indistinguishable from her *subjective* reality. There is, after all, nowhere else from which to sense the world except from the subjective point of view, but that point of view is always embedded into the world itself. As Marx concludes, and the conclusion is neuroscientifically sound, 'The nature which develops in human history – the genesis of human society – is man's *real* nature; hence nature as it develops through industry, even though in an *estranged* form, is true *anthropological* nature.'[11]

Ways of seeing and of sensing tell us about the dynamics that

[10] Marx, 'Private property', viii.
[11] Marx, 'Private property', ix.

shaped human experience and the human perception of reality. What it *felt* like to be there and then, if we can attain such an analysis, will tell us about the subjective reality of power structures, social stratification, institutional systemisation of routine and ritual, and the vagaries of identity and belonging. Our sources are such mundanities as the reported taste of food at high table and low; accounts of the smell of effluent in the noses of the urbane, and of the perfumed in the nostrils of the poor; testimony of the pious on the sight of the Host at the altar, and of the pleasure seeker on the sight of the flesh at a burlesque; the revels of festival goers in a soundscape of music, and the complaints of bourgeois locals about noise pollution. In sum, as Classen has demonstrated, 'sensory values are social values, sensory relations are also social relations'.[12]

In some ways, Marx's observations came after a long line of kindred observations that, the predominance of the five senses notwithstanding, placed the essence of being human in a sixth sense, an inward sense, a *common* sense.[13] In English, we use the phrase 'common sense' as if to mean something generally understood, but it is worth pausing to reflect on the literal meaning of the word 'sense' here. It is understanding but not born of knowledge; rather, it is something simply perceived to be. Since Descartes at least, but certainly also for ages before, there has been a notion of a form of judgement that is at the heart of the human self, that understands and processes the sensory information from the traditional senses, and which provides motivation for action. Whether this overarching sense that understands is located in the head or the gut, or the soul, it is generally given a power of relating the objective world to the self (itself a contingent category), and giving movement and meaning to the human experience of the world. Hence, the twelfth-century Cistercian reformer Bernard of Clairvaux's association of each of the five senses with types of love, each pairing deriving ultimately from the nature of the soul.[14] As Richard G. Newhauser has summarised it, with reference to medieval times, 'sensation was not just guarded, but guided'. Then,

---

[12] Classen, *Worlds of Sense*, 136.
[13] Hallett, *Senses*, 7.
[14] R.G. Newhauser, 'Introduction: The sensual Middle Ages', in R.G. Newhauser [ed.], *A Cultural History of the Senses in the Middle Ages* (London: Bloomsbury, 2014), 5.

as now, both the translation of sensation through cognition and the evaluative output of this process are 'interpretive', not simply natural.[15]

That such a mind–affect–sensation triad might also apply to Descartes cuts across the grain of received wisdom that Descartes separated mind and body, soul and soma. While there are major consequences of Cartesian dualism (summarised below with reference to pain sensation), it should be noted that Descartes himself had a complex view of the relation of sensation to the soul. Key to this was his observation that things that happened to the body were happening to *him*, or, in other words, his self-perception was not indifferently detached from the body's machinery. Rather, the mind was sympathetically situated in such a way as to identify with the body. The Cartesian human, in Descartes' own terms, was a union of body-mind, not a divided pilot and vessel.[16]

The presence of such an inner sense alerts us to the historical instability of what we know as the senses, which are limited to five. The inner senses – common sense, imagination, memory – as well as the spiritual senses, were all in play for centuries. There is no historiographical utility in acknowledging that past epistemologies have numbered many more than five senses, only to dismiss the observation because these epistemologies were 'wrong'. On the contrary, what people *knew* to be correct influenced the kinds of practices in which they engaged and the kinds of evaluations they made about the world around them. It matters that Aristotle thought common sense was located in the heart, but that it later moved to the brain.[17] For the same reasons, it matters when contemporary political theorist Erin Manning exhorts us, without irony, 'to stray from a commonsense reading of the senses'.[18] The process of knowledge transformation, through which we can chart the journey of common sense from heart to head, is also a process of practice transformation, through which we can chart the changes in affective evaluation of the world. Also, Manning reminds us, the

---

[15] Newhauser, 'Introduction', 12.

[16] R. Descartes, *Mediation on First Philosophy* (1641; Cambridge: Cambridge University Press, 1996), 56.

[17] Aristotle, *De Anima*, 425a27–432b29.

[18] E. Manning, *Politics of Touch: Sense, Movement, Sovereignty* (Minneapolis: University of Minnesota Press, 2007), xiv.

effects of sensation are bodily, a point to which I will return under the heading of 'Neurohistory'.

Senselessness

What we now might call a failure in empathy has, at other times, been construed in much more moralistic terms. Historically, various categories of people or profession have been adjudged susceptible to *callousness*, which is not merely a quality that fails to detect the emotional disposition of others, but rather is incapable of so detecting. Callousness is, on the face of it, a sensory shortcoming. It employs the image of hardened skin on a hand or foot that is incapable of *feeling* a stimulus. An accusation of callousness, however, is rarely a charge of sensory shortcoming. Rather, this lack in sensibility is connected to emotional shortcomings and moral consequences. The typical figure of callousness is the surgeon, whose exposure to blood and pain was thought to render him unfeeling and therefore morally suspect.[19] Butchers, whose occupations depended on a failure to make an emotional connection with the animals they slaughtered as well as a disconnect between blood and the feeling of disgust, were also thought to be callous. Colloquially at least, their professions disqualified both from jury service in matters of life and death, for they were thought much more likely to convict. It does not matter so much that this point has no historical grounding in fact. It matters only that it has historical grounding in vernacular knowledge, for interactions with such professions were influenced by it.[20]

The connection between callousness and moral suspicion was echoed in a long-standing relationship between practices of childhood callousness and cruelty in adulthood. From at least the time of Thomas Aquinas, echoed in the art of William Hogarth and the lectures of Immanuel Kant, and repeated often throughout the late eighteenth and nineteenth centuries, cruelty to animals as a

---

[19] The veracity of such claims depends on historical circumstances. See M.S. Pernick, 'The calculus of suffering in nineteenth-century surgery', *The Hastings Center Report*, 13 (1983): 26–36.

[20] The observation possibly originates with Mandeville's *Fable of the Bees* (1714). For a detailed account of the myth and its influence, see L.G. Stevenson, 'On the supposed exclusion of butchers and surgeons from jury duty', *Journal of the History of Medicine and Allied Sciences*, 9 (1954): 235–8.

child was supposed to lead to criminality in adulthood.[21] Hogarth, in the 1750s, famously connected puerile torture routines with animals to the commission of murder and the unchecked scientific curiosity that permitted anatomical dissection. Civilisation itself was threatened by people who could not *feel*. The answer was to make children aware of the tender mercy required of their dominion over dumb animals, so that they might then recognise the suffering of other people around them. The relationship between cruelty to animals in childhood and violence and aggression in adulthood is still cited today, and is known as the 'graduation hypothesis'.[22] There have never been (indeed, one wonders how there could be) controlled studies to confirm this relationship, but a firm belief in its truth has led to many political, legislative and social interventions to prevent callousness in the population.

We should not look at the rise of the animal welfare movement, for example, as a natural development in the evolution and social progress of civilisation, but as a particular historical judgement about the senses and the emotions, and the ways in which practices and value judgements associated with them ought to be controlled.[23] To identify an upholder of animal welfare as the possessor of a moral disposition is to express the conflation of sensitivity, sympathy (or empathy), social practice, and the objects to which social practice refers (animals). Contrariwise, to identify an 'unfeeling' person, unable to access the machinery of compassion, is to identify a failure of sensation, emotion and, therefore, morals. In civil society, the word *feeling* has tended to encompass all three of these facets, and finds its synonym in the word *humanity*. The fact that, since at least the eighteenth century, the label for the human species taken as a whole has been bound up with a sensory and affective quality ought to be of great interest to historians of emotion.[24]

---

[21] Boddice, *History of Attitudes*, 25–120.
[22] For example, J. Wright and C. Hensley, 'From animal cruelty to serial murder: Applying the graduation hypothesis', *International Journal of Offender Therapy and Comparative Criminology*, 47 (2003): 71–88.
[23] Boddice, *History of Attitudes*; R. Preece, *Brute Souls, Happy Beasts and Evolution: The Historical Status of Animals* (Vancouver: UBC Press, 2005); E. Griffin, *England's Revelry: A History of Popular Sports and Pastimes, 1660–1830* (Oxford: Oxford University Press, 2005).
[24] See Haskell, 'Capitalism'; N.S. Fiering, 'Irresistible compassion: An aspect of

Yet, as Corbin reminds us, we have to be aware of who is making our sources. Often, judgements about the insensitiveness of an actor, replete with emotional and moral bluntness, came from people who, in Corbin's words, 'had to mark the distance which separated [them] from [their] subject'.[25] Moreover, when such things are written down we have to assess the intended audience, which might typically be assumed to be of the same stamp of the author. The result is not necessarily, therefore, a true representation of the sense/emotion/moral substance of a historical actor or society in general, but the socio-cultural judgement of another historical actor about that substance. In order to reach a kind of verification, we need also to hear from those labelled insensate, cruel and immoral. Unfortunately, such actors speak far less frequently to the historical record than do their denouncers. I have been lucky enough to find some, but this may justly be called the privilege of the modernist. For those who seek further back in time, there may be less hope.

Nevertheless, one can adopt a position of critical awareness and reflexivity when dealing with the dynamics of interpersonal judgement in historical sources. As Corbin points out, any historian can take the 'precaution' of knowing 'the representations of the sensory system and the ways in which it functioned' in any given period.[26] Evidence follows the logic of its time, and there are few periods that do not give up the secrets of emotional or sensory theory through medical texts. In short, we can understand social dynamics of behaviour and judgement by understanding shifting epistemologies of the senses and the emotions. What is *known* at any given time will inform how an actor practises at that time, how he feels, how he treats a social superior or inferior, and how he will evaluate the pleasant or malodorous smells, urbane or dishevelled sights, or refined or humble cuisine. Essential here is that we can attain an understanding of *evaluation*, for it is here and only here that we can understand what sensation and the affects associated

    eighteenth-century sympathy and humanitarianism', 37 (1976): 195–218; M. Barnett, *Empire of Humanity: A History of Humanitarianism* (Ithaca: Cornell University Press, 2011); B. Taithe, 'The "Making" of the Origins of Humanitarianism?', *Contemporanea*, 3 (2015): 489–96.
[25] Corbin, *Time*, 187.
[26] Corbin, *Time*, 189.

with the objects of sensation mean. Therein lies the history of experience.

We must, for example, know to suspect our simple recognition of words, which may have changed their meaning beyond all recognition. As Constance Classen reminds us, taste 'once meant "to touch"', a fact evidenced in the German word *Taste*, which is a push-button. Scent, she goes on, meant 'to feel', whereas hear meant 'to look'.[27] If this is not compelling reason enough to force us to enter into the worlds of knowledge and ideas that structure reality at different times and places, Classen's following observation surely is:

> many of the terms we use in English to refer to emotions and the intellect have a sensory basis. *Sad*, for example, once meant sated, while *glad* originally meant shining. *Sagacious*, in turn, comes from the Latin for keen-scented, while *sage* comes from the Latin for taste. Even Descartes' pronouncement of intellectual exclusivity, 'Cogito ergo sum', literally means 'I put in motion together (*coagitare*) therefore I am'. Insofar as thought depends on language, therefore, the sensory foundations of many of the words we think with demonstrate that we not only think *about* our senses, we think *through* them.[28]

But what should by now be clear is that, whatever the broad stability of the existence of a relationship among senses, emotions and intellect, the precise configuration of that relationship is far from stable. And, of course, it is the conjecture of historians of emotions that instability about what we think about this relationship will also be reflected in how we sense it, and how we feel it.

Pain, the brain and the neuro turn

The conjecture above is underwritten by borrowed knowledge from neuroscience about the 'plastic' nature of synaptic development. Not all historians of emotions are taking the 'neuro turn', and indeed there are some who would draw attention to the distinctions between, even contradictions of, the history of emotions

---

[27] Classen, *Worlds of Sense*, 8.
[28] Classen, *Worlds of Sense*, 8–9; on the political usage of 'sagacity', see R. Boddice, 'The historical animal mind: "Sagacity" in nineteenth-century Britain', in Smith and Mitchell [eds], *Animal Minds*, 65–78.

and neurohistory.[29] It is important to take a brief diversion into neurohistoriography (which might be a new coinage), for it seems likely that the neuro turn is only going to become more prominent in the humanities and social sciences, and in history in particular.[30] Since neither neurohistory nor the history of emotions has a fixed methodology or orthodoxy of practice, there is room to try to sketch their coming together, even though certain elements may risk pulling them apart.

The fundamental principle of neurohistory is that culture writes to nature. Though Monique Scheer is not an ardent proponent of the field, she nevertheless hit on a key aspect of it when she said that where 'fMRI [functional magnetic resonance imaging] scans show the neural correlates of emotion, then they must be read as images of a "used" brain, one molded by practices of a specific culture'.[31] In fact, the expression 'culture writes to nature' contains a nature/culture duality that neurohistorians could and probably should reject. But it does throw up an image that makes the central theoretical argument easy to grasp. If the brain is imagined as a fixed biological entity, with determined physical and chemical processes going on in it, and if these things that go on have gone on for as long as humans have been recognisable as humans, then there can be no true history of the brain, or its processes. But if the brain is imagined as a biological organ that is in part *made* by the world it is in, then two things happen: the world takes on a remarkable new importance in our understanding of who we are, and the brain becomes historical because it is a contextual object.

Some historians are interested in the second of these things for its own sake. They see the brain itself as an object of study, and they want to know how it works and how it has worked. Such historians are rare, even if their colleagues in the neurosciences are legion. For most historians who are familiar with this approach, however, it is a combination of both that appeals, with an eye to the potential for new histories of experience. Neurobiology's object of

---

[29] See especially McGrath, 'Historiography'.
[30] See in particular F. Callard and D. Fitzgerald, *Rethinking Interdisciplinarity across the Social Science and Neurosciences* (Houndmills: Palgrave, 2015); D. Fitzgerald and F. Callard, 'Social science and neuroscience beyond interdisciplinarity: Experimental entanglements', *Theory, Culture & Society*, 32 (2015): 3–32.
[31] Scheer, 'Emotions': 219.

study is the whole human, for the body, the brain, the senses and the emotions all fall under its remit. Its most recent developments directly impact the history of emotions in a way that makes the neurosciences impossible to ignore for historians. While many will be uncomfortable with this, the rapprochement and active engagement of the humanities and the human sciences is already well underway, and there is good reason to hope for a unity of purpose in our studies.

At one time the study of the nerves and the brain was about the uncovering of the body's internal mechanics. The secret to the senses and the emotions, to pain and suffering, to psychological disorders and mental illness, all were thought to dwell in the specific functional qualities and layout of the body's instruments: nerves, spinal cord, brain. Add to these instruments hormonal secretions such as adrenalin and cortisone, chemical messaging, opioid and cannabinoid systems, and the immune system, and over time a picture emerged of the human as a chemical–mechanical entity that responded to stimuli in predictable ways. The human machine was revealing its secrets, slowly but surely. Where secrets remained, depending on one's point of view, either time would reveal them, or else there lay the *deus ex machina*.

The problem for neuroscientists since at least the 1960s has been the observation that the human does not necessarily behave in predictable ways. There is no absolute stimulus/response relationship that enables us to reduce the human to its mechanics. From this point onwards, neurobiological research in a number of areas has sought to explain the vicissitudes and variations of human experience, looking for the ways in which our realities are constructed as outputs of the brain, rather than the brain simply processing the stimuli of an externally present reality. Put another way, no movement, no sensation and no bodily encounter with the world correlates automatically with a set experience.

This might seem counter-intuitive. If I hit my thumb with a hammer, it is going to hurt, you might argue, and I will not keep on doing it: stimulus, experience and action in predictable relation. But it is precisely such banal examples that neuroscientific research now tends against. It matters when, how and why I am hammering, how many times I have done it before and under what circumstances. An experienced carpenter who has hammered his thumb a thousand times would probably not experience the same sense of pain and anxiety in this moment as, for example, a child wielding a hammer for the first time, or a magician who depends on her manual dexterity for her living. Similarly, there are many well-documented cases of gunshot victims who do not recognise that they have been shot.[32] In the moment, and sometimes for a long time afterwards, they report no pain. The reasons for this are manifold, and we shall come to them. Suffice it to say that neuroscientists tend now to agree with historians that experience – our reality in a given moment – is constructed in the brain, and depends on a wealth of instantly processed information, some of it biological, but much of it cultural and contextual.

We can go further still, however, and say that neural and synaptic development in infancy seems to have a significant impact on the way in which stimuli are experienced in later life. A science of touch has demonstrated that infants exposed to the reassuring touch of a parent in early life go on to have decreased risk of anxiety, chronic pain, depression, as well as decreased risk of what might seem like socio-economic diseases, such as heart disease, obesity and so on.[33] Conversely, infants exposed to significant pain go on to have increased risk of anxiety disorders in later life and are far more likely to suffer from chronic pain syndromes.[34]

The dynamic interaction of touch as a meaningful act – a caress, a punch – directly impacts the way the body develops its physiological stress responses. Cortisol, the body's stress hormone, is useful as an immune response in case of injury, but too much for too long and the body is effectively waging war on itself.[35] We are being physically made, *constructed*, after birth. And insofar as we are being physically made, we are also being affectively made: the emotions do not exist immaterially, but are part of the development of brain function. Moreover, after decades of research that attempted to locate emotional functions to specific parts of the brain, associating

[32] P. Wall, *Pain: The Science of Suffering* (New York: Columbia University Press, 2000), 5–7.
[33] M. Meany, 'Maternal care, gene expression, and the transmission of individual differences in stress reactivity across generations', *Annual Review of Neuroscience*, 24 (2001): 1161–92; I.C.G. Waever *et al.*, 'Epigenetic programming by maternal behavior', *Nature Neuroscience*, 7 (2004): 847–54; cf. Manning, *Politics of Touch*, xi.
[34] G.G. Page, 'Are there long-term consequences of pain in newborn or very young infants?', *Journal of Perinatal Education*, 13 (2004): 10–17.
[35] See Melzack, 'Evolution'.

fear with the amygdala, to name just the most common refrain, neuroscientists have since cast doubt on what they are looking at when they are looking at fMRI scans of emotional activity in human brains.[36] As Lisa Feldman-Barrett and her team have discovered, however, there is every reason to believe that the whole of the brain is recruited in the construction of emotional experience, and that much of the synaptic development required to make that constructive process happen takes place after birth.[37]

Neuroplasticity involves an understanding of the brain, reached in major part through experimentation using fMRI, which transforms what we understand about the sensory body and the meaning of experience. While fMRI techniques have recently endured a significant challenge to their veracity,[38] some of the findings of neuroscientific research have provided elegant explanations for human experience (especially painful experience) that remain highly promising. We can summarise the reversal in our knowledge of the brain thus: since the time of Descartes (at least), neurological sciences laboured under the key assumption that the brain processed the body's afferent experiential sensations, causing a variety of responses which can be labelled 'action'. In other words, the brain's role in experience was to receive sensory information from the periphery and respond: the periphery (skin) signals it is cold, the action centre instructs to move nearer the fire; the periphery (nociceptors in foot) signals pain, the action centre issues an instruction to pull the foot out of the fire; the periphery (ocular sensors in the eye, pain fibres running through the body and to the spinal cord) signals fear, the action centre responds by seeking help and relief. All the while different chemical cascades are being automatically triggered in response to sensation, washing the brain and the nervous system in neurostimulators or neuroblockers that colour the brain's picture of what is going on. In this scenario, the meaningful experiences of cold, burning pain and the fearful sight

[36] See Plamper, *History of Emotions*, 209–12; A. Eklund, T.E. Nichols and H. Knutsson, 'Cluster failure: Why fMRI inferences for spatial extent have inflated false-positive rates', *Proceedings of the National Academy of Sciences of the United States of America*, 113 (2016): 7900–5.

[37] In addition to the other works by Feldman Barrett cited in this book, see J. Beck, 'Hard feelings: Science's struggle to define emotions', *The Atlantic*, 24 February 2015, which reviews Feldman Barrett's work.

[38] Eklund *et al.*, 'Cluster failure'.

of a physical injury all exist objectively. They are relayed from the world to the brain, which takes appropriate action. Insofar as the brain makes judgements about these experiences, it does so with the limitation that cold, pain and fear are objective values that exist in the world.

This view of sensation, judgement and action has been overturned, and the scene can be re-written as follows. Experience is efferent, not afferent. It is an *output* of the brain. Whatever sensory signals the brain receives are not, in and of themselves, experience, but simply sensation. Experience of them has to be *made* in and by the brain. Judgement is part of this output. So, the periphery (skin) signals a drop in temperature, which the brain interprets, leading *perhaps* to the qualitative judgement 'I am cold', the action for which is to move closer to the fire. The periphery (nociceptors in the foot) signals *injury*, not pain, which the brain *could* interpret, based on a whole host of factors, including experience and context, as pain, and the action centre issues an instruction to remove the foot from the fire. The periphery (ocular sensors in the eye, nerves running through the body and to the spinal cord) signals the presence, the image, of injury – a blistered and bloody foot – which the brain *might* interpret as frightening, leading to the seeking of help and relief. In each case, the experience of cold, pain and fear is created in the brain. These are translations of the value-free sensations of temperature and injury, and the sensations associated with the wound after injury.

In each case here I have added a note of circumspection. The reason for this is the key to understanding why this interpretation of experience as brain output is probably correct. People do not experience objective values in the same way. In a room heated to 21 °C, some will be hot, some will be cold, some will be just right. The insoluble problem is that everyone is correct about how they feel about the temperature. Similarly, and more dramatically, experiences of injury are not uniform. Even among people whose nervous systems are functioning 'normatively', the same injurious stimulus results in different types and levels of pain, including no pain at all, and different reactions to that experience, from stoic tolerance to an absolute abandonment to agony.[39]

As for fear, what can be stated with some certainty is that objects

[39] Wall, *Pain*, 59–78.

that arouse fear have to *become* objects of fear through teaching and experience. Those things that are typically thought to be scary in some primal way, such as snakes and spiders, have been shown to be observed neutrally by infants, who must learn the fearfulness of these creatures from others.[40] Even the fearful sight or feeling of one's own injured body can, in certain circumstances, be a point of indifference. I will come back to this particular point shortly, but I first want to dwell on why we might seem to be instinctively afraid of and pained by our own injuries. The relevance of all of this for historians will become clear in due course.

How and why we come to be in pain when we are injured – and indeed, if we come to be in pain at all – holds an illustrative key to understanding neuroplasticity, for it illustrates how people conceive of themselves as bodies, or how we can say, when something is happening to our bodies, that it is happening to *us*. The essential ingredient to an understanding of how pain, or other sensory experience, works is to disassociate experience with anything intrinsic to objects in the world. No matter what the state of damaged nerves in the periphery of our bodies, our pain is not inherent to this damage. Instead, neuroscientists now understand individuals to have a 'neuromatrix' that produces a 'neurosignature' of the body. This is the 'image' or 'pattern' of our bodies that we understand or interpret as our *selves*. The neurosignature is always there and is genetically programmed, but it is also plastic. The neurosignature makes experience out of the sensory information the brain receives from the periphery. This information both feeds and makes the neuromatrix according to a whole raft of variables. Sensory inputs – from the skin, from optic and auditory sources – account for some of these variables. These are intermixed with affects and emotions, themselves made in and through culture and cultural experience.

Body parts themselves have designated meanings or values ascribed to them, as do their organisation into gestures, movements and postures. And as we have seen, many of these movements and positions are themselves responses to cultural prescription and experience. All are processed together in the brain and, in the language of Ronald Melzack, who first imagined the neuromatrix, arranged into a symphonic output that adds up to what we know

---

[40] Smail, *Deep History*, 137.

of as our body-selves.[41] This is how we know, when we are damaged, that the damage is *ours*. The disruption of the neurosignature imprint of the neuromatrix is registered as an anomaly. Depending on our context and experience, that anomaly might well arouse fear. It is one of the attendants of pain.

The major significance of these theories is that they give credence to highly individual experiences of reality that have mystified researchers who might have expected to find reality in the objective, material world. Those suffering from phantom limb pain, for example, perplexed physicians for centuries.[42] A phantom limb is experienced as present, and sometimes extremely painful, even though the limb in question is missing. This is now understood as a result of a disruption of the neurosignature.[43] Signals that are expected from the missing limb do not arrive. The response is a pattern of neural activity that can be experienced as burning pain in the missing limb. After all, the neuromatrix of the body-self still contains the limb that is physically absent. Moreover, the neuromatrix might command the missing limb to move, a command sent with increasing amplification because there is no modulating response from the periphery. This is often experienced as muscle cramp in the absent limb. Though there is still some debate about this, it is generally thought that these pains and experiences are not to do with the site of the injury, but to do with the brain's output.

To a person with phantom limb pain, both the experience of the missing limb and the pain in it are real. Treatment involves attempting to modify the neurosignature so as to change that reality. In other words, the solution pertains to brain plasticity. Work in this regard has led to evidence that individuals can purposefully

[41] Melzack, 'Evolution'.
[42] D.B. Price and N.J. Twombly, *The Phantom Limb Phenomenon: A Medical, Folkloric, and Historical Study: Texts and Translations of 10th to 20th Century Accounts of the Miraculous Restoration of Lost Body Parts* (Washington DC: Georgetown University Press, 1978); J. Bourke, *The Story of Pain: From Prayer to Painkillers* (Oxford: Oxford University Press, 2014), 153–4; J. Bourke, 'Phantom suffering: Amputees, stump pain and phantom sensations in modern Britain', in Boddice [ed.], *Pain and Emotion*, 66–89; W. Witte, 'The emergence of chronic pain: Phantom limbs, subjective experience and pain management in post-war West Germany', in Boddice [ed.], *Pain and Emotion*, 90–110.
[43] Melzack, 'Evolution'; cf. A. Vaso, H.-M. Adahan, A. Gjika, S. Zahaj, T. Zhurda, G. Vyshka and M. Devor, 'Peripheral nervous system origin of phantom limb pain', *Pain*, 155 (2014): 1384–91.

control parts of their brains that have become associated with physical pain. Similar experiments have shown that the brain activity associated with motor functions can be reproduced even without making the associated movement. One can, in effect, experience playing tennis in the mind. Under controlled circumstances, neuroscientists are exploring the extent to which they can provide evidence for something we talk about casually all the time. Can we control our emotions, our affective responses to sensory stimuli and the brain activity associated with movement? The answers point to a high capacity for control.[44] The implication is that our experience of the world is, to some extent, subject to our autonomous control. Even where it is not, reality as we perceive it is an output of the brain. This kind of observation suggests a programme of revision in the history of medicine to take the painful experiences of past actors into account as truth statements concerning the historical contingency of pain. In various ways I have forcefully argued for the re-evaluation of pain in historical sources, as well as pain in contemporary medical practice, as an emotion.[45] Nowhere does the history of emotions and the history of the senses, in conjunction with the neuro turn, have the potential to combine in such fruitful ways.

Why do I call pain an emotion? Taking a cue from Nikola Grahek, I could formulate it another way: if pain is not attended by emotion it is not pain at all, for without affective evaluation, there is only injury, or inflammation, or exclusion.[46] We know this from studies of people with pain asymbolia, a rare condition characterised by an individual's inability to feel pain. Importantly, this is not an anaesthetic condition. The sensations of touch, heat, crushing and so on are all perceived by a person with pain asymbolia, but the affective evaluation of these sensations is inactive. Under fMRI scanners, the brain is shown to detect sensory stimuli to do with injury, but the

---

[44] F. Zeidan et al., 'Mindfulness meditation-related pain relief: Evidence for unique brain mechanisms in the regulation of pain', *Neuroscience Letters*, 520 (2012): 165–73; A. Cair, 'Regulation of anterior insular cortex using real-time fMRI', *Neuroimage*, 35 (2007): 1238–46; R.C. deCharms et al., 'Learned regulation of spatially localized brain activation using real-time fMRI', *Neuroimage*, 21 (2004): 436–43; S. Haller, N. Birbaumer and R. Veit, 'Real-time fMRI feedback training may improve chronic tinitus', *European Radiology*, 20 (2010): 696–703.

[45] Boddice [ed.], *Pain and Emotion*, 1–10; Boddice, *Pain: A Very Short Introduction*.

[46] N. Grahek, *Feeling Pain and Being in Pain*, 2nd edn. (Cambridge, MA: MIT Press, 2007).

part of the brain that would be expected to indicate the affective part of pain experience is missing. People with this condition might not recognise the threat of injury, or dangerous situations, because they are indifferent to injury. It follows from this that when they are injured, they do not protect the injury. They do not limp, or avoid using a broken arm. The physiological signs of recovery that keep people in pain in order to allow the body to heal are not processed by the brain affectively. Hence, people with pain asymbolia tend to live short lives.[47] Wear and tear in their bodies is exaggerated. Nonetheless, they cannot be said to 'suffer' in a meaningful way. No affect, no pain.

The confirmation of the importance of affective processing in the brain in pain states is confirmed, at the other end of the scale, by experiments on pain where there is no physical injury at all. Social exclusion tests, principally carried out by Naomi Eisenberger and her team, have shown that the feeling of being left out carries very similar neural affective responses to the feeling of being physically injured.[48] Being bullied, ostracised or bereaved, in essence, are similar affective stimuli to physical injury in most people. To be in pain, therefore, does not depend on a mechanical or somatic disruption at all. When the trajectories of these two strands of research are intertwined, we can conclude that the meaningfulness of pain is derived affectively. In turn this means that the meaning of pain is contextual. It helps us understand how pain can be pleasurable, according to context;[49] how it might be a sign of divine movement or extreme piety;[50] and how it might be avoided altogether, when our affective attention is otherwise engaged. For historians, this is truly transformative, for we can no longer trust what have typically been the signs of pain, namely weapons or the instruments

---

[47] Wall, *Pain*, 50–1.
[48] N.I. Eisenberger, 'Does rejection hurt? An fMRI study of social exclusion', *Science*, 302 (2003): 290–2. See also, G. MacDonald and L.A. Jensen-Campbell [eds], *Social Pain: Neuropsychological and Health Implications of Loss and Exclusion* (Washington DC: American Psychological Association, 2011).
[49] See, for example, J.R. Yamamoto-Wilson, *Pain, Pleasure and Perversity: Discourses of Suffering in Seventeenth-century England* (New York: Routledge, 2013).
[50] See, for example, M. Berbara, '"Esta pena tan sabrosa": Teresa of Avila and the figurative arts', in J.F. van Dijkhuizen and K.A.E. Enenkel [eds], *The Sense of Suffering: Constructions of Physical Pain in Early Modern Culture* (Leiden and Boston: Brill, 2009): 267–97.

of torture, or wounds and injuries. Instead, we have to interrogate such signs in context, read against the testimony of those who claim not to be in pain in what look to be painful circumstances, and of those who claim to be in pain even where there is no obvious sign of pain. We can follow Sara Ahmed's reflexive observation:

> I become aware of bodily limits *as* my bodily dwelling or dwelling place when I am in pain. Pain is hence bound up with how we inhabit the world, how we live in relationship to the surfaces, bodies and objects that make up our dwelling places. Our question becomes not so much what *is* pain, but what *does* pain do.[51]

Pain is in the world, characterised by our emotional evaluation of what is *happening* to us. It is not, as is so commonly parroted, a human universal. Because it is evaluative, pain is not reducible to physiology alone. Without the dynamic process of coming to understand the meaning of what is happening, without the attendant contingencies of fear, anxiety or misery, pain does not exist.

On the other hand, where there is fear, anxiety or misery, we might look also for pain, giving new life to accounts of painful experience that have not necessarily always been taken at face value. The relation of the body, the emotions, the mind and the senses has often been most clearly elaborated by human accounts of illness, disease or the encounter with medicine in general. One could, for example, trace a historiography of hysteria from antiquity to the present, which would make for a thick catalogue of conditions that would variously arrange the disorders of body and mind according to a wide variety of concepts that organise them. In antiquity, for example, hysteria referred literally to the wandering of the womb within the body, causing the intemperate passions of the sufferer. This wholly physical hypothesis could, however, have sensory cures, as Jerry Toner has noted: 'A fetid fumigation was placed under the woman's nose to repel the ascending uterus, whereas an aromatic was applied to the vagina to attract it downwards.' While Toner observes that the concept of internal bodily mobility was a 'metaphor for the dangers posed by any kind of female social mobility', we ought not to doubt that ancient medics did in fact believe the womb to be peripatetic, that bodily disruption could be witnessed in passionate disturbances, and that sensory applications could

---

[51] Ahmed, *Cultural Politics*, 27.

restore the parts to their proper places.[52] This is not to deny the metaphor, but rather to re-emphasise the extent to which female instability was concretely embodied.

Later accounts of hysteria re-stated the relationship of body, passions and senses in different ways, but the relationship did remain intact. By the time of nineteenth-century clinical investigations into hysteria there was somewhat less emphasis on the actual movement of the womb, but there were nevertheless frequent connections drawn between female sexual deviancy and bodily and mental disorders. Put another way, frowned upon practices such as masturbation or promiscuous sexual activity – an overburden of physical stimulation that highlighted the dangers of certain kinds of touching or contact – could lead to passionate outbursts and physical seizures alike. Tempering the sexual appetite could lead to a diminution of both physical and emotional signs of hysteria.

The corollary to this is to take seriously hysteria as a culturally situated and therefore contextually authentic expression of pain. Its particular form of expression can be thought of as a prescriptive script, the following of which made treatment more likely. This is not to say that such a script was consciously performed, but that it was part of contingent emotive processes where hysterical acts were connected to social pain. While certain medical points of view would point to hysteria as an 'imaginary' complaint, and even point to the quackery used to treat hysteria as proof of its detachment from 'real' medical conditions, when viewed as an emotive process the efficacy of those treatments make sense. To garner medical intervention based on a bodily practice equates to authoritative recognition and corroboration of a medical problem: emotive success. In and of itself this was doubtless a form of relief.

It has become newly important in such figures of pathology and cure, therefore, to make a serious commitment to exploring how far remedies actually worked. In what Javier Moscoso has called the 'moral economy of hope', historians of experience and cultural historians of medicine take seriously contemporary research into the placebo effect and ask how historical iterations of this might have been

---

[52] J. Toner, 'Introduction: Sensing the ancient past', in J. Toner [ed.], *A Cultural History of the Senses in Antiquity* (London: Bloomsbury, 2014), 4.

brought about.[53] There is nothing magical or mystical in placebo, though it is true that we do not understand fully what causes variations in the effect over time and in different subjects.[54] Our bodies come replete with endogenous systems of pain relief that can be understood as both natural analgesics and affect modulators. Some analgesic drugs work by stimulating our own pain-killing systems, and placebo can be thought of in much the same way. If both doctor (or person imbued with medical authority) and patient believe a certain procedure, drug, application or practice will effectively lessen pain, there is a good chance that it will. To study the sensation of pain in historical context is therefore to study the particulars of affective meaning-making in context. To study pain-killing in context is to study the connection between culturally bound beliefs in the medical efficacy of certain drugs or procedures, in combination with what we know about the functioning of inbuilt systems of relief.

Neurohistory

The employment of experimental research, a lot of which has taken place in medical contexts, is complemented by research in evolutionary biology, which also collapses the nature/culture dyad. The key argument for historians is that evolutionary adaptations that took place through natural selection came bundled with other uses that went beyond the initial reason for the adaptation's selection. Individual examples of this are called 'exaptations'. One such exaptation is feathers, thought to have been selected as useful for regulating body temperature, which have had the ultimate additional advantage of being good for flight.

Exaptations are not limited to this kind of physical trait, however. Culture itself can be considered as such. Larry McGrath gives the example of sex as an exaptation, for example. Procreation would be the evolutionary reason for the selection of traits that make sex part of human life. But, as he points out, sex also 'secures social bonds

---

[53] J. Moscoso, 'Exquisite and lingering pains: Facing cancer in early modern Europe', in Boddice [ed.], *Pain and Emotion*, 16–36, at 31.
[54] K.T. Hall, J. Loscalzo and T.J. Kaptchuk, 'Genetics and the placebo effect: The placebome', *Trends in Molecular Medicine*, 21 (2015): 285–94; A. Tuttle *et al.*, 'Increasing placebo responses over time in U.S. clinical trials of neuropathic pain', *Pain*, 156 (2015): 2616–26.

and reproduces cultural desires', both of which are beyond the natural-selection explanation for sex, but which have themselves become factors in additional selection.[55] The conclusion to be drawn is that culture is a product of evolution and, moreover, becomes a part of the 'natural' world in which further adaptations are selected. The brain, and whatever the brain produces, is not exempt from these forces. McGrath summarises as follows: 'For practitioners of neurohistory, the repeated behaviors comprising cultural relations reciprocally influence the brain's plasticity – a process called the "Baldwin effect." Neurons are wired to a social context. Changes in culture take place within and through the brain's continuous evolution.'[56] There is also an essential dynamic to be added here, which is to say that the brain's continuous evolution takes place within and through cultural change. They are each other's cause and effect.[57]

Let us pull together these threads and see why they are so relevant for the historian, and for the historian of emotions in particular. If cultural relations literally *make* the brain – think of millions of new synaptic connections being made in the crucible of everyday interactions – then we cannot presume to understand what past experience of different cultures was like. We certainly cannot presume that our own experiential register is appropriate for judging how it felt to be a historical actor. That doubt is further enhanced by the neurobiological knowledge that tells us that missing limbs feel present, and by experiments that show how experiences can be processed in the brain even if they are not objectively happening in the world. To compound this further still, we must not only think of human evolution in terms of what is commonly known as 'evolutionary time'. Human life is constantly evolving, at a micro-evolutionary level, so that we cannot assume the neurological development of a child in contemporary New York City follows the same course as a child in eighteenth-century New York. Cultural adaptation and innovation, including technological change, radically alters what humans do and how humans interact. Such changes in practice and exchange inevitably effect how the

---

[55] McGrath, 'Historiography': 4.
[56] McGrath, 'Historiography': 4.
[57] It is important here to stress dynamism, rather than find fault with a 'loopy' causality; cf. J.T. Burman, 'History from within? Contextualizing the new neurohistory and seeking its methods', *History of Psychology*, 15 (2012): 84–99, at 91.

brain develops. We are, in a profound sense, our worlds. We are biocultural.

Think of these observations in terms of the possibilities for emotional experience. What does a new technology – the printing press, the steam engine, the Internet – do to change us at a neurological level, and what are the effects of that change? Likewise, what does the hitherto unknown ingestion of caffeine, alcohol or opium do? It is possible, as Daniel Lord Smail, McGrath and others have pointed out, to think of such things as psychotropic stimulants that come with psychotropic practices: the printing press implies new practices of reading; the steam engine implies new practices of work, travel, time-keeping and more; the Internet implies new practices of communication, organisation, identification and so on. The ingestion of new chemical compounds in the stuff of food, drink and drugs implies new social configurations, not only of production and supply, but also of consumption.

According to McGrath, 'Examining the shifting landscape of psychotropic practices lies at the heart of neurohistorians' ambition to bring together biology and culture.'[58] But if 'the conditioning of the nervous system [is] the principal means through which institutions are established and extended over long expanses of space and time', then we must also seriously entertain the inverse proposition: that the establishment of new institutions and new practices is the principal means through which the nervous system is conditioned.[59] The project laid out by Smail in 2008 worked towards this, and it obviously intersects with the history of emotions in a profound way. It not only explains how new emotions might emerge (and disappear), but also the extent to which the neurological complex that lies at the heart of emotional output is directly hitched to social practices and social institutions.

It behoves me here to appraise the neurohistorical project as Smail constructed it, in order to make it both useable and even more palatable to historians of emotions. The principal stumbling block is that Smail adheres to a basic-emotions model that is unappealing to historians of emotion. In what follows I want to show how we can – must – extricate neurohistory from this model and, in so doing, leave Smail's vision otherwise largely intact. Smail first

[58] McGrath, 'Historiography': 5.
[59] McGrath (quoting Fuller), 'Historiography': 5.

positions himself within an evolutionary understanding of the emotions that foregrounds a stable biological human being, stating: 'Many of the things we do are shaped by behavioral predispositions, moods, emotions, and feelings that have a deep evolutionary history.' With this he commits analytical errors that have stunted the reception of neurohistory. He goes on:

> These body states are not ghostly things flitting mysteriously through consciousness. Recent work in neuropsychology and neurophysiology has shown that they are physiological entities, characteristically located in specific parts of the brain and put there by natural selection. Some of them, including emotions, are relatively automated, no different from the other areas of life governance – basic metabolism, reflexes, pain, pleasures, drives, motivations – that are routinely handled by the brain in all hominoids.[60]

On the face of it, this might sound fair enough, but the historian of emotions would probably object to the idea that emotions and pain, among other things, have been 'put there' by a natural force, and operate basically automatically. Smail does qualify all of this in due course, but with 'nature' and automation looming large this suggests a pre-cultural background to the human being, which always begs the question of what a human being without culture is. Further evidence for this biological determinism is found in the statement that 'hormones and neurotransmitters ... help determine how feelings actually feel', and the insistence on a 'universal biological substrate that simply cannot be ignored'.[61] Why not? What if we reject this substrate entirely? In a world of brain plasticity, how relevant is it, and how universal can it really be said to be when the thing that gives meaning to existence is so culturally bound? Smail himself gives us cause to ask the question, for he points out that 'behaviors that are shaped by predispositions and emotions are often plastic, not hardwired'. And this means that even the 'universal biological substrate' has its nuances: 'Basic social emotions are almost certainly universal. Nonetheless ... they do different things in different historical cultures.'[62] He goes on to point out, emphatically and rightly, the futility of any 'quest to identify "human nature"', since 'biology and cultural studies are fundamentally

---

[60] Smail, *Deep History*, 113.
[61] Smail, *Deep History*, 113–14.
[62] Smail, *Deep History*, 114.

congruent'.⁶³ Both disciplines agree that there is nothing 'essential or primordial about things like race or identity', which depend in large part on feelings of belonging or not belonging.⁶⁴

The problem with this analysis remains one of teleology. It is a methodological weakness with basic-emotions analysis that has more or less dogged everyone who has propounded it. Starting with a known concept of 'disgust', usually in English, the physiological and gestural signs of this concept are mapped onto people of other cultures who, when representing similar physiological signs and expression, are said to be 'disgusted', even if the local concept in question is worthy of a rich conceptual analysis of its own and does not bear any contextual or experiential resemblance to 'normative' representations of disgust in anglophone contexts. To concede that social emotions 'do different things in different historical cultures' makes it meaningless, even an obfuscation, to say that, 'disgust' is nevertheless 'universal', irrespective of its different contexts, signs and experiences. To quip, 'Same disgust, different object', as Smail does, is to impose a preferred and a priori conceptual definition on a physiological process that does not, in fact, need to be defined by the label of its associated emotional experience in some cultures.⁶⁵ Bare physiology does not carry any meaning. The analysis is, perhaps, the legacy and hangover of twentieth-century physiological experimentation that determined to locate the emotions in physiological processes. More or less explicitly, then, this kind of analysis identifies a physiological process with the emotion itself, which is confusing if it is then necessary to talk about emotions as dynamic experiences dependent on cultural context.

Clearly, at this point, 'emotions' means two different things, and this pinpoints the tension in Smail's work. An emotion, for historians of emotions, cannot be reduced to its physiological process, and we should probably resist this kind of slippage. A physiological process associated with specific expressions of disgust is, if we follow Reddy, in a dynamic relationship with the cultural prescriptions for what is disgusting. To call it automatic is to use another shorthand that obscures the degree to which physiological reactions are culturally bound by what stimulates them, and culturally influenced by

[63] Smail, *Deep History*, 125.
[64] Smail, *Deep History*, 124.
[65] Smail, *Deep History*, 115.

codes of expression that in turn modulate or modify them. There is always translation, always a process. Even what some scholars call 'basic' is negotiated, whether by effortful self-management that is conscious or by the kind of self-management that occurs *as if* automatically, and inevitably, for humans in culture. For Smail, 'A neurohistorical perspective on human history is built around the plasticity of the synapses that link a universal emotion, such as disgust, to a particular object or stimulus, a plasticity that allows culture to embed itself in physiology.'[66] McGrath simply entertains the possibility of a radical rejection of the universal emotion by proposing that the existence of the aforementioned plasticity undermines or contradicts allusions to the universal.[67]

Given Smail's emphasis on the vast array of ways in which different cultures can 'exploit' physiological stimuli, it is difficult to see why the basic emotion model is retained. We ought to be able to re-work the following statement of Smail's to better represent the fact that human nature *is* human culture: 'Given the plasticity of such emotions as disgust, the interaction between universal cognitive or physiological traits and particular historical cultures is never simple.'[68] Historians make life difficult for themselves when they begin with transhistorical categories of analysis and then try to account for an all-too-evident historicism within them. By simply removing the word 'universal' from this quote, and by adding quotation marks around the word 'disgust', we have a useable appraisal of the problems facing historians of emotion and neurohistorians alike: 'Given the plasticity of such emotions as "disgust", the interaction between cognitive or physiological traits and particular historical cultures is never simple'. By untethering ourselves from the basic-emotions mooring, we likely also find ourselves better equipped to begin tackling them.

This position also makes for a more consistent approach to the other aspects of Smail's configuration of a neurohistorical agenda. As he says, just because the capacity for a certain physiological state is universal, it does not mean that we are all bound to have it. Hormones need receptors in the brain in order to have effect, and the presence of specific receptors often depends on 'development

---

[66] Smail, *Deep History*, 115.
[67] McGrath, 'Historiography': *passim*.
[68] Smail, *Deep History*, 115.

and experience', which in turn depend on 'cultural norms'.[69] Moreover, what one *does* because of a physiological state is not determined by the physiological state. Smail identifies this truth, but seems at first to represent the relationship between physiology and behaviour as a one-way street: 'Human behavioral norms, suitably internalized, allow one to ignore or override the predispositions one may have toward doing things or the emotions experienced while doing them.' To exemplify the point, he notes, 'Few people cave in, on the spot, to the feelings of lust they might occasionally have toward someone who is not their partner.'[70] True enough. But the modification of behaviour necessarily also modifies the physiological state. The physiological state that is experienced, in context, as lust, might quickly become a source of longing, of shame and guilt, of unrequited love and of grief. The cascade of experiences related to behavioural modification does not take place against a stable background of physiological lust, and nor can we assume that all of the emotional experiences in this sequence are preceded by their respective physiological indicators. We are always in an emotional two-way street. Smail, in turn, acknowledges this. In fact, it is a guiding principle for neurohistory: 'cultural practices can have profound neurophysiological consequences'.[71]

Some historians have already begun to explore such questions.[72] Most recently, Julia Bourke applied neurohistorical methods to anchoritic guidance writing, specifically *De Institutione Inclusarum* (*c.*1160) of Aelred of Rievaulx. She views the guide as a 'means' by which an anchorite could pursue 'an emotional aim – that of mystical union, in which the anchorite is subsumed by the divine'.[73] Not unusually, for a neurohistorian, textual practices are analysed for the psychotropic effects: 'All reading shapes a reader's interior

[69] Smail, *Deep History*, 115.
[70] Smail, *Deep History*, 116.
[71] Smail, *Deep History*, 117.
[72] See, for example, C. Berco, 'Perception and the Mulatto body in Inquisitorial Spain: A neurohistory', *Past and Present*, 231 (2016): 33–60; E. Russell [ed.], 'Environment, culture, and the brain: New explorations in neurohistory', *RCC Perspectives*, 6 (2012). For a critical appraisal, see the five articles in 'Focus: Neurohistory and history of science', *Isis*, 105 (2014): 100–54.
[73] J. Bourke, 'An experiment in "neurohistory": Reading emotions in Aelred's *De Institutione Inclusarum* (*Rule for a Recluse*)', *The Journal of Medieval Religious Cultures*, 42 (2016): 124–42, at 126.

world to some extent, whether the reader is aware of this or not.' In this case, 'Devotional reading ... is a conscious effort to use the act of reading written text to construct a spiritually significant internal space and to fill that space with useful images and affective states in service of a religious goal.'[74] Here I would add a nuance to this not untypical neurohistorical quest for the interior. If reading practices shape a reader's interior world and if, as we see from medical research into affective pain experience, experience is an output of the brain, then the distance between interiority and exteriority is collapsed. The shaping of the interior world is the shaping of the world. To be subsumed by the divine is not experienced as an entirely interior phenomenon. The divine, in this instance, exists. In particular, effortful production of *caritas* (translated here as 'compassion') is connected to studies on the effortful direction of empathy in contemporary neuroscientific experimentation, with the observation that practice, in both senses (doing and repetition), led to a more automatic response over time.[75]

Lynn Hunt proposed a similar approach to a re-casting of the French Revolution, first observing that, '*Experience* is not a neutral term'.[76] The self that experiences is not reducible either to a completely incoherent entity, awash in discursive threads and entanglements, or a completely coherent, rational thing. Drawing from neuroscientific accounts of what comprised the self, and the functioning of experience, Hunt cast the historical net anew. The self 'is not a physiological substance', but it is based in 'matter'. The self is 'not simply a discursive effect', but 'an activity'.[77] The brain 'arranges, categorizes, and manages experience, consciously or unconsciously, creating over time the cohesion and continuity that we call identity, which is never fixed and yet is real, not to mention crucial for survival in the world'.[78] She might have gone further. To say that the brain 'arranges, categorizes, and manages experience' is to imply that experience exists out there, to be in some way sorted out by the brain. It would be better to say that the brain itself constructs experience, based on its arrangement,

---

[74] Bourke, 'Experiment': 126.
[75] Bourke, 'Experiment': 132.
[76] Hunt, 'Revolution': 672.
[77] Hunt, 'Revolution': 673.
[78] Hunt, 'Revolution': 673.

categorisation and management of stimuli from the world. There is no experiential feeling inherent in events, in objects, in relations. They all have to be made.

Hunt pursues a complex relationship of conscious and unconscious, rational and emotional, without quite collapsing these distinctions. A loose reference to 'hardwiring', a reference to something neurologically permanent in the human, the historicity of her argument notwithstanding, allows her to suggest that selves have a universal capacity for 'empathy'. Individuals are not isolated beings, but social ones. What is more, this social essence is inscribed in the biology of individual bodies. McGrath in particular is critical of the way Hunt dispenses with an emphasis on self-regulation and suggests that neurohistorians in general have jettisoned the role of 'the active contributions of historical actors' in brain activity. They are, he claims, relying on an 'automatic conception of affect', where 'psychotropics generate direct affects via the brain independent of cognitive input'. The risk, he states, is that 'biochemical alteration risks becoming unmoored from the significance that historical actors attribute to their affective experiences'.[79]

Hunt's neurohistorical intervention is an explanation of an earlier work.[80] As Burman has pointed out, Hunt's neurohistorical turn provides the explanatory model for the emergence, in the French Revolution, of 'socially directed individual feeling' en masse: sympathy, in context, or empathy, if the universalism of the analysis is to be given its full political charge. In short, Hunt's argument about the effects of the new literary form of the epistolary novel, which allowed for the practice of emotional projection across social divides and beyond the confines of immediate kinship and community, is explicable by a turn to neurobiology. In Burman's words, 'the new literary form parasitized an already-existing human capacity and extended it to apply beyond the circle of close relations; that it provided a new way to make felt individual meaning at the social level.'[81] Hence the need, in Hunt's later piece, for the reference to hardwiring. Yet, as we have seen, such language carries a large risk of over-extrapolation from a universal biological substrate. If we are truly to set about doing neurohistory in order to find out what it felt

---

[79] McGrath, 'Historiography': 6.
[80] L. Hunt, *Inventing Human Rights: A History* (New York: Norton, 2007).
[81] Burman, 'History ': 89.

like to be a historical actor, hardwiring always presents us the easy option of inferring experience in the past by filtering it through our own in the present, using presentist psychological categories. That is precisely what Febvre warned against. Moreover, it misses an obvious trick.

What are we really doing when we are doing neurohistory, or the history of emotions? Our end is not a history of the brain, or a history of the nervous system (at least, for most of us). Our aim is to find out how experiences felt and what they motivated. We are investigating emotions as causes and as effects. We are looking at emotional 'landscapes', as it were, to reach a better understanding of why societies function in the ways they do, radically different from one another, and changing over time. In sum, our neurohistorical gaze is not directed at the 'history from within', but on the worlds made by interactions between worlds and within. The history of *e-motions*, outwardly projected movements, is literally what we are looking for. To that end, what the neurohistorical insight tells us is simply this: when a historical actor says 'it felt like this', we do not have to translate that into a contemporary psychological figure; we do not have to take it as metaphor; we must not dismiss it as the fluff of the historical record. On the contrary, if experience is historical because the brain is culturally made – an exaptation – then we must take historical actors at their word. To do that, affective statements have to be read in context, against other affective statements, against the languages of the body, or gesture, of interaction and intercourse, and against the sensual worlds in which historical actors moved and existed. In this, at the very least, we can follow Hunt:

> Revolution, modernity, bourgeois society, our own era of globalization – these cannot just be imposed by an economic system, a political structure, or a discursive web of representations, whether textual or, for that matter, visual. They must be learned, lived, embodied, and felt within individual selves.[82]

The neurohistorical approach warns us, fundamentally, that we probably do not know and cannot assume what is was like to be there, in a historical moment. We cannot hope to explain it in *our* terms, according to *our* experiential frame of reference. But

[82] Hunt, 'Revolution': 678.

we can, through nothing more exciting than rigorous historical research, explain it in the terms of historical actors themselves as connected networks of individuals.[83] We can reconstruct their experiential frame of reference, including those situated practices that would have driven synaptic development and those psychotropic influences that would have washed the historical mind. If past experience seems unfamiliar, strange, seemingly implausible, but empirically verifiable, then our powers of historical analysis and explanation promise to expand dramatically.

Genetics and epigenetics

Genetic programming and genetic dispositions are contemporary hot topics. How we are is how we are written in our DNA. At best that is a partial statement. Genetic expression is dependent on a range of factors, chemical and environmental, as well as cultural. There is little evidence that behaviour is genetically programmed. We are not, and certainly our emotions are not, reducible to our DNA.

Few historians have incorporated genetics into their historiographical practice. Smail has, as part of his broader 'deep history' project, and he walks a fine line when working out exactly where historians should enter the genetic debate. At what point can we say that evolutionary biology is not the principal agent of change, but culture is? That there is a line, is clear enough:

> Genes alone are not enough to build deep grammar or a theory of mind in the absence of specific developmental experiences. These developmental experiences are not only environmental; they are also cultural. In this way, culture can actually be wired in the human body. Since cultures change, human psychologies, in principle, can differ greatly from one era to the next.[84]

So far so good, but Smail leaves room for concessions in the direction of evolutionary psychology, in the laying down of 'basic fears, urges, and other predispositions'. This still chimes, however, with circularity, and begs the question precisely of experience. He asks: 'Are you, like most people, somewhat scared of the dark? Our dis-

---

[83] Burman, 'History': 96.
[84] Smail, *Deep History*, 131.

tant ancestors must have been scared of the dark. Those who acted more cautiously at night managed to out-reproduce their fearless peers, and this slight selection pressure resulted in the cognitive module for fear of the dark that you eventually inherited.'[85] This is immediately followed by a piece of reasoning that undermines the implication that night fear was somehow predisposed, basic, a naturally inscribed caution: 'Enough evidence ... has now been collected to show that australopithecines and archaic humans actually had good reason to be scared of the dark.'[86] A good reason? In this alone we see that *experience* of things that go bump in the night would have led to a nurturing environment where the perils of darkness were passed along. It is much easier to imagine fear of the dark perpetuated by such nurturing behaviour, based on learning of the perils of night predators, than it is to imagine a Lamarckian mechanism of transmission based on 'having good reason' in the first place. Moreover, Smail's claims to the contrary notwithstanding, many people in 'modern social and demographic conditions' – that is, people in civilisation – have tangible and entirely justifiable reasons to remain afraid of the dark.[87]

Smail would likely agree with this alternative explanation, if pressed, since his argument otherwise tends in that direction. In his striving for balance, it is not always clear where a neurohistorian should draw the line between biological, genetic fixity and cultural development. Would it not be better to assume the latter until or unless an alternative can be found? As Smail says, 'a neurohistorical approach suggests the possibility of significant changes over time in the social distribution of cognitive modules as an effect of cultural, not biological, inheritance.'[88] Insofar as psychologies change from context to context, and insofar as human culture is exaptive, so we can chart the micro-evolutionary history of the emotions among humans as biocultural beings.

[85] Smail, *Deep History*, 139–40.
[86] Smail, *Deep History*, 140.
[87] Smail, *Deep History*, 140. The all too reasonable and tangible perception of threat at night was given polemical treatment in a reaction against the post-modern turn in the social sciences by Laura Lee Downs in her article, 'If "woman" is just an empty category, then why am I afraid to walk alone at night? Identity politics meets the postmodern subject', *Comparative Studies in Society and History*, 35 (1993): 414–37.
[88] Smail, *Deep History*, 144.

One could also go further along the genetic route. New research in epigenetics has the potential to impact historiography in profound ways. As geneticists continue to build their understanding about the ways in which the experience of parents can effect gene expression in their offspring, the more alive we become to the possibility of epigenetic history. We are not dealing here with the inheritance of acquired characteristics in a Lamarckian sense, or in the sense of substantial changes in DNA that become heritable. Rather, epigenetics looks at the protein packaging of genetic material, and the effect on gene expression of environmental and experiential impacts on this packaging. We are beginning to understand that extreme experiences, especially prolonged ones, such as famine, warfare and poverty, can have an effect that is bequeathed to offspring that impacts gene expression and the body's physiological stress reaction.[89] Though it would be difficult to say exactly how such effects would alter experience at the individual level, we might be able to see signs of them at the societal level, looking at aggregate changes in the ways in which associations are formed and interpreted and experience is mediated and recorded.

As genetics takes a social turn, so historians can turn to it. The history of stress, for example, seems to offer a fruitful avenue of exploration, for the concept has both emotional and physiological connotations, which are necessarily connected.[90] As mentioned above, we know that the experience of pain in infancy directly affects the way in which the body handles physiological stress and the production of cortisol in later life, and that infant pain is correlated with the occurrence of adult anxiety disorders.[91] The development of the phenotype does not follow a simple computer program or the determined sequences of genetic code.[92] How we

[89] R.K. Silbereisen and X. Chen [eds], *Social Change and Human Development: Concepts and Results* (London: Sage, 2010); E. Jablonka and M.J. Lamb, *Evolution in Four Dimensions: Genetic, Epigenetic, Behavioural, and Symbolic Variation in the History of Life* (Cambridge, MA: MIT Press, 2005).

[90] The history department at the University of Tampere in Finland is rapidly becoming a centre for such work, much of which is currently only in Finnish. See, for example, V. Kivimäki, *Murtuneet mielet: Taistelu suomalaissotilaiden hermoista 1939–1945* (Helsinki: WSOY, 2013).

[91] Page, 'Long-term consequences'.

[92] See, for example, N. Véron and A.H.F.M. Peters, 'Tet proteins in the limelight', *Nature*, 473 (2011): 293–4.

are expressed as individuals has a lot to do with the world in which we find ourselves. Epigenetic influences promise to further develop this study, as we hone the possibilities for biocultural history that has emotions at its heart.[93]

In sum, neuroscience and genetics are arming historians with tools they can apply to the historical record and to the history of experience at the most fundamental level. The sensory world of the past leads us to a substantial historicisation of human feeling, which is to say, human *being*. These approaches also provide us with the tools we need to challenge those who posit a timelessness in human emotions. Where once there might have been only the most tenuous connection between the historian and the neuroscientist, they now look set to become sympathetic intellectual allies.

---

[93] See, for example, P. Cheung and P Lau, 'Epigenetic regulation by histone methylation and histone variants', *Molecular Endocrinology*, 19 (2005): 563–83.

7

SPACES, PLACES AND OBJECTS

Architecture of the emotions

On the main floor of the Jewish Museum in Berlin there is a door to a void: a space enclosed by twenty-metre-high walls, but narrowly open to the elements at the top. I had been, in daytime, and stood in this structure, known as the Holocaust Tower. I had been unmoved, one of many in the space, looking upward and wondering what I was supposed to feel. Daniel Libeskind, the architect who designed the museum, himself claimed that such voids, of which there are various within the building, represent 'that which can never be exhibited when it comes to Jewish Berlin history: Humanity reduced to ashes'.[1] According to the museum, 'Many visitors experience a feeling of oppression or anxiety inside the Holocaust Tower.'[2] Clearly, the design is supposed to evoke something. The visitor is exposed to the elements, but thoroughly enclosed. Openness is a distant promise in an otherwise claustrophobic environment.

It was light on my first visit. There was the comfort of other people, talking, taking pictures, brandishing guidebooks, reading the official account of what the space we were standing in was supposed to do. I went back, therefore, some months later, without trepidation. It was winter, and dark outside. I took a guest to the Holocaust Tower. As the door opened, a shaft of light illuminated the people standing inside, but as the door closed it became

---

[1] Quoted in R. Bianchini, 'Daniel Libeskind: Jewish Museum – Part 2', www.inexhibit.com/case-studies/daniel-libeskind-jewish-museum-part2/, accessed 18 November 2016.

[2] Jewish Museum, Berlin, www.jmberlin.de/en/libeskind-building, accessed 18 November 2016.

instantly and absolutely black. I was immediately disorientated. Nobody was speaking. I no longer knew how many people were around me, or where they were. I no longer knew where the door, the only exit, was. An overwhelming feeling of panic overtook me. I was rooted to the spot, desperate, in fact, that someone would come or go, so as to reveal to me the location of the door. After what seemed too long an impasse, the shaft of light lit up the room once more, and I bolted through it.

Such is the power of designed space; but how does this power work? The building, in this case, came with an explicit script of which I was aware. I had not read the script the first time, but the second, under different conditions, I read it all too well. The image in my mind, planted there beforehand, was the gas chamber, the crematorium, a killing room. The power of suggestion, in tandem with the power of circumstance and the effectiveness of the architecture, produced emotive success. It is the most profound experience I have had in a museum.

So far in this book the critical dynamic processes of emotional prescription and expression have been somewhat limited to interactions among humans. The agents of emotional prescription can be described as institutional, but the implicit assumption is that they are maintained not merely by their own inertia, but also by the people who guide and control them. The world humans live in, however, is a more complex fabric than this. Our networks and interactions take place in lived spaces and places, against backdrops of real buildings and edifices, and involve all manner of objects: mundane, precious, artistic and otherwise. The architecture of emotive dynamics is, in a tangible sense, partly located in the physical architecture of the world around us. Insofar as spaces, places, buildings and objects are themselves historical, their character and the ways with which they interact become centrally important in understanding the particularities of emotional style in context.[3] We might well ask, 'where are emotions?', or, literally, 'how are

---

[3] Much of the impetus here comes from studies in social geography. See, for example, G. Bruno, *Atlas of Emotion: Journeys in Art, Architecture and Film* (New York: Verso Books, 2007); H. Jones and E. Jackson [eds], *Stories of Cosmopolitan Belonging: Emotion and Location* (London: Routledge, 2014); L. Bondi, J. Davidson and M. Smith, 'Introduction: Geography's "emotional turn"', in J. Davidson, L. Bondi and M. Smith [eds], *Emotional Geographies* (Aldershot: Ashgate, 2005), 1–16.

emotions *built*?' What is the relationship, moreover, between emotions and space?[4] The obvious jumping-off point here is Michel Foucault's studies of the prison and the school as places in which social interaction is prescribed by the configuration of institutional space. A building embodies the power structures of society. It literally puts people in their proper place and guides the ways in which social intercourse takes place.[5] By such reasoning, an architectural plan can have an emotional regime in mind. The 'atmosphere' of a space is determined by the logic of its own construction. The culturally located side of the emotive process is embedded in the very fabric of the construction. Emotional expression is literally bounded according to which side of the bars, or which side of the desk, a person finds himself. Behaviour is limited by the clear demarcations of *what* a person is according to *where* he is.

It is not, and perhaps this goes without saying, as simple as this. As we have seen with other forms of emotive process, prescription does not determine behaviour, though it does shape how behaviour is received. Architectural intent tends not to map onto how people feel once the building is, for want of a better word, alive. Prescriptions can be transgressed in any number of ways, with spaces being used for purposes other than those for which they were intended, and the internal logic of architectural and spatial planning disrupted by users whose practices cut against the grain or resist the flow imposed on them. Prescriptions can also be plural, even contradictory.[6] Drawing from memory, my school rules were centred on what a pupil could do in the space, and what they could not: walk on the left; do not run in corridors; do not play in cloakrooms; no ball games; no long skipping ropes, etc. So many imperatives, all

---

[4] For introductions to the topic, see G. Lehnert [ed.], *Raum und Gefühl: Der Spatial Turn und die Neue Emotionsforschung* (Bielefeld: Transcript, 2011); J. Davidson, M. Smith, L. Bondi and E. Probyn, 'Emotion, space and society: Editorial introduction', *Emotion, Space and Society*, 1 (2008): 1–3; A. Reckwitz, 'Affective spaces: A praxeological outlook', *Rethinking History*, 16 (2012): 241–58; K. Vallgårda, 'Affekt, følelser og rum – historiefaglige perspektiver', *Temp: tidsskrift for historie*, 5 (2015): 175–83.

[5] M. Foucault, *Discipline and Punish: The Birth of the Prison* (New York: Vintage, 1995).

[6] M. Pernau, 'Space and emotion: Building to feel', *History Compass*, 12 (2014): 541–9, at 543.

apparently issuing from the building itself, as if contravention of these rules would turn a safe space into an unsafe space; from order, chaos. Authority, as we all probably know, is not as simple as that and, when one feels nobody is looking, or even if somebody is, from a spirit of defiance, all such rules are readily broken. Transgression itself notwithstanding, the feelings associated with transgression are still pegged to the expectations prescribed by the space in question. In Jane Hamlett's words, 'The spatial, physical world, then, represents an important dimension of emotional experience. Enclosure or confinement in space is also fundamental to emotional life in that its arrangement often determines the positions of bodies and their relationships to each other.'[7] Architectural historians have described such spaces as 'activity arenas', a label that captures the ways in which people practise in spaces, in tension with, or in conformity with, the expectations inherent in space design and its attendant agencies of authority.[8] Roy Kozlovsky has suggested that a more focused study of the ways in which architecture is implicated in emotive processes will complicate Reddy's 'binary model of spaces of emotional orthodoxy and emotional refuges';[9] indeed, this complication has been exemplified in such diverse arenas as the Italian courtroom and the chambers for divorce hearings in Denmark.[10] As hinted at above, a prescriptive space can become a refuge if and when nobody is looking. Moreover, buildings and other constructed spaces tend not to be single-use, but in a variety of ways host a plurality of communities and dynamics, with prescriptions changing from room to room, and perhaps throughout the day.

[7] J. Hamlett, 'Space and emotional experience in Victorian and Edwardian English public school dormitories', in Olsen [ed.], *Childhood*, 121. See also Reckwitz, 'Affective spaces': 254.
[8] E.C. Cromley, 'Transforming the food axis: Houses, tools, modes of analysis', *Material Culture Review*, 44 (1996). See also R. Kozlovsky, 'Architecture, emotions and the history of childhood', in Olsen [ed.], *Childhood*, 100; A.A. van Slyck, *A Manufactured Wilderness: Summercamps and the Shaping of American Youth, 1890–1960* (Minneapolis: University of Minnesota Press, 2006), xxxi; S. Brooke, 'Space, emotions and the everyday: The affective ecology of 1980s London', *20th Century British History*, 28 (2017): 110–42.
[9] Kozlovsky, 'Architecture', in Olsen [ed.], *Childhood*, 100.
[10] Seymour, 'Emotional arenas': 177–97; K. Vallgårda, 'Divorce, bureaucracy, and emotional frontiers: Marital dissolution in late nineteenth-century Copenhagen', *Journal of Family History* (forthcoming).

Kozlovsky himself has shown the possibilities, looking at children's playgrounds, hospitals and schools in the shadow of World War II. The apparent 'freedom' of play is circumscribed by the spaces in which it takes place, and Kozlovsky highlights deliberate attempts to direct childhood obedience while carrying off the illusion that 'discipline' emanated 'from within the children'.[11] Aesthetics are implicated in building design as part of the dynamic of social practice. Literally, of course, aesthetics refers not to beauty but to sensation. Post-war reformers saw the possibilities of forming the emotions through a channelling of both. School spaces opened up the possibility for movement – the body in motion as expressive of artistic feeling – that would free children from their 'fears, inhibitions and aggression'.[12]

The feeling that built space could free people from fear was of great moment in the period immediately after World War II. In the new Federal Republic of Germany, the building of government buildings in Bonn was fraught with conceptual and symbolic uncertainty, about how to represent the power that inhered in the State without risking evoking fear in the citizenry before its edifices. As Philipp Nielsen has argued, the government's conception of a population 'not cowering before power, but ... identify[ing] with it on an emotional level' played a large part in the design of government architecture in the new capital. The State was to 'confront its citizens with humility', which it could do through the austerity and apparent temporariness of its new structures, to stave off anger, fear or resentment among the people.[13] Whether it really worked – whether people really did sense the humility of the architects of democracy through the spaces in which they served – is open to interpretation. The question, and the strategy, however, are part of a larger body of work that explores the place of emotions in the making of a new democracy, with particular reference to the formation of the emotional disposition of newly minted democratic citizens.[14] It is a research impetus that has been recognised in

[11] Kozlovsky, 'Architecture', in Olsen [ed.], *Childhood*, 102.
[12] Kozlovsky, 'Architecture', in Olsen [ed.], *Childhood*, 112.
[13] P. Nielsen, 'Building Bonn: Democracy and the architecture of humility', *History of Emotions – Insights into Research*, January 2014, www.history-of-emotions.mpg.de/en/texte/building-bonn-democracy-and-the-architecture-of-humility, accessed 21 November 2016.
[14] T. van Rahden, 'Clumsy democrats: Moral passions in the Federal Republic', *German*

other contexts, in different political and cultural situations, with much promise.

The central claim, that 'city planning aims at the creation of emotions', is coupled with the additional claim that such planning is 'based on emotion knowledge specific to a certain time and place', where a physical reality is constructed so that it 'stabilizes and perpetuates' this emotion knowledge. These were Margrit Pernau's claims about Mughal-era Delhi, and they come with the standard caveats.[15] Prescriptive intent is limited only to the group implicated or valued by the designer. The emotional experience of the excluded in such space is always doubtless different. Moreover, neither political dynamics nor cultural configurations are stable, resulting in changes in the ways designed spaces are perceived, sensed and felt. The historicity of emotion knowledge is materially built into the landscape. It is all around us.

In an astonishing analysis, Geoff Lehman and Michael Weinman have shown how profoundly true this is for perhaps the most iconic piece of architecture in western civilisation: the Parthenon in Athens. Their aim is to get at what the Parthenon's designers intended, but in the process they have to unravel centuries of interpretation, based on having experienced the building in different ways. Lehman and Weinman carefully build an argument about the building's embodiment of the ideas of harmony and symmetry, of beauty and truth, of the rational and the irrational, so as to embody fundamental Greek ideals that would be available to those who beheld the structure at the level of the senses. The Parthenon's capturing of the measurable and the unmeasurable, of different elements that make a whole, makes the structure an ontological challenge that, through its proportions, refers to the human body and the human being, to the rationality of mathematics and to the irrationality of harmony, to music and to dance, and to movement, of the body and of the soul. Questions of proportion, symmetry, harmony and measurement are, Lehman and Weinman admit, 'theoretical', and of a 'mathematical sort', but they are also 'a question of direct experience. A viewer or worshipper in the

---

History, 29 (2011): 485–504; N. Verheyen, *Diskussionslust: Eine Kulturgeschichte des 'besseren Arguments' in Westdeutschland* (Göttingen: Vandenhoeck & Ruprecht, 2010).
[15] Pernau, 'Space': 546.

presence of the Parthenon experiences the building as an ontological whole, and at the same time is engaged, directly and intuitively, by an interplay of related parts whose proportional relationships function as a kind of visual analogue of the effects of harmony in music.'[16]

Nevertheless, Lehman and Weinman have to work hard to recover this analysis from diverse sources, and part of the problem is that those who have viewed the Parthenon over the centuries, after the context of its construction and classical heyday, did not experience the building in this way. As knowledge shifts and slips, as culture changes, so experience follows. Is there, then, a general theoretical framework for understanding how space and emotion are related? From a historical point of view, such an approach is still in development, but there are clear beginnings. Andreas Reckwitz built upon Gernot Böhme's theory of 'atmospheres' to capture the 'affective mood which spatial arrangements stir in the sensual bodies of their users', that connect 'private practices with their homes, political practices with their bureaucratic offices, parliament buildings, rough streets or marching fields, economic practices with their factories, creative lofts of shopping malls, subcultural sexual practices with their darkrooms and cruising areas or educational practices with their classrooms and libraries'.[17] It is not that affects are simply projected from space to people, but that affects are formed 'when a space is practically appropriated by its users':

> Atmospheres are thus always already connected to a specific cultural sensitivity and attentiveness on the part of the carriers of practices, a specific sensitivity for perceptions, impressions and affections. Routine practices mostly rely on perfect matches between atmospheres and sensitivities similar to the ideal fits between habitus and field that Pierre Bourdieu mentions. ... Such spatial environments constitute crucial constellations for social and cultural reproduction in general and the reproduction of affective relations in particular.[18]

---

[16] G. Lehman and M. Weinman, *The Parthenon and Liberal Education* (New York: SUNY Press, forthcoming). I thank the authors for generously allowing me to read the manuscript ahead of publication.
[17] Reckwitz, 'Affective spaces': 254.
[18] Reckwitz, 'Affective spaces': 255. G. Böhme, *Atmosphäre: Essays zur neuen Ästhetik* (Frankfurt am Main: Suhrkamp, 2000). See also, B. Anderson, 'Affective atmospheres', *Emotion, Space and Society*, 2 (2009): 77–81.

Without putting it in quite the same terms, I pursued this agenda myself in my analysis of the affective atmosphere of banality in the late nineteenth-century physiological laboratory, where everyday scientific practices in spaces designed specifically to concentrate the mind on the mundaneness of physiological work helped to eliminate any ethical or aesthetic doubts. Disgust was not an option for the physiological functionary.[19] Yet – and this is the key – the intentions of builders, architects and designers is only ever part of the story. The practical appropriation of building users, mentioned by Reckwitz, has the potential to re-imagine affective or atmospheric space. Even in the most elaborate designs and with the best of intentions, as with the Parthenon, ultimately the atmosphere is not *built in*, but rather emerges only through the dynamic of *use*.

This begs further questions. What if there is not a 'perfect match' between atmosphere and sensitivity, habitus and field, feeling and feeling rule? What happens in unstable spaces, liminal spaces and spaces where purpose and authority are contested? What happens in re-purposed places, at the boundaries of competing influences, where the emotional landscape carries different representational weight for different people and, sometimes, for the same people at different times? This question has so far received little attention, though an approach has been formulated on a much bigger canvas. Our focus must zoom out, to imagine the specific sites of emotive contestation that takes place within emotional regimes, especially where those regimes are unstable.

Emotions in place

The rise of global history, coming hard on the heels of imperial history, has ushered in a new challenge to historiography in general, but this challenge is of great moment to the history of emotions in particular. From the outset it has been clear that emotions history does not comfortably follow national boundaries, though

---

[19] Boddice, *Science of Sympathy*, 75–86. See also T. Schlich, 'Surgery, science and modernity: Operating rooms and laboratories as spaces of control', *History of Science*, 45 (2007): 231–56; S. Shapin, 'The house of experiment in seventeenth-century England', *Isis*, 79 (1988): 373–404; O. Hannaway, 'Laboratory design and the aim of science: Andreas Libavius versus Tycho Brahe', *Isis*, 77 (1986): 584–610.

nationalism of course remains of great interest. Research into national *feelings*, or of emotional communities at the level of the nation, have already produced fruitful studies, and will doubtless continue to foster new research. William Reddy's own formative work was based on the emergence of a modern nation state, and the model he provided exemplified how one might explore the currents of emotional belonging and non-belonging at this level.

Yet the question remains about what happens when national interests overlap, or when the nation encompasses people and communities who do not formally belong to it, or whose status is otherwise than citizenship. There are many studies that explore such phenomena from the point of view of human relations, political dynamics, social systems, identity, institutions, economics and so on. So far, very few histories of emotion have risen to the challenge of emotional identity at the intersection of ideas of place. Kyra Giorgi has mapped the conceptual difficulties of emotional translation when emotional concepts will not translate, comparing Portuguese, Czech and Turkish examples, but the challenge increases in cases of emotional encounter among different national cultures.[20]

Stephanie Olsen's 2014 study of the emotional formation of future British citizens in the first generation of compulsory schooling, and in the era of high imperialism in the three decades before World War I, ably demonstrates the forces at work in orientating the child's moral compass by orientating its emotional compass. Whatever agency children had for themselves in their emotional formation, the influence of their context, which was characterised by a consistency of message in the juvenile periodical press and across youth organisations of many different stripes, was undeniable. Fascinating though this is for the national context, with its paradoxical conclusion that the same emotional identity can explain both the mass military voluntarism of 1914 and its opposite – the retreat to security in home and hearth – the analytical drama lies in the translation of British metropolitan strategies of emotional formation to colonial India. Here the specificity of emotional context according to place is highlighted precisely by the vagaries of compatibility when strategies of emotional education were exported.

---

[20] K. Giorgi, *Emotions, Language and Identity on the Margins of Europe* (Houndmills: Palgrave, 2014).

Local languages, customs, religions, politics and, most importantly, the subaltern status of British subjects as compared with British citizens, necessarily forced changes into the message of formal and informal educational attempts, as well as a realisation among colonial reformers that emotional and moral characters were contingent. To educate the emotions therefore involved a sensitivity to the vagaries of place.[21]

This empirical account was followed, in association with Kristine Alexander and Karen Vallgårda, with a theoretical exposition that also picked up Alexander's own work on internationalism within the Girl Guides movement, and Vallgårda's investigations into the emotional encounters of Danish missionaries in India.[22] The premise here was that none of the existing theoretical tools in the standard list of history-of-emotions jargon, be it 'emotional communities', 'emotional regimes' or 'emotional styles', fully addressed how any given emotional repertoire was formed in the first place, let alone the competing interests within the politics of emotional formation in given places and spaces. Importantly, this introduced in a substantial way the category of age as critical for understanding the process of emotional identity formation. Moreover, it strongly emphasised the critical politics of place and space that exemplify sympathetic and competing influences that children encounter, and which they must accommodate in order to successfully manage emotive processes. All sites, from nebulous entities such as the nation to specific locales such as the playground, schoolroom or parlour, become sites of competing influences for the emotional identity of the child. Olsen, Vallgårda and Alexander label these places of intersection 'emotional frontiers'.[23]

[21] S. Olsen, *Juvenile Nation: Youth, Emotions and the Making of the Modern British Citizen, 1880–1914* (London: Bloomsbury, 2014), esp. 117–36; S. Olsen, 'Adolescent empire: Moral dangers for boys in Britain and India, c.1880–1914', in H. Ellis [ed.], *Juvenile Delinquency and the Limits of Western Influence, 1850–2000* (Houndmills: Palgrave, 2014), 19–41.
[22] K. Vallgårda, K. Alexander and S. Olsen, 'Emotions and the global politics of childhood', in Olsen [ed.], *Childhood*, 12–34; K. Vallgårda, *Imperial Childhoods and Christian Mission: Education and Emotions in South India and Denmark* (Houndmills: Palgrave, 2015); C. McLisky, D. Midena and K. Vallgårda [eds], *Emotions and Christian Missions: Historical Perspectives* (Houndmills: Palgrave, 2015); K. Alexander, *Guiding Modern Girls: Imperialism, Internationalism and the Girl Guide Movement* (Vancouver: UBC Press, forthcoming).
[23] Vallgårda, Alexander and Olsen, 'Global politics', in Olsen [ed.], *Childhood*, 22–6.

It makes sense, given Reddy's overt use of a geographical metaphor in 'navigation' to ground emotive processes in specific places and spaces. Both Reddy and Rosenwein acknowledge the overlapping of emotional communities or regimes, but do not explore in detail the high stakes of such points of overlap, especially among those large groups who cannot be fully said to conform or to have rejected the prescribed emotional norms of a given community or regime: children. The emotional frontier is the literal and physical site of emotional navigation, and while all historical actors might be said to be always on some emotional frontier or other, the visibility of such places is more tangible when those actors are young, and especially when those actors are in places that have competing political and/or social interests in their emotional identity or fealty. The evidence of an emotional frontier can be derived from competing literature of other prescriptive documentation that makes alternative emotive demands of actors. This might be in one place, such as the colonial schoolroom, where, for example, academic and devotional expectations might clash; or it might be between two places, such as school and home, or church and home, where the source of emotional prescriptions are culturally incommensurate. Accessing the navigation strategies of actors at the frontier is challenging, and perhaps lends itself most clearly to modernists who can take oral testimony. But ego documents and other written sources do make analysis possible in other periods, allowing historians to uncover the ways in which historical actors handled the high stakes of emotives, struggling to find themselves in unstable landscapes of emotional prescription; dissembling perhaps, but often feeling emotional kinship in multiple directions, being pulled apart.[24]

Before this concept of the emotional frontier emerged, I had described such an experience of being pulled in different directions, not knowing what or how to feel, as 'emotional crisis'.[25] This is both an individual and a collective phenomenon, but it seems

---

[24] Two particularly salient examples are K. Vongsathorn, 'Teaching, learning and adapting emotions in Uganda's child leprosy settlement, c.1930–1962', in Olsen [ed.], *Childhood*, 56–75, and J. Brauer, 'Clashes of emotions: Punk music, youth subculture and authority in the GDR (1978–1983)', *Social Justice*, 38 (2012): 53–70.

[25] Boddice, 'Affective turn', 158–63.

particularly ripe for study in those places where competition for emotional formation – those sites where the emotional frontier is most acutely detectable – is fragmented. Global forces, encounters, exchanges, transfers and translations make for ambiguity of both emotional concepts and experiences, the negotiation and navigation of which ought to make for dynamic histories in which the crucible of identity formation is most clearly visible through the evaluation of a whole palate of emotional practices tied to place.

Associationism

The first psychologists, going back to the late nineteenth century, developed an understanding of the ways in which objects came to be associated with emotional and affective dispositions and responses. There is nothing intrinsically meaningful in any object, but the way in which an object is constructed in a space, placed into a narrative, associated with something beyond itself, and with past experiences, all endow said object with meaning. This meaning is construed individually, but may, in an emotional community, be construed similarly across the collective. The way in which an object is associated with a value across a community is confirmed in ritual, in discourse and in collective action and practice with the object. The easiest way to see this in action is in religious communities, where, for example, a chalice, a reliquary, a holy book, etc., is immediately understood to stand for a certain meaningful representation of the common feeling of faith. Such objects serve as familiar entry points to shared feelings. The people who share those feelings tend, in the abstract, to associate the objects in question with the feeling itself, as if to put the source of emotion in those objects.

For those who would prescribe patterns of feeling in a given community, the ritual association of objects with desired emotions is a positively sought mechanism for ensuring the stability of the community in question. As Milner as described, when discussing the Reformation Mass, such objects were combined with other indicators of emotional prescription, discursive and practical, to ensure a contained and predictable response. What is more, there is evidence that such prescription was a planned, conscious ordering of the kinds of experience desired by the Church:

the use of objects, words and actions to manipulate, exploit or control the processes of causation and agency that lay outside an impressionable body[,] in order to prevent harm or bring about benefit[,] point towards a highly rationalized system that was aware of the stakes involved in human experience.[26]

We can also be certain, however, that long-standing associations exist irrespective of the prescriptions of authority, according primarily to individual experience or to the collective memory of the experience of the past. By no means are such associations limited to the religious world. Julie-Marie Strange, for example, noted the affective resonance of the father's chair in late Victorian and Edwardian working-class homes in Britain. These chairs – material embodiments of fatherly space – 'facilitated physical proximity and multisensory intimacy'; they 'were instrumental in the non-verbal navigation of feeling'. Not only did the father's chair serve to gender domestic space, it also typified its 'emotional dynamics'.[27] Such an analysis might be extended to the everyday stuff of life in any period or place, where commonalities of belongings, designs and orientation of lived spaces helped cement identities and affective relations, both with the material itself and among the people who used it.

Memories – which may not only arise from direct personal experience, but also from an awareness of the experiences of others that 'live' in the everyday understanding of the world – also extend to what is painful and/or feared. The instruments of surgery, for example, were highlighted by both David Hume and Adam Smith as having the power to arouse terror and dread, not because of anything intrinsic to those instruments, but because of their anticipated use. Hume wrote:

> Were I present at any of the more terrible operations of surgery, 'tis certain that even before it begun, the preparation of the instruments, the laying of the bandages in order, the heating of the irons, with all the signs of anxiety and concern in the patients and assistants, wou'd have a great effect upon my mind, and excite the strongest sentiments of pity and terror.[28]

[26] Milner, *Senses*, 347.
[27] J.-M. Strange, *Fatherhood and the British Working Class, 1865–1914* (Cambridge: Cambridge University Press, 2015), 100–3.
[28] Quoted in P. Mercer, *Sympathy and Ethics: A Study of the Relationship between Sympathy and Morality with Special Reference to Hume's Treatise* (Oxford: Clarendon Press, 1972), 31.

Hume therefore places the mechanism of sympathy in the material world, not in any intrinsic quality of the human mind: 'No passion of another discovers itself immediately to the mind. We are only sensible of its causes and effects. From *these* we infer the passion: And consequently *these* give rise to our sympathy.'[29] Smith agreed that since the 'immediate effect' of the 'instruments of surgery' was 'pain and suffering, the sight of them always displeases us'.[30]

Curiously, however, in such cases it is possible to see how the associations of certain objects outlive changes in the things those objects actually do. In Thomas Eakins' depiction of *The Clinic of Dr Gross* (1875), for example, the surgeon is shown, mid-operation, wielding a bloody scalpel. The painting, based on direct experience of the painter, shows an operation for osteomyelitis of the femur. An audience of medical students look on dispassionately, even bored. In the background, however, the surgical subject's mother turns away in terror or horror, being unable to bear the sight of the bloodied hand and surgical steel. The context, essential to an understanding of the tension in the painting, is that the surgery is being conducted under anaesthetic, still a relatively new reality at that time. The patient therefore feels no pain. Moreover, new surgical techniques mean the patient is undergoing a relatively minor procedure, whereas in previous decades he might have undergone an amputation. Such a painting demonstrates the lag of popular sentiment behind scientific progress, showing clearly that the mother's terror is out of place. It calls for an emotional re-appraisal of the association of blood and scalpel, so that those objects equate to a march of civilisation. Unwittingly, however, Eakins' painting had the opposite effect, generally arousing emotional responses similar to the cowering woman, rather than nodding approval at dispassionate surgical advances. Critics, not uncommonly in this period, worried about a growing body of influential men whose tender passions were blunted or calcified, and asserted their own fine sentiments by recoiling at the sight of blood.[31]

The argument about the emotional effects of a work of art is also germane to this discussion, for in the case of Eakins' painting, the critical response was given *as if* the viewers had seen a real

---

[29] Mercer, *Sympathy and Ethics*, 31.
[30] Smith, *Moral Sentiments*, 45.
[31] Boddice, *Science of Sympathy*, 65–71.

surgery. The reaction was to the sight of blood, and of the scalpel, but of course viewers were only seeing paint applied this way and that, in various colours. Paintings came, in the late nineteenth and early twentieth centuries, to drive theoretical explorations of the emotional encounter with art. The question centred on whether an object could, in and of itself, carry any emotional weight, or whether the apparent emotion emanating from an object had first to be put there by the viewer, who then received the reflection of that emotion *as if* it had come from the object itself. This relation of object and emotion drove early discourse about empathy, which could be construed not as an emotional connection to something outside of the self, but rather as the perception of something external that was, in fact, entirely produced by an individual. Such is the basis for wider thinking about the paradox of empathy: whatever its appearances of transmission and reception between affective entities, there is in the end only the neurological output of the individual. Concordance can be checked and confirmed, but the feeling of experiencing something outside oneself is, all things considered, an illusion of the self, by the self.[32]

This reasoning can be applied to objects in general, which, in context, appear to be loaded with emotional weight, but which, out of context, signify nothing. John Styles explored this phenomenon with regard to the more than 5000 objects in the London Foundling Hospital archive that originally accompanied infants given up to the hospital between the years of 1741 and 1760. A repository of sorrow, shame, hope and love is, when viewed as a repository, just a collection of bric-a-brac. But when stories of loss, grief, hardship, poverty and desperation are re-introduced to such objects, in the context of giving up a child, they reassume a pathos that can be hard to bear. Here, and in similar cases, we must be cautious. Our own empathy runs ahead of us, and the pathetic weight we feel at the prospect of giving up a child dominates how we view such objects, at the risk of missing vital nuances in intent and meaning, of the difference between the banality of symbolic inventory and the sentimentality that inhered in certain mementos. This can only be recovered through knowledge of the historical context.[33]

[32] Burdett, '"Subjective inside"'.
[33] J. Styles, 'Objects of emotion: The London Foundling Hospital tokens, 1741–60',

Object orientation and satisfaction

In Sara Ahmed's 'cultural politics' of emotion, it is impossible to disentangle emotion and sensation, and the objects with which both are associated. Emotions 'circulate' among the objects, places and spaces associated with the senses. If we accept the premise that emotions are situational, that is, they happen because of *things*, then even if we made a sweeping concession to the universalists and declared certain emotions to be fundamental to human *being*, we could not make a similar concession to the circumstances of their arousal, their causes or their effects. What arouses fear, or lust, or disgust, is a matter of the meaningfulness of a situation, an object, a set of walls and so on, and not a determined response to objects with universal characteristics. Reading with Ahmed, emotions are not aroused by anything inherent in the objects that arouse them, but by the way in which we encounter and evaluate them. This notion of an encounter throws together sensation and emotion in a form of 'contact' that 'generates feeling', which involves 'thought and evaluation'.[34]

At the forefront of this formulation is the inescapable observation that emotions are *sensed* in a world of interactions with other beings and objects. To that end, our emotional worlds are social worlds, for it is impossible to imagine an emotional life isolated from a world. Even if we could propose the isolation of an individual from all interaction with people, that individual would have to be *somewhere*, and that place and its characteristics would be encountered as it were socially. Feelings, in Ahmed's estimation, are the 'effects of circulation', or of encountering objects (including other people) in context. In the process of circulation, we sense what is ours and what is not ours – what is 'inside' and 'outside' – from the point of view of experience.

Emotions, in this way, *make* what Ahmed calls the 'surfaces or boundaries' that distinguish me from you, and us from the material world. Moreover, it is not emotions themselves that are out there, circulating in social spaces, but the 'objects of emotion' through

in A. Gerritsen and G. Riello [eds], *Writing Material Culture History* (London: Bloomsbury, 2014): 165–72; see also, M. Zytaruk, 'Artifacts of elegy: The Foundling Hospital tokens', *Journal of British Studies*, 54 (2015): 320–48.

[34] Ahmed, *Cultural Politics*, 6–8.

which emotions are themselves formed.[35] In this way, Ahmed more or less undermines notions of emotional contagion as the transmission of a discrete emotion itself, and also speaks to the social embeddedness of sympathy or empathy, even if we grant that the capacity for empathy is inbuilt. One has to *know* – and the knowledge here is not explicit or conscious, or not necessarily so, but rather ingrained, learnt, practised, prescribed – how to interpret an emotional dynamic in order to enter into it. Even then, one enters into it not *as* the other experiences the emotion, but *as if* one does: the father is dead; the daughter is in grief; I know what death is, and also the meaning of the ties that bind; I understand the reason for grief; I can enter into the realm of grief; I grieve *with* the daughter. Such a list is too tidy, too easy and too *sequenced* to represent a process that, in the event, seems simply to happen. But it is an impressionistic account of how empathy works and how social emotions are formed in the dynamic among objects.

In Ahmed's words, the immediacy of sensations – like the instant sensation that somebody is upset – fools us into thinking that they are unmediated by experience. We take the aggregate of our experience of reading the surfaces of emotional situations everywhere with us, and our reactions to the emotions of others, which we simply seem to sense, are always part of a 'process of recognition'.[36] Social emotions take place according to shared emotional practices, and their great myth is that they allow us literally to share an experience. This feeling, of going through the same emotional process as others, is reassuring and satisfying, and has been thought to be key to the functionality of civilised social life. Similarly, where there appears to be a barrier to shared experience, and where ways of life meet at the emotional frontier, there may be what Arlie Russel Hochschild calls an 'empathy wall', an 'obstacle to deep understanding of another person, one that can make us feel indifferent or even hostile to those who hold different beliefs', or those whose emotional disposition simply does not compute, for us.[37]

Moreover, as Ahmed points out, there are many times when

---

[35] Ahmed, *Cultural Politics*, 10–11. For an interesting take on object orientation and the re-invocation of recorded emotions, see J. Willenfelt, 'Documenting bodies: Pain surfaces', in Boddice [ed.], *Pain and Emotion*, 260–76.
[36] Ahmed, *Cultural Politics*, 25.
[37] Hochschild, *Strangers*, 5.

one might assume one knows what other people are experiencing, only to discover that one was completely wrong. Discovering such a discontinuity of experience can be disturbing and destabilising. I remember watching M. Night Shyamalan's *The Sixth Sense* for the first time, among a large group of people whom I did not know. While I assumed that we were all experiencing the same suspenseful feelings of not knowing what was happening in the film, several of the audience, it later transpired, had seen it before. Subsequent conversation revealed that these people were watching *us* watching the film to try to gauge at what moment (if at all) we would work out that Bruce Willis' character was in fact already dead. They were in on their own shared experience, which was in the realm of comedy, while the rest of us assumed we were all sharing an experience of suspense and contained horror. The discovery of the rupture felt something like betrayal, or at the very least mockery. Our little society divided into camps along the lines of those who were in on the joke and those who were excluded. Exclusion, ultimately, was based on a trick that highlighted the limitations of empathy and its corruptibility.

Our relationship with others and with things is complex and has a complex history. The quest for satisfaction, which could be the orientating factor in a new sensory historiography, can be its own hindrance. Lauren Berlant has documented the ways in which post-war optimism or hope and the activities associated with them represent meaningful attachments to 'unachievable fantasies'. The 'object-ideas' at the centre of modern desire for the 'good life' are, in Berlant's argument, precisely the things that stand in the way of fulfilment. They paradoxically enable people to get through lives in permanent crisis while being instrumental in the formation and perpetuation of that crisis. She talks of the 'historical sensorium that has developed belatedly since the fantasmatic part of the optimism about structural transformation realized less and less traction in the world'. In short, as the wished-for dreams of the would-be upwardly mobile became less realisable, so they loomed ever larger in the imagination and in people's affective interaction with the world, to the point where coping with the precariousness of failing to achieve these dreams, while not letting them go, becomes an 'accomplishment'.[38]

[38] L. Berlant, *Cruel Optimism* (Durham, NC: Duke University Press, 2011).

The contradictions that seem to inhere in this history of desire (its modern history at any rate) run deep and have broad implications. For her part, Sara Ahmed develops a negative construction whereby happiness is actually oppressive, used to 'redescribe social norms as social goods', keeping many – women, black or LGBTQ people – unhappy and locked into the happiness regime.[39] But one could also construe it the other way and show how some profoundly miserable-sounding practices – religious asceticism, flagellation – might have been sources of happiness, for happiness was associated with those things. We can postulate a radical disjuncture between sensation and the evaluation of sensation, precisely because evaluations are culturally and contextually situated. What it means to be struck with a strap, therefore, depends on the meaningful attitude of the bare skin being struck. In a theatre of punishment, or retribution, where control is absent and fear is present, or omnipresent, the sensation of the lash would probably be painful and difficult to endure. It is not too difficult to imagine, however, a more amorous theatre, with an atmosphere defined by complicity and safety, trust and control, where the sensation of the lash is pleasurable in extremis.[40] Which is to say that pain is not intrinsic to sensation, but to evaluation, and that happiness and unhappiness, as evaluations, are not attached to fixed associations but to embedded associations.

One might imagine, as Aldous Huxley did in *Brave New World*, an emotional regime in which the power of emotional prescription is so pervasive that the population evaluates itself as happy against its interests, while under the influence of a psychotropic drug recognised as part of normal practice. The diminution of free will, critical thought, range of choice, etc. come to be the associations of happiness, from which we as readers are supposed to recoil in horror. But these reflections cast a light on our own happiness, begging us to question what it is that makes us happy, or, perhaps more pertinently, what it is that we *desire* that we *think* will make us happy. Money, love, revelation, a house, a spouse, a dog, a child, a car, an *objet d'art*: there is nothing intrinsic in any of these objects that emits or guarantees happiness. In the attainment of them,

---

[39] S. Ahmed, *The Promise of Happiness* (Durham, NC, and London: Duke University Press, 2010), 2.
[40] Moscoso, *Pain*, 137–64.

many feel let down by the reality and may even miss the yearning for the thing now attained.

So what is it that imbues objects with their power of association? The answer to that, which is, of course, endlessly complex and rich, reveals the dynamic of power behind happiness. The yearning itself, the quest to become happy, which is an emotional state distinct from happiness, does not come from within. How could there be a *natural* yearning for this or that association? To discover who directs the yearning, and the extent to which we are alienated from that powerful agency, is to begin to relinquish that yearning by seeing it for its ultimately political nature. Perhaps in the act of relinquishing we may find happiness. Or we may find that happiness does not really exist, but instead discover the power of *satisfaction*.

In Ahmed's project these things are part of being politically active in the present, but we can orientate a search for happiness – or the happy sense – to the past by much the same means, and this sense does not need to be labelled 'happy' either. The power structures that define when people are satisfied with their lives are open to investigation. Who or what defines the terms of conformity? What practices are evaluated as happy-making, or satisfying, which we might call complicit conformity, and why? Such questions automatically also suggest their opposites, namely, what constitutes non-conformity and what are its consequences? What practices make unhappiness or result in a lack of satisfaction, which we might call non-complicit conformity? Ahmed is clear about this: 'The question "what does happiness do?" is inseparable from the question of how happiness and unhappiness are distributed over time and in space. To track the history of happiness is to track the history of its distribution. Happiness gets distributed in all sorts of complicated ways. Certainly to be a good subject is to be perceived as a happiness-cause, as making others happy. To be bad is thus to be a killjoy.'[41] In short, the sense of being happy, or satisfied, or content, or of simply *fitting in*, has to do with the prescriptive practices and objects defined by institutions or personalities that hold power within a given community or regime.

The sense of satisfaction of an individual, in general, relates to the aggregate of all the emotive processes going on in that

[41] Ahmed, *Happiness*, 19–20.

individual over the course of time. Following on from this, the sense of satisfaction of a society can be said to be an aggregate of each individual's sense of satisfaction. Where individual complicit conformity to prescriptive emotionology is high, and where this is mirrored in the social interactions of individuals writ large, then the society might be described as 'happy'. Where individual non-complicit conformity, or outright non-conformity, is high, and where this causes fractious or fearful interactions across society, then the society might be described as 'unhappy'.

Given that we live in a present where politics have increasingly moved towards metrics of happiness and satisfaction to gauge the success of political regimes, it seems germane for historians to have both the theoretical wherewithal to challenge the apparent naturalness of such 'happy society' claims, and to express their scepticism through studies of the sense of satisfaction in the past.[42] After all, a happy society does not necessarily accord with any particular kind of regime or community, but rather with the degree to which those who make prescriptions, and the way in which they are made, facilitate the complicit conformity of society. One could find examples of stable periods in regimes of every stamp where, in broad strokes, we might conclude that people were 'happy'. There is no obvious or timeless correlation of happiness or satisfaction with social democracy, or of unhappiness with tyranny. Satisfaction does not naturally accord with the number of human 'rights' available to a society, though we can measure how such an accordance might come about. Rather, degrees of satisfaction inhere in the integrity of the everyday practices of satisfaction within a given regime at a given time.

In the 1980s Thomas Haskell approached this subject from the point of view of what he called the 'ethical shelter', which circumscribed those issues about which ethical concern could be discussed while also drawing an exclusion line around those issues that could not be broached.[43] Haskell was seeking an answer for the highly limited aims of eighteenth-century humanitarianism (why did it pursue an end to the slave trade, and to cruelty to animals, but not the massive wealth inequalities and their social consequences within Western polities?), but his argument is highly relevant for

---

[42] See chapter 1, note 72.
[43] Haskell, 'Capitalism'.

historians who wish to understand how a sense of satisfaction might be attained in historical context, when a contemporary view would seem to make it unsatisfactory in the extreme. Haskell theorised that in order to take action to correct a perceived wrong, there had to be both the necessary conditions to be able to sense the wrong *as* a wrong in the first place, and a readily available set of practices that could be employed to correct this wrong. This set of practices had to be at hand to a degree that it might have become unethical not to have employed them. Where these conditions were not met, the 'wrong', as we might perceive it from the vantage of hindsight, could remain outside the ethical shelter.

Reformers in the early decades of the nineteenth century might therefore have sensed a great deal of satisfaction about the end of the slave trade (even if this did not mean the immediate end of slavery) and about the introduction of Acts of Parliament against cruelty to animals (even if this did not make any great difference to the aggregate of suffering among animals); they will have rested easy in the knowledge that society was 'happier' for these changes, even though the lot of the vast majority of the population had not changed at all. Moreover, historians are able to point out in such terms that it is often only relatively small numbers of a given polity who are counted when considering the extent to which satisfaction prevailed. In nineteenth-century Britain this might be said to fall along the lines of independent citizenship, where a highly satisfied group could be found among men of a certain social standing. Since these men drove the political narratives that framed social prescriptions for proprietary actions – in effect, social practices – and defined what constituted gentlemanly behaviour – ethical and bodily practices – so they made the terms by which society had to conform. It would be fascinating, for example, to re-cast this age not as the Age of Reform, but as the Age of Dissatisfaction. For political and social change, and with it emotional and moral change, came from a *sense* of injustice in the ways in which the prescription makers did not represent the interests – the *feelings* – of the population. This sense of rightness and wrongness will occupy us in the last chapter.

8

MORALITY

An emotional basis for morality?

Since professional historians have tended to reject easy formulations about learning from the past, or history repeating itself, they have often been left stammering when asked to justify what history does, or what it is worth. On good days, of course, most historians can justify what they do, at least to themselves, but an air of suspicion has tended to linger over so-called 'soft' sub-fields of history that are not thought to get to the real meat of historical significance. For decades, this meant powerful white men, their politics, the institutions of politics and the delicacies of diplomacy, were 'real' history, and everything else was a kind of academic fluff. Such ring-fencing of historical importance has long since ceased. Gender history, the history of race and ethnicity, the history of class, the history of the body and of sex: all these have, to a large extent, ceased to be sub-fields of history and have become part and parcel of what every historian needs to know and needs to do. The dynamics revealed by these approaches tell us something about social and cultural relations that 'great man' narratives did not.

For all the change, there was a risk that the history of emotions would become a mere sub-field, of little importance to the grander historiographical project. It seemed to risk being limited to the study of individuals, and, as we have seen, faced seemingly insurmountable territorial challenges from those sciences who laid a more obvious claim to the emotions as a field of study. Talking about feelings, from a certain point of view, meant missing the real stuff of history: namely, reason and action. This book has dealt with many of the extra-historical problems of emotions research and the perception of emotions as something transhistorical. In sum, the emotions looked from certain vantage points to represent layer upon layer of irrelevance for the historian. Already it should be clear why this perception is wrong in so many ways: emotion is part of reason; emotions take place through action. But we are left with the nagging question, once all the finer details are settled: what's the point? In a 2009 article Ville Kivimäki and Tuomas Tepora addressed this in a more straightforward way than most historians have managed. 'Why do emotions matter?' they asked, in the context of research into the emotional attachments behind the motivations for male fighting and violence in World War II. Do we not have sociology, psychology, power relations and social dynamics to make sense of why people act the way they do (or did)? Having made an extraordinary argument that it was love, not hate, that made men fight, they conclude with a programmatic statement that I will pursue further here:

> We think that to study emotions in their wide-ranging historical contexts helps to understand how various social and cultural practices create mentalities, experiences, interaction, and behavior. Emotions shape, intensify, and transmit cultural meanings. Their analysis shifts the focus to individuals in their attempt to give meaning even to the most devastating historical experiences. Human identities and communities are based on emotional ties of love, attachment, trust, and desire, and suffice to say, their opposites, with the objects and patterns of such emotions varying historically and situationally. Any history of emotions therefore addresses the dynamics, functions, and consequences of this tangled web of interpersonal and communal relations. In the process, the complexity of human experience is recreated.[1]

This, in short, puts emotions at the heart of what it means to be human, and therefore at the heart of historiographical interest. Far from being merely irrational noise, emotions are the fundamental meaning-making phenomena in human life. They are part of cognitive processes, undergirding social relations, colouring in reasoned discourse and providing a sense of what hurts and what pleases, what feels good and bad, and what feels right and wrong.

These observations seem to hold good regardless of where and

---

[1] V. Kivimäki and T. Tepora, 'War of hearts: Love and collective attachment as integrating factors in Finland during World War II', *Journal of Social History*, 43 (2009): 285–305, at 297.

when we look at emotional phenomena among humans. The operation of the emotions changes quite radically, but there can be no question that the meaningfulness or, to put it another way, the *value* of experience is and has always been established by or filtered through what experience *felt* like. If there is a fundamental framework for the emotions, across time and space, it is this. Yet it should by now be clear that this knowledge of the frame tells us nothing about the picture within it, for it is always fleshed out in context. Whatever is going on at the level of human biology, brain activity and so on, is happening in an environment that is itself shaping those biological processes. There is, at the risk of repetition, no nature/nurture divide, only biocultural dynamics. The effort required to emote is the working of body-minds in culture. As Reddy stated, it 'is here, rather than in some putative set of genetically programmed "basic" emotions, that a universal conception of the person, one with political relevance, can be founded'.[2]

Political relevance, yes, for what humans strive to feel is closely aligned to, or resistant to, the power structures that lay out prescriptions of what humans *should* feel. But I also want to say that in this general universal framework there is also moral relevance. In Reddy's estimation, emotives always come loaded with a degree of failure, the extent of which determines a person's feeling of accord with the emotional regime, and therefore with the politics of the emotional community. But what is a feeling of accord except a sense of appropriateness, or a feeling of rightness or wrongness? The prescription of emotional repertoires necessarily comes loaded with moral value, experienced as a moral sense. To emphasise this, I think, gives the history of emotions a real weight of purpose. For beyond an exploration of the meaning and structure of human experience, which is compelling enough, lies a deeper exploration of the value of human experience. The history of morality is already a large field, but the history of emotions promises to open up a new front, analysing how morality is experienced, and the ways in which moral economies are formed, entrenched, destabilised and changed.

I will come back to the specific term 'moral economy' presently, but first it is necessary to build the case for emotions as the basis of morality. I do not want to set out a philosophical agenda here,

---

[2] Reddy, *Navigation*, 105.

though I will out of necessity have to refer to one. Rather, I will attempt to lay out some common ground about what morality is when it is encountered at the level of experience, rather than in the abstract. Without doubt, moral codes can be written down, transmitted, debated and contested, all in abstract terms. Morality, as a major branch of ethics, is self-evidently a part of abstract reasoning, and it seems as though questions of right and wrong can be determined, as it were, beyond the emotional realm. I want to bracket all of this, for the following reasons.

First, morality in the abstract – a moral code, a philosophical treatise – does not necessarily lead to acceptance on an individual or societal level. Being punished, socially or through the more formal channels of penal justice, does not automatically equate to an internal conception of having done wrong. Indeed, there are countless examples of justice systems that seem themselves to be on the wrong side of morality, with those punished by it seen as victims rather than as justly treated. I could write a moral treatise today that exhorted people to avoid throwing cucumbers on Tuesdays, for it is immoral to do so, but unless I could really persuade people to internalise the wrongness of this activity, nobody would credit it. Perhaps, over time and with sufficient control over the instruments of violence, police and justice, I could punish people so severely that Tuesday cucumber throwing would, as a matter of common sense, become unwise. And from unwise it might eventually become internalised as wrong in itself. But, if all this were possible, all I would have proven is that the moral code in and of itself would have been worthless without the social and cultural instruments of power and influence that give meaning – in this case punitive meaning – to the code.

Second, historians have become mistrustful of any debate that is framed by an assertion of neutrality, objectivity or timelessness. Perhaps some will be surprised to hear this of neutrality and objectivity, but the lessons of history's flirtation or, in some cases, full embrace of post-modernism have been widely appropriated. Moreover, historians themselves have written histories of objectivity that have laid bare the affective work that has to be done in order to profess an objective position.[3] The historian can hardly preach that all historical actors were contextually and culturally bound

[3] Daston and Galison, *Objectivity*.

and then claim a position of neutrality for himself. Empiricism and the burden of evidence can still lead us to narratives that are true, but constructing the truth of the past cannot be divorced from the process of construction and production, and the situatedness of the historian.

When historians look over the fence at philosophers, they therefore look with some scepticism at truth statements that stake transcendent claims. Statements from contemporary philosophers about the precise definition of morality (or emotion, for that matter) are treated by historians no differently to similar statements from philosophers of the past. That is, they are contextualised, weighed against other claims and used to understand something about the moment that has produced them. Any historian whose research was defined by a concrete understanding of timeless morality would be engaged in the most ludicrous pursuit of anachronism.

Putting the content of philosophy to one side, then, I want to turn instead to one of its essential frameworks. While I do not want to engage ethicists about ethics, I do want to engage them about where ethics come from. There is a grand history of philosophy, with a strong emphasis on the Scottish Enlightenment, which has emphasised the emotional basis of morality, and a contemporary philosophical tradition that follows this principle.[4] It is theoretically compelling, but has the added advantage of being empirically researchable. As such, it supplies an agenda for historical research that can unlock the real potential for the history of emotions.

Moral economies, affective communities

At this point it is necessary to return to the theoretical and methodological jargon, the assemblage of neologisms, of the history of emotions and ask whether it sufficiently permits historiographical practice. It is my contention that something is lacking, not so much in the theory that underlies talk of emotional communities, emotional regimes and emotional practices, but in the academic

---

[4] For the contemporary tradition see C. Bagnoli [ed.], *Morality and the Emotions* (Oxford: Oxford University Press, 2012) and J. Prinz, *The Emotional Construction of Morals* (Oxford: Oxford University Press, 2008). For the historical philosophical tradition see Gross, *Secret History*: Aristotle, 63–4; Hobbes, 45; Hume, 130; Smith, 169–79.

territorialism that is implicit in them. Coming up with new analytical labels is part and parcel of what historians do, but on closer reading it seems we already have a superfluity of labels in the history of emotions, many of which carry significant conceptual overlap. The field has undoubtedly been stretched by the debates aroused by the introduction of these terms, and the theoretical explication of them has been revealing (even though it seems the reception of these explications has been limited). But the conclusion I draw from these explications is that there is nothing particularly new in their contents, and that we might perhaps give priority elsewhere.

In 1995 Lorraine Daston wrote 'The moral economy of science' to find a way to express the ways that science 'depends in essential ways upon highly specific constellations of emotions and values'.[5] To make sense of this, in what paved the way for a further decade of work on the affective practices of science and scientists, Daston appropriated a term from E.P. Thompson and radically altered it. The 'moral economy', as Daston reconstructed the term, effectively does the work of the 'emotional community'; it understands the way in which the evaluation of affective behaviour is part of power dynamics, and therefore forecasts the 'emotional regime'. It also ties affective behaviour to activities, thereby forecasting 'emotional practice'.

The moral economy undergirded and permitted specific ways of knowing, and therefore tied emotional practices to knowledge systems, reason to affect, even where those forms of knowing explicitly denied any form of emotive content. The moral economy explicitly is not about individual psychology, and indeed rejects psychologism altogether. Moreover, the moral economy can be pluralised, to make sense of competing or sympathetic collectives or communities that do not entirely share a set of affective practices. In short, Daston's moral economy pre-dates most of the jargon coined by historians of emotion, does most of the work of that jargon and loads it with the quality of *value*, which the other analytical categories lack, or tend to lack. So what is the moral economy, in detail?

Daston's version of the moral economy was explicitly and rigorously defined. Since so many other people prior to Daston have used exactly this phrase, it was essential that the terms were

[5] L. Daston, 'The moral economy of science', *Osiris*, 2nd series, 10 (1995): 2–24, at 2.

made plain.[6] In general, a moral economy is defined thus: 'a web of affect-saturated values that stand and function in well-defined relationship to one another'. The word 'moral' refers to 'the psychological and the normative', to the valorisation of objects and actions (practices) with emotion. The word 'economy' has nothing to do with *the* economy, in a financial and labour sense, but rather refers to a regularised 'system' that is 'explicable but not always predictable' (like a regime).[7] This is then elaborated:

> A moral economy is a balanced system of emotional forces, with equilibrium points and constraints. Although it is a contingent, malleable thing of no necessity, a moral economy has a certain logic to its composition and operations. Not all conceivable combinations of affects and values are in fact possible. Much of the stability and integrity of a moral economy derives from its ties to activities ...[8]

In sum, a moral economy is circumscribed by prescription and the possibilities of practice. The relationship of affects, values and their associated practices are limited by a range of what is considered possible or – and this is key – acceptable within a given framework of relations and collaborations. A moral economy is 'a *Gefühls-* as well as a *Denkkollektiv*'.[9] What she calls 'ways of feeling' are absolutely intertwined with 'ways of seeing, manipulating, and understanding'.[10] The value of knowledge and the affective practices that give expression to such a value are not, in the end, separable. Though she did not cite the Stearns, this seems to be an expression of emotionology; however, it superadds the element of value to prescribed norms, which sets out what might be at stake in a given system. Only by understanding the 'moral' element of emotional prescription can we understand why people follow norms, or why they struggle to resist them. This introduces the element of power,

---

[6] Daston's usage is in contradistinction to Robert E. Kohler or Bruno Strasser, who both borrowed from E.P. Thompson. Those moral economies 'regulate authority relations and access to the means of production and rewards of achievement'. See R.E. Kohler, *Lords of the Fly: Drosophila Genetics and the Experimental Life* (Chicago: University of Chicago Press, 1994); Strasser, 'Experimenter's museum'.
[7] Daston, 'Moral economy': 4.
[8] Daston, 'Moral economy': 4.
[9] Daston, 'Moral economy': 5.
[10] Daston, 'Moral economy': 5.

as in a regime, but pre-empts the question of whether such power must rest on overt political forces. Moral economies emphasise the 'power of the microscopic, internalized Foucauldian sort', which can be expressed as 'self-discipline' rather than through 'coercion'.[11] In this, Daston seems to pre-empt Reddy's 'emotives', though she is less interested in individual effortful self-expression than in what happens at the communal level of social interaction and practice. Self-discipline, after all, takes place within the framework of the moral economy, and is therefore never detached from it. The individual's modes of expression are irrevocably and dynamically related to the collective norms that circumscribe the limits of practice. But, of course, both the plurality of moral economies and the latitude within a given moral economy to forge expression and practice, leave room for potential change. Crucial for historians of emotion, therefore, is the notion that 'moral economies are historically created, modified, and destroyed; enforced by culture rather than nature and therefore both mutable and violable; and integral to ... ways of knowing'.[12] This applies even when a given moral economy purports to be enforced by nature or by natural law. Indeed, such a cultural wolf in natural sheep's clothing may have made for some formidably strong moral economies, especially in the high days of social Darwinism.

Within history-of-science networks, Daston's moral economy article has been enormously influential, having been cited several hundred times. I have used it myself in order to give structure and coherence to my own study of the scientific affective practices of the first generation of Darwinists, broadly conceived, in my book *The Science of Sympathy*.[13] There are clear traces of its influence in other attempts to try to extend the study of the history of emotions within scientific bowers, notably the special issue of *Isis* edited by Paul White on 'the emotional economy of science', which preserved at least half of the label, but which pursued much the same ends as Daston.[14] In it, White called for the study of the 'ways in which the emotions might be studied as objects and as agents integral to

[11] Daston, 'Moral economy': 6.
[12] Daston, 'Moral economy': 7.
[13] Boddice, *Science of Sympathy*, esp. 15–16.
[14] P. White [ed.], 'Focus: The emotional economy of science', *Isis*, 100 (2009).

scientific *practice*: the principles of observation, experiment, and theory, and reciprocally, the practices of the self'.[15] And of course, those practices are overlaid with evaluative judgments that bespeak normativity, or the category of the 'moral', broadly conceived.

Javier Moscoso, when talking about the complex pre-history of placebo and the virtues of treatments that were bound both to medical authority, personality and cultural values, framed the discussion by the 'moral economy of hope'.[16] Doubtless, Daston was the reference point here. In a significant move, the foundation of a new research school on moral economies in modern societies at the Max Planck Institute for Human Development in Berlin, and connecting with the three Berlin universities, promises to deliver more than twenty new PhDs on the subject over the coming few years. Though it is by no means prescribed what is meant by moral economies here, the fact that this school is embedded within the Center for the History of Emotions provides at least some conceptual association with Daston's work, which has been required reading.

The reach of the moral economy beyond the history of science is somewhat limited. Anthropologist Claire Wendland used the concept to help analyse her study of Malawian medical students and their confrontation of poverty in medical practice.[17] Didier Fassin considered the broader implications of Daston's re-working of the label, in an attempt to reconcile her definition with Thompson's, noting that Daston had denuded the moral economy of its 'political dimension'.[18] In my reading, she had actually got to the heart of the way political dynamics are embedded or sewn into quotidian practices. It was a much more sophisticated imagining of political relations and the soft working of power in context than the more overt political oppositions of class struggle.

Given its potential importance for the history of emotions it is vital that insubstantial disciplinary barriers are breached. A slight hindrance to this was Daston's own decision to drop the term,

---

[15] P. White, 'Introduction', in White, 'Focus': 792–7, at 793.
[16] Moscoso, 'Facing cancer', in Boddice [ed.], *Pain and Emotion*, 31.
[17] C.L. Wendland, *A Heart for the Work: Journey Through an African Medical School* (Chicago: Chicago University Press, 2010), 196.
[18] D. Fassin, 'Les économies morales revisitées', *Annales. Histoire, Sciences Sociales* (2009): 1237–66.

perhaps because of its slipperiness in relation to its other deployments. Its influence, however, was foundational for Daston's even more important contribution, with Peter Galison, in her 2007 book *Objectivity*, which at time of writing has been cited more than 1600 times. In *Objectivity* Daston and Galison refine the semantics of morality and ethics in a bid to understand the ways in which a notion of the self is arrived at through specific contextually bound practices that are connected to ways of knowing:

> The mastery of scientific practices is inevitably linked to self-mastery, the assiduous cultivation of a certain kind of self. And where the self is enlisted as both sculptor and sculpture, ethos enters willy-nilly. It is useful for our purposes to distinguish between the ethical and the moral: *ethical* refers to normative codes of conduct that are bound up with a way of being in the world, an ethos in the sense of the habitual disposition of an individual or group, while *moral* refers to specific normative rules that may be upheld or transgressed and to which one may be held to account.[19]

The theory is easily applied to other collectives, beyond the scientific world, to professional, confessional, social, political or any other type of group. As Daston and Galison point out, it is 'perhaps conceivable that an epistemology without an ethos may exist, but we have yet to encounter one'.[20] An individual who internalises a particular ethos, who understands and lives by the values inherent in a system of knowledge/practice, and who is also efficacious 'in securing knowledge' through and for that system, is described as having 'epistemic virtue'.[21] This analysis, which is the basis of *Objectivity*, is in effect a re-statement of the 'moral economy of science', though the habitus of the group is now understood as an ethos, while the moral sense attaches to those who are exemplary in their individual practices within those ethical bounds.

In a recent issue of *Osiris*, Daston's contribution to the affective nature of scientific practice looms especially large, centred around the observation, from *Objectivity*, that 'all "epistemology is rooted in an ethos, which is at once normative and affective – or affective *because* normative"'.[22] But here the phrase from *Objectivity* of

---

[19] Daston and Galison, *Objectivity*, 40.
[20] Daston and Galison, *Objectivity*, 40.
[21] Daston and Galison, *Objectivity*, 40–1.
[22] Dror *et al.*, 'History': 14n.

'epistemic virtue' does not have any great traction with the editors in their attempt to say something about the history of emotions in the history of science. Instead, the editors connect Daston and Galison's appraisal of 'objectivity', along with Jessica Riskin's 'sentimental empiricism' and Amir Alexander's 'tragic' mathematics, to 'emotional style'.[23] They thereby perform some unnecessary translation work, for they end up putting the 'interobjectivity that is related to the interplay of humans, artifacts, and spaces', together with its more apparent 'intersubjective' elements, into a category coined by Stearns and Stearns in 1985 that, at least in its early development, failed to penetrate deeply into affective experience or practice. The analytical category that in fact pertains to these observations is Daston's own – the moral economy – for unlike 'emotional style' it substantially drills down to the power dynamics that inhere in normative practices and scientific methods, as well as getting at the complex relationship between expression and experience in the construction of the scientific self.

Perhaps more importantly, the moral economy explicitly weighs emotions (or affects) as part of individual and collective cognition. Patterns of thought that bolster everyday practices, formalised into epistemologies that justify multi-layered worldviews, are not separable from affective experience, even and perhaps especially when they are represented as separate.[24] That was the great epistemological conceit of objectivity that Daston and Galison so thoroughly explored, unveiling science's concept of reason coming from a 'neutral' place as a kind of quintessential view from *somewhere*. Both philosophers and neurobiologists have abandoned the binary division of reason and emotion, or cognition and affect, and demonstrated by various methods that emotions are part of reason, just as reason is experienced and expressed through emotive states. The risk, especially with respect to intellectual history, is that the history of emotions is rejected for failing to grasp intellectual history or the history of ideas at all. By emphasising the conjunction of thought-collective and emotional-collective in a moral economy, we can actually penetrate to the heart of what gives certain ideas their power, their influence and their capacity to make change or resist it.

---

[23] Dror *et al.*, 'History': 14.
[24] On this, see also S. Ahmed, 'Affective economies', *Social Text*, 22 (2004): 117–39.

When Thomas Kuhn introduced his argument about the structure of scientific revolutions he exposed the extent to which ideas need to be reinforced by power, influence and institutions in order to have legs. Bruno Latour added substantial weight to this position in his research on contemporary scientific practice and the ways in which institutional settings and interpersonal dynamics circumscribe what can happen and therefore what can *be*.[25] But there was still a missing link in understanding how these 'atmospheres' came into being in the first place. The innovative notion of looking at the affective web of interrelated practices provides this dimension of explanation, for it connects isolated moral economies to the broader moral economies of society in which they must exist.

Though there is room for idiosyncrasy in a small moral economy, a kind of esoterica at the level of interpersonal and interobjective practice, seldom in history have institutional atmospheres been completely isolated from the socio-cultural realm more broadly conceived. Elsewhere I have described this phenomenon as like a set of *matryoshka* dolls, where the largest doll must contain every other doll, each of which will be smaller than the last, with subtle differences of marking and scale.[26] They are fundamentally connected, but each can be considered whole by itself, from a certain point of view. This model of culture, society, institutionalisation, power, collective thought and practice, and the impact this has on individual emotive processes, has the potential to connect the history of ideas and the history of society. Viewed in this way, the history of emotions in the idiom of the moral economy has the potential to work at the very heart of what historians do. With full recognition of the mutability of experience and the historicity of the body and the brain, but with research grounded in archival empiricism and the laboratories of neuroscientists, the study of moral economies promises to be a meta-narrative for the post-postmodern age in historical scholarship.

The moral sense

I deliberately held back a discussion of the moral sense in the chapters on the senses and experience, though it could easily have

---

[25] See chapter 4, note 3.
[26] Boddice, *Science of Sympathy*, 15–16.

been included there. I reserve it for this terminal point because of its overriding importance for the history-of-emotions project considered as a whole. The history of emotions and the history of the senses taken together collapse the old distinction between thinking and feeling and begin to construct a meaningful holism when approaching the experiences of the past. Equally inseparable from this holistic approach are the social and cultural evaluations that run through the human experience-making system. As we have seen, there is no pain without an affective evaluation of its meaning; there is no neutral sensory experience that is somehow outside of the sphere of social and cultural measurement. Rights and wrongs can be codified and introduced in abstract terms, but rights and wrongs are experienced – always – as sensory and affective as well as intellectual phenomena. In fact, if anything gives way in the ordinary historical experience of justice and injustice, it is abstract reasoning. Morality is at our fingertips, in our guts and potentially anywhere in the sensory/affective world made by the brain, in its interaction with other world-making brains. As Classen argued as long ago as 1993, 'sensory relations are ... moral relations'.[27]

Structures of power, the dynamic interaction within and across social boundaries, and constructions of taboo – the moral economy, if you will – are made through the sensory and emotional particularities of a given place at a given time. Various scholars have found evidence of this in different settings, such as Nicky Hallett's documenting of life in early modern Carmelite convents. What she found in studying the 'power structures in such communities' was an invariable 'encounter' with 'moral ecologies as well as gendered ideologies', where '[a]ttitudes *to* nuns might be expected to shape their attitudes to themselves'.[28] The convent as sensorium was both indicator and formational of the nun's moral economy, in terms of what defined conformity and non-conformity. 'By imbuing sensory values with social values', Classen states, 'cultures attempt to ensure that their members will perceive the world aright.'[29] In other words, the moral compass exists in the realm of *feeling*, which can finally be defined as a concept that includes emotions and sensations. And of course, where members of a culture do not perceive the world

---

[27] Classen, *Worlds of Sense*, 137.
[28] Hallett, *Senses*, 21.
[29] Classen, *Worlds of Sense*, 137.

aright, they will feel out of place, or out of time, and society will judge them for it. The results of this will either be called justice or injustice, leading to a dominant recapitulation of the status quo of the moral economy, or to an upheaval that recognises the rightness of those who seemed to be out of step.

This puts recorded material on all manner of sights, sounds, smells and tastes, as well as all forms of bodily contact, in conjunction with the practices that are implied by these senses, in play as plausible sources for the history of morality and justice. Take, for example, the history of the senses in religious contexts over the *longue durée*. Susan Ashbrook Harvey made the following observation about the importance of smell in the early Christian church: 'For the late antique Christian, odors served to effect changes in moral condition, to discipline the body towards a more perfectly fashioned existence, to instruct on the qualities and consequences of human and divine natures, to classify and order human–divine relation and interaction in explicitly Christian terms.'[30] To be clear, nothing in a smell could intrinsically alter a person or a community's moral condition, but the applied meaning of given smells could. Harvey calls this the 'olfactory imagination', but the process of associating smells with conditions is as much a form of practice as anything else we have encountered. The making of affective meaning as an output of the brain is made possible through olfactory practices that connect smells to values. Moreover, it does not really matter where one looks in the history of organised religion (the sphere of the history of morality par excellence, at least before the twentieth century), we find that similar processes of translation – translating sensory input into meaningful and evaluated outputs – takes place. But the meanings of sensory inputs change radically.

As Milner discovered, at the core of any 'analysis of social discipline and the tensions of confessional statecraft' was the observation that 'the perceptive was the political and the moral'.[31] Crucially, the Protestant mistrust of, or outright antagonism towards, Catholic ritual sensory practices in sixteenth-century England did not result in a form of practice that was sensorially neutral, or entirely lacking. Rather, the Protestant ritual sensorium was re-evaluated, literally,

---

[30] S.A. Harvey, *Scenting Salvation: Ancient Christianity and the Olfactory Imagination* (Berkeley and Los Angeles: University of California Press, 2006), 3.
[31] Milner, *Senses*, 345.

so that moral meaning was hitched anew to specific sensibilities and untethered from old ones. But the experience of religious ritual – feeling pious, sensing grace, experiencing divine justice, etc. – was still a *sensory* experience. Whether one felt themselves moral or felt themselves to be among the elect, the moral sense – driven by the sensorium in general, in combination with affective and cognitive practices, including reason – has always been at the heart of being human. The rider to this observation, naturally, is that this being has been anything but constant.

All of this is of great moment for the discipline of history, for this way of researching the world's past gives us a key to understanding justice as historical in a way that makes the study of justice the province of historiography.

CONCLUSION

Over the course of this book I have tried to gauge from where the history of emotions came, why it is important and where we are now. In various ways, especially with reference to the turn to the neurosciences, genetics and to the question of morality, I have tried to suggest the potential routes for our historiographical future. By way of conclusion I want to re-state what is at stake in the history of emotions, and to emphasise what must happen in the coming years if the approach (currently a plural here would be more appropriate) is to prove to be analytically and substantially useful for doing historical research, and be broadly accepted in the discipline of history and beyond.

There are three essential steps, in my estimation. First, we need to read across historical periods and be open to the porous nature of disciplinary boundaries. Second, we need to be much better at reading across language barriers. These two things are about making theoretical and methodological debates more constructive and more coherent, and about the avoidance of repetition or needless re-invention. Third, these theories and methods need to be taught, and taught well, so that students begin to practise the history of emotions as undergraduates. The effectiveness of this teaching will depend to a large extent on scholars new to the field being able to make sense of what I once called a 'loose canon' of works and approaches, and on students being able to condense an amorphous set of debates and discussions into a notion of best practice, however unstable and subject to imaginative development. In many ways it is my hope that this book provides a key to unlocking these possibilities.

Period problems

Concerns about periodisation in the discipline of history are not, of course, limited to the history of emotions, but they are starkly in evidence in the formative years of this particular historiographical development. There are run-of-the-mill reasons for this as well as some esoteric developments that have put modernists and medievalists apparently at odds. It is, of course, not unusual that medievalists and modernists do not really engage with each other's historical work, but in the formative period of theory development in the history of emotions, each set of scholars came up with approaches to the history of emotions that would work with their own peculiar materials and historiographical traditions. In an ideal world, historical methods would work for any period, but any medievalist will tell you that there are different pressures and limitations when dealing with medieval sources, just as any modernist will aver that it is sometimes difficult to place limits on the number of sources, which seem to continue to expand as digitisation projects make everything more readily available.

What created a particular problem was Barbara Rosenwein's perception that the history of emotions was being orientated around modernist preoccupations with the emergence of the nation state, and an unfortunate tendency to buy into a hackneyed cliché about pre-modern societies being 'child-like', before becoming more 'adult' – meaning restrained – in civilised modernity.[1] That misgiving has been echoed by others, notably Damien Boquet and Piroska Nagy, who raised serious concerns about the focus of (particularly French) social and political science that had, by marking out the rise of liberal democracy as the rise of rationalism, identified emotions as both simply irrational and as forces opposed to modern civilisation.[2] This had the effect of infantilising the medieval past as well as forcing emotions into modern categories of 'authenticity'. As they point out, the relationship between an emotional feeling and an emotional expression is very complicated, involving all manner of social codes, rituals, performances, etc., and there-

---

[1] Rosenwein, 'Worrying': 823–5.
[2] D. Boquet and P. Nagy, 'L'historien et les émotions en politique: entre science et citoyenneté', in D. Boquet and P. Nagy [eds], *Politiques des émotions au Moyen Âge* (Florence: Sismel, 2010), 5–30.

fore the authentication of emotions takes place in the context of situated practices.

To write all this off as irrational or child-like is clearly an absurd reduction.[3] The danger of psychologism – the very danger pointed out by Febvre in the founding statement of the history of emotions – still lurks, and even if it is not associated with modern *historians*, it is associated with modern *social scientists* in general. Modern psychological categories, or, to put it even more strongly, the closed book of psychological knowledge concerning what emotions are, still threaten to derail the history of emotions in the most fundamental way by privileging contemporary epistemology over the lived experience of past actors.

There is, to be sure, clear evidence that certain kinds of psychologists are not listening to historians, or taking seriously their claims about situated emotional practices and relations. Even in the conclusion to Boquet and Nagy's volume mentioned above, the psychologist Bernard Rimé felt it necessary to point out that Boquet and Nagy were wrong to say that there is no absolute definition of what emotions are. This was followed by a brief statement of everything that tends towards the inculcation of iconoclasm among historians of emotion, about a 'prototypical definition of emotion', which, despite infinite variety and complexity in practice, could nevertheless be boiled down to the following: an abrupt modification of the situation with physiological and expressive responses, modification of the consciousness and an inclination to action. And under the wheels of this categorical juggernaut went the preceding 300 pages of scholarship that historicised and particularised emotions in social, ritual and political contexts, and which did not necessarily fit at all with the model of psychological abruptness.[4]

This is not the only such attempt to restore timeless and unchanging categories onto the emotions. In an otherwise splendid volume on sympathy in the eighteenth century, the purpose of which was to directly challenge what might be meant by emotional authenticity, a chapter by psychologist W. Gerrod Parrott undermined the entire work by introducing 'ur-emotions', which are nothing more than nuanced recapitulations of Ekman's 'basic emotions', and

---

[3] Boquet and Nagy, 'L'historien', in Boquet and Nagy [eds], *Politiques*, 20–5.
[4] B. Rimé, 'Les émotions médiévales. Réflexions psychologiques', in Boquet and Nagy [eds], *Politiques*, 309–32, at 311–12.

have something in common with Rimé's emotional 'prototypes'. The tautological arrangement of fundamental emotion concepts, in English, which then determine the search for those emotions in any culture or period, is haunted by the same methodological and ethnocentric flaws as the search for basic emotions. It also predetermines that the category 'emotion' is settled and universal, at root. Remarkably, the book's editors praise this piece for pointing out the 'underlying features common to humans in all emotional displays', while allowing for 'the influence of environment', ignoring all the work on emotional practice and emotional ethnography, not to mention social neuroscience, that have brought such universal foundations into disrepute. If modern historians themselves refuse to engage with the developments in biocultural studies, then the expression of such crude dualism will inevitably live on. All the evidence of cultural variation of the expression and experience of emotions will remain the mere dross of context on the unchanging human body, with its fixed definitions of different emotions, with equally fixed notions of what those emotions do.[5]

It is doubtful, and here one must have some sympathy with the claims of Rosenwein and others, that such a piece of work would have been included in a volume on medieval or ancient emotions. The implications of its inclusion in a work of modern history only further raises the suspicion that modern historians are not taking seriously enough the evidence being supplied by historians of emotions from other periods. Indeed, the charge lies open that modernists are happy to cherry-pick their definitional categories from psychology, without critical engagement. Clearly, then, problems from other disciplines remain, not so much unwelcome trespassers as they are blocks to genuine interdisciplinary collaboration on common, or at least negotiable, theoretical ground. Those blocks, it must be said, do look as if they are situated within modernist historiography. The expression of these problems merits further attention and scrutiny. I will begin with Rosenwein's issues with Elias in particular.

First of all, Rosenwein objected to the emergent popularity of

---

[5] W.G. Parrott, 'Psychological perspectives on emotion in groups', in D. Lemmings, H. Kerr and R. Phiddian [eds], *Passions, Sympathy and Print Culture: Public Opinion and Emotional Authenticity in Eighteenth-century Britain* (Houndmills: Palgrave, 2016), 20–46; editors' introduction to the same volume, 8.

Norbert Elias' *Civilizing Process*, which had been co-opted by modernists as a true picture of how the unrestrained, unchecked and barbarous courts of the medieval world had been slowly transformed, through a process of the consolidation of power, into bastions of controlled emotions and refined courtly manners. That Elias overlaid his historical narrative with a compound of biological, psychological and sociological theory (to confirm how changes in emotional restraint were fixed from one generation to the next, while still allowing for further 'progress') gave further credence to the medieval-as-child thesis, and irked Rosenwein all the more. In Elias' thesis, the degree to which emotions became subject to restraint was proportional to the extent to which emotions could burst violently forth, as if by 'hydraulic' action. Hence the peaceable existence of modern civilisation, punctuated by extraordinary outbursts of violence at the level of the State.

Rosenwein could demonstrate that Elias and others were wrong about the emotions in medieval times, but she complained that nobody else was working over the *longue durée* in such a way as to offer a substantial challenge to the Eliasian thesis. She has supplied much corrective work in this regard, aiming to illuminate the life of emotional expressions (she is less interested, or less able to access, experiences) in medieval periods and show that in many ways the structure of emotional relations and the restraints on expression were not so different to those in modernity.[6] For certain, the kinds of emotional expression available to medieval actors *were* significantly different, and crucially they also underwent rather dramatic changes from generation to generation within the medieval period, and from place to place. So far so good, but it still seems to me that modernists (who dominate the study of the history of emotions in terms of numbers) are not really reading Rosenwein's empirical and substantial work. They know about emotional communities, but they do not acknowledge the historiographical complaint out of which the theory of emotional communities was born.

This connects to the second strand of Rosenwein's complaint, for emotional communities were opposed in the first instance, explicitly, to William Reddy's emotional regimes. The problem with emotional regimes in Rosenwein's eyes, as we saw in chapter 3, was

[6] This was the agenda of Rosenwein, 'Worrying', which was fulfilled in Rosenwein, *Generations*.

that they seemed inextricably to be linked to modern formations of State power, and therefore an analysis of an emotional regime could only really work for modern history. It was, in effect, another way of saying that the structure of emotionology in pre-modern times was not just different in degree, but different in kind to the structure of emotionology in modernity. By instituting the emotional community, Rosenwein tried to find a way to talk about societal prescriptions of emotion norms that avoided alluding to the State as an organising principle. The problem again is that modernists have not really understood the distinction that Rosenwein was trying to make, and they use both emotional regime and emotional community interchangeably, without getting to the heart of what either of them actually means. As with Benedict Anderson's coinage of the 'imagined community', usage has become a commonplace convenience, devoid of substantial analytical purpose, but readily recognised as a conceptual tool somewhere near the top of the historiographical list of useful jargon.

These divisions ought now to be put to bed, with a more careful use of terminology brought about. We can and should retain Rosenwein's argument that modernists should engage with the long run of history, and not be so assured that life was begun anew in the eighteenth century. However, we might also be reassured that some of Rosenwein's complaints were perhaps overstated to begin with, and have perhaps also been remedied in the years since she made them.

First of all, the work of Elias does not seem to have become the watchword for emotional change among modernists that Rosenwein feared. Insofar as the history of emotions has expanded rapidly, it has tended to dial in to narrowly focused studies that are, if anything, averse to theory. There have been so many fora in recent years to discuss what the history of emotions actually is, with many of them failing to do the preparatory reading or seek engagement with the already decades-long debates in the field, favouring instead a notion that the field still needs to be substantially invented. There has been growth in content, therefore, but little development in theory.

Secondly, and perhaps more importantly, Rosenwein might have missed the point about Elias' work in the first place, which was really a masterpiece of irony. Published in 1939 in Germany, at the high-point of everyday brutality, fear, paranoia and repression, the end point of civilisation did not look, to Elias, very civilised at all. The process had only cast a thin veil over barbarism, to the point that the finer points of debate about *courtois* behaviour in medieval times looked refreshingly quaint and comparatively civilised in comparison to the violent abuses of modernity. Anyone who uses the *Civilizing Process* as a theoretical or explanatory model has to recognise the time and place of its production, and see it as the damning indictment of modernity that it was surely designed to be.

What Elias does usefully do, and a reason why we might keep hold of it, is something that Rosenwein understates in her theory of emotional communities. Elias' understanding of the importance of power is critical in understanding where emotional prescriptions come from, how they are tacitly or implicitly enforced, and what kinds of effort on the part of individuals and communities are required to conform to (or resist) them. An emotional community, in order to cohere, must have a power dynamic in it somewhere. Rosenwein does acknowledge this, given the prominence of kings and aristocrats in her narratives of emotional community formation, but given Reddy's subsequent statements about the broad applicability of the term 'emotional regime' to any community where there is a structure of power, surely Rosenwein's complaint that this refers only to nation states must melt away.

The problem is that both these conceptual labels are sufficiently in play to carry a certain mark of identity, even though, as mentioned above, there is no great evidence of theoretical sophistication as a whole in the field. It is for that reason, and for the sake of a more inclusive approach to the long run of history over many different periods, I suggest we abandon both for the 'moral economy' discussed in chapter 8. Not only does it stress the emotional practices that inhere in a community, but it also points to the ways in which those practices are evaluated and according to what authorities. As an analytical category, the moral economy also has the added advantage of allowing us to talk about emotions, passions, feelings and so on, in the language of historical actors, rather than imposing a contemporary language of emotions into times and places where it does not fit.

This shift in register, or else one like it, seems to me necessary if we are to be able to read across the period boundaries that define us as ancient historians, medievalists and modernists. The history of emotions actually offers a possibility of re-drawing the boundaries of historical periodisation, to see disjuncture and continuity afresh. We must have analytical tools that do not preference contemporary categories, and those tools need to be flexible enough to accommodate the great shifts in the history of experience that come over long periods of time, and comparing place to place. The advantages of so doing for something like the history of emotions are manifest. For while we are sometimes tracking dramatic and acute changes in moral economy, often we are charting much longer-spun alterations that put the history of the human body and human brain at the forefront of our research.

The coming rapprochement of the history of emotions with neurohistory, coupled with the development of the latter's extremely long- and short-term foci, will demand that we are able to study the biocultural human in succinct historical moments and across great eras of historical time. That speaks to the second aspect of disciplinary openness here: namely, our willingness as historians to work with other disciplines that have not always tended to make comfortable bedfellows. While William Reddy has stated that it is not necessary for historians to become experts in neuroscience, we are nonetheless behoved to have some idea about what is going on, and not only so that we can be alive to the potential benefits such research has for our own historical enquiries.[7]

The psychological essentialism mentioned above notwithstanding, we have also seen, for example, that historians have been among the leaders in challenging sweeping assumptions in the biological and psychological sciences, especially where they have been unreflectively gendered, raced, ethnocentric or tautological. Moreover, the overwhelming evidence that emotions have a history, at every level, from expression, to gesture, to experience itself, has led us into a much closer dialogue with neuroscientists who are aware of the extent to which brains are inscribed and experience constructed according to cultural formations. They are in a position to be able to show us how the brain works, how synaptic development happens and what it looks like when we go through an emotive process. In turn, historians are able to show neuroscientists the significance of emotional formation in context, the ways in which social evaluation and the structures of moral economies help organise, stratify and make meaningful human existence.

[7] Plamper, 'Interview': 248.

At the heart of such a relationship is the common understanding that experience, as a constructed output of the brain, is both embodied and transformative (constitutive) of the body. In the greatest traditions of empirical research, we do not define emotions (basic, 'ur', prototypical, universal linguistic concepts or otherwise) first and then go in search of them. Rather, we look at what happens, in the brain and body and in culture and society, and draw conclusions about what we find. This basic scientific premise applies equally to neuroscience as to history. Our disciplinary borders are open, if only we would cease defining in absolute terms the conditions of entry.

The most fruitful collaboration I can imagine is one in which the sciences of how things work are conjoined with the sciences of what things mean. This too includes disciplinary openness to genetic research, and an understanding of the meaningfulness of the human sack of DNA. While some geneticists, Richard Dawkins chief among them, have pooh-poohed the rise of epigenetics as overstated and ultimately unimportant to the story of human evolution over the very long run, historians are in a position to offer a corrective.[8] Epigenetic knowledge might help historians understand the meta-structure of changes in moral economy in societies that have undergone dramatic or traumatic changes on a wide scale: Europe after the Great Plague; World War I, followed immediately by the Spanish Flu pandemic; the Holocaust; the Blitz; famines and civil wars in any number of countries. In times of such widespread stress there are social, cultural and political ramifications, as well as physiological impacts on individuals that affect how social interaction works. New emotive prescriptions are thrown up by new socio-political formations, but they are experienced by bodies and minds newly forged, at least in part in the existing population, and wholly new in those children born in the midst of, or in the aftermath of, trouble.

There is enormous potential for historians to understand meta-social changes in new ways with these new tools, just as there is potential for geneticists to learn from historians what aspects of cultural innovation might have fed back into the process of human

[8] J. Webb, 'The gene's still selfish: Dawkins' famous idea turns 40', BBC News, 24 May 2016, www.bbc.co.uk/news/science-environment-36358104, accessed 15 December 2016.

adaptation. As Daniel Lord Smail and others have suggested, if historians are really interested in human beings over time, then their notion of what time is considered relevant, and what aspects of the human are considered worthy of study, are long overdue an expansion. The history of emotions, with its broad temporal coverage and loaded with a disciplinary porousness, promises much in this regard.

Language

It was not so long ago that an English-speaking academic historian might have been expected to be able to read at least one classical language, in addition to the language of civilisation (French) and the language of scholarship (German). The flow of ideas before World War I was much less troubled by national boundaries than it is now, even though we live in an era in which academics in most disciplines in non-anglophone areas are under no illusions about the importance – primarily for their careers – of publishing in English. The sad fact about the rise to prominence of English as the de facto international language of the academy is that native speakers of English have been able to let their own linguistic skills lapse. Moreover, other languages, especially those in Continental Europe, are being overlooked in favour of English. The result is that much good scholarship justifiably published in languages other than English is overlooked by the international scholarly community.

The loose community of scholars in the history of emotions has felt this linguistic impasse particularly severely. In the great expansion phase of the discipline in the first decade and a half of the twenty-first century, groups and individuals working around the world have each contributed developments to the discipline as a whole, but there is little sense that ideas are being cross-pollinated across language barriers. Germans are not, as a rule, reading the French, and vice versa. The French are not, in general, reading (or presenting) in English. Natives of anglophone countries are not, in general, reading anything *but* English. And the rest are under a heavy burden that unless they publish in English their words will not reach very far at all. The only way the Spanish are likely to discover Italian works on the history of emotions, for example, is if those works are in English, and vice versa.

CONCLUSION

In other fields the linguistic divisions might be tolerable. When historiography was divided largely along national lines, it was fairly obvious that an anglophone historian of France would need to be up on the French literature, just as a French historian of the Italian Renaissance would need to be able to navigate Italian. The languages in which works were written were matters of convenience, but not barriers to collective understanding. The history of emotions is different precisely because it has, at least so far, resisted being carved up along national lines. While in practice this may in fact be happening (the Germans do German history of emotions, the French do French history of emotions), everyone's intent at least is to contribute something beyond a minor addition to the history of their respective nation states. The history of emotions might be said to be thematic, but I think even that description underplays its fundamental importance in getting to the heart of what human experience in history has been all about. This is such an important task that it surely makes sense for us to pool our theoretical and methodological insights, not to mention learning from each other's empirical research and debating the kind of emotional-change narratives that are emerging.

Practically, this is difficult and not a short-term fix. The major fault lies with anglophone scholars who cannot go beyond English, but pointing this out will not afford them sudden competence in other tongues. To place the burden on non-anglophone scholars to get their work translated into English seems unfair, and does not solve the fundamental problem. In the first instance, the best we might hope for is awareness and acknowledgement. Not being able to read in a language other than our own ought not be a hindrance to knowing about relevant work in other languages. At present, it seems that most people do not even look. The bibliography to this book purposefully represents works in five languages, without translation, precisely because I think very few scholars in the field will be unable, when presented with the works in context, to understand what they are about. As a reference point, this is at least a start. From there, once it is acknowledged that works exist in languages beyond English, it will be much more difficult to justify ignoring them in historical analysis.

Teaching

The linguistic chauvinism of anglophones can ultimately only be undone in the classroom, and that has to be a long-term solution to academic infertility. Historians can contribute to this, by encouragement if by no other means. But there is a more specific point about teaching with which I wish to end this book.

So far, only a few courses around the world have been developed for undergraduate and graduate students in the history of emotions. The largest centres of excellence in history-of-emotions research have not contributed greatly to the dissemination of its theories, methods and findings in the classroom. The Max Planck Institute in Berlin has a small teaching programme for doctoral students, and members occasionally teach at the various Berlin universities. The Australian Centre for Excellence in the History of Emotions has focused on European emotions between 1100 and 1800, but found little scope for teaching this subject in Australian universities. There is a closer connection between teaching and research in both the US and the UK, but courses in the history of emotions depend greatly on the degree of experience of the individual teacher, and range from being in-depth reviews of the field to seemingly experimental attempts to take on something new. All should be applauded for the effort, but what they have in common is a lack of common ground to introduce the subject.

While I hope this book will fill that need in certain respects, not least in terms of its review of what is currently out there and what the landscape of debate and possibility looks like, there are further requirements if the subject is to be taught effectively. Cross-disciplinary team-teaching needs to be co-ordinated, but first it needs to be possible. What are the administrative difficulties facing humanities students hoping to receive credits in neurobiology, and likewise in the reverse direction? The issues are not insurmountable, but this kind of pedagogical collaboration will likely take bureaucratic effort, and it will need to be repeated many times before the history of emotions is substantially established in such a way as to effectively represent the direction of scholarship in the field.

Such team-teaching might not be possible everywhere, but even where it is not, students can still be given a good grounding in the history of emotions. Key to this grounding is practice. Reading about theories and methods will get a student only so far: we should be pushing students to *do* the history of emotions, and not worry about frontloading their papers with the jargon that has been so prolifically created. If there is currently a deficiency in the field, it is in the lack of empirical works that substantiate the stated aims of the field's ancients. Confidence that this can be done, as with the leading edges of research in most areas of history, will be generated by students going out and doing it. They should be let off the leash, allowed to go and find histories of emotions for themselves. Our canon is too small to rely on revisions and critical commentaries. The whole of historical time is up for grabs. The next generation of students should be enabled to grab it. Essential to this is that they are not taught as if an orthodoxy of theory and method already exists. For all of the debates, discussions and options presented in this book, the field is still wide open, still pregnant with possibilities for innovation in theory and practice, and still awaiting its master historian.

SELECT BIBLIOGRAPHY

The list compiled here refers to works that directly address or impact the history of emotions. It is not a guide to emotions research in the broader sense, although of course there are necessary overlaps with other disciplines where those disciplines have directly impacted what historians do. The bibliography is, broadly speaking, up to date as of April 2017 and goes further where it has been possible. The list is simply organised alphabetically by author.

While it is tempting to break things thematically and historically, this would probably just make the bibliography more difficult to use. The reader will therefore find some historical works about emotion intermixed with historiographical works about the history of emotions. In a way this serves to demonstrate the connectedness of recent research to its historical sources, as well as demonstrating implicitly that the latest research will, sooner or later, also become part of a long narrative of changing understandings of what emotions are and what they do. Given the proliferation of works in the history of emotions, this might be the last time that it is conceivable to supply a comprehensive list. Even now, there are countless works that have begun to incorporate the history of emotions without being explicitly works about the history of emotions, which suggests the beginnings of the field's establishment within the mainstream of historical practice.

To introduce some kind of parsimony to the list, I have included only those works that are direct contributions to the understanding of the emotions in history, or which could be used for such. Where the whole of an edited volume or journal issue is devoted to the subject, I have only listed the work *in toto*. The bibliography is not a complete list of every reference cited in this book; in fact, it is far from it.

Two other notes: the bibliography, though largely of works in English, attempts to be representative of works in the history of emotions in other languages (notably French, German and Spanish). Where these works have been translated into English, only the English translation is listed.

Otherwise, it is assumed that these works will be of substantial use even to those without reading proficiency in those languages. And finally, the bibliography attempts to provide equal coverage to works focusing on different periods. One of the central dynamics within the history of emotions (and within the discipline of history in general) is the lack of communication, or lack of harmony, among modern and pre-modern scholars. By making no discrimination about what gets listed here, it is to be hoped that students of the history of emotions can begin to approach the field as a whole, and not necessarily as a secondary choice coming only after the decision to work in modernity, the medieval or antiquity.

Adams, T. [ed.] (2012), 'Devotion and emotions in the Middle Ages', special issue of *Digital Philology*, 1.
Ahmed, S. (2004), *The Cultural Politics of Emotion*, Edinburgh: Edinburgh University Press.
Ahmed, S. (2004), 'Affective economies', *Social Text*, 22: 117–39.
Ahmed, S. (2010), *The Promise of Happiness*, Durham and London: Duke University Press.
AHR Conversation (2012), 'The historical study of emotions: Nicole Eustace, Eugenia Lean, Julie Livingston, Jan Plamper, William M. Reddy, and Barbara H. Rosenwein', *American Historical Review*, 117: 1487–531.
Ambroise-Rendu, A.C., Demartini, A.E., Eck, H., and Edelman, N. [eds] (2014), *Émotions contemporaines: XIXe–XXIe siècles*, Paris: Armand Colin.
Arellano, J. (2015), *Magical Realism and the History of the Emotions in Latin America*, Lanham, MD: Bucknell University Press.
Arnaud, S. (2015), *On Hysteria: The Invention of a Medical Category between 1670 and 1820*, Chicago: University of Chicago Press.
Arnold, J.H. (2008), 'Inside and outside the medieval laity: Some reflections on the history of emotions', in M. Rubin [ed.], *European Religious Cultures: Essays Offered to Christopher Brookes on the Occasion of his Eightieth Birthday*, London: Insitute of Historical Research.
Assmann, A., and Detmers, I. [eds] (2016), *Empathy and its Limits*, Houndmills: Palgrave.
Badinter, E. (1980), *L'amour en plus: Histoire de l'amour maternel, 17–20 siècles*, Paris: Flammarion.
Bailey, J. (2012), *Parenting in England, 1760–1830: Emotion, Identity, and Generation*, Oxford: Oxford University Press.
Bailey, M., and Barclay, K. [eds] (2017), *Emotion, Ritual and Power in Europe, 1200–1920*, Houndmills: Palgrave.
Bain, A. (1859), *Emotions and the Will*, London: John W. Parker and Son.
Bain, A. (1894), *The Senses and the Intellect*, 4th edn, London: Longmans, Green, and Co.

Barclay, K. (2011), *Love, Intimacy and Power: Marriage and Patriarchy in Scotland, 1650–1850*, Manchester: Manchester University Press.

Barclay, K. (2013), 'Love and courtship in eighteenth-century Scotland', in K. Barclay and D. Simonton [eds], *Women in Eighteenth-century Scotland: Intimate, Intellectual and Public Lives*, Farnham: Ashgate.

Barclay, K. (2014), 'Sounds of sedition: Music and emotion in Ireland, 1780–1845', *Cultural History*, 3: 54–80.

Barclay, K. (2016), 'Emotions, the law and the press in Britain: Seduction and breach of promise suits, 1780–1830', *Journal of Eighteenth-century Studies*, 39: 267–84.

Barclay, K., Reynolds, K., and Rawnsley, C. [eds] (2017), *Death, Emotion and Childhood in Premodern Europe*, London: Palgrave Macmillan.

Bantock, G.H. (1986), 'Educating the emotions: An historical perspective', *British Journal of Educational Studies*, 34: 122–41.

Barton, R. (2005), 'Gendering anger: *Ira, Furor* and discourses of power and masculinity in the eleventh and twelfth centuries', in R. Newhauser [ed.], *In the Garden of Evil: The Vices and Culture in the Middle Ages*, Toronto: Pontifical Institute of Mediaeval Studies.

Batic, G.C. [ed.] (2011), *Encoding Emotions in African Languages*, Munich: Lincom Europa.

Beard, G.M. (1881), *American Nervousness: Its Causes and Consequences*, New York: G.P. Putnam's Sons.

Beljan, M. (2015), 'Aids-Geschichter als Gefühlsgeschichte', *Aus Politik und Zeitgeschichte*, 65: 25–31.

Bell, C. (1806), *Essays on the Anatomy of Expression in Painting*, London: Longman, Hurst, Rees, and Orme.

Biess, F. (2009), '"Everybody has a chance": Nuclear angst, civil defence, and the history of emotions in postwar West Germany', *German History*, 27: 215–43.

Biess, F., and Gross, D.M. [eds] (2014), *Science and Emotions after 1945: A Transatlantic Perspective*, Chicago: Chicago University Press.

Blauvelt, M.T. (2007), *The Work of the Heart: Young Women and Emotion, 1780–1830*, Charlottesville: University of Virginia Press.

Boddice, R. (2011), 'The manly mind? Re-visiting the Victorian "sex in brain" debate', *Gender and History*, 23: 321–40.

Boddice, R. (2012), 'Species of compassion: Aesthetics, anaesthetics, and pain in the physiological laboratory', *19: Interdisciplinary Studies in the Long Nineteenth Century*, 15.

Boddice, R. (2014), 'German methods, English morals: Physiological networks and the question of callousness, c.1870–81', in H. Ellis and U. Kirchberger [eds], *Anglo-German scholarly networks in the long nineteenth century*, Leiden: Brill.

Boddice, R. (2014), 'The affective turn: Historicizing the emotions', in

C. Tileagă and J. Byford [eds], *Psychology and History: Interdisciplinary Explorations*, Cambridge: Cambridge University Press.
Boddice, R. [ed.] (2014), *Pain and Emotion in Modern History*, Houndmills: Palgrave.
Boddice, R. (2016), 'Vaccination, fear and historical relevance', *History Compass*, 14: 71–8.
Boddice, R. (2016), *The Science of Sympathy: Morality, Evolution and Victorian Civilization*, Urbana-Champaign: University of Illinois Press.
Boddice, R. (2017), 'The history of emotions', in L. Noakes, R. McWilliam and S. Handley [eds], *New Directions in Social and Cultural History*, London: Bloomsbury.
Boddice, R. (2017), *Pain: A Very Short Introduction*, Oxford: Oxford University Press.
Boddice, R. (2018), 'Experiences', in J. Reinarz [ed.], *A Cultural History of Medicine*, vol. 5, London: Bloomsbury.
Boddice, R., with Smail, D.L. (2018), 'Neurohistory', in P. Burke and M. Tamm [eds], *Debating New Approaches in History*, London: Bloomsbury.
Bonneuil, N. (2016), 'Arrival of courtly love: Moving in the emotional space', *History and Theory*, 55: 253–69.
Boquet, D. (2005), *L'ordre de l'affect au moyen âge: autour de l'anthropologie affective d'Aelred de Rievaulx*, Caen: CRAHM.
Boquet, D. [ed.] (2008), 'Histoire de la vergogne', special issue of *Rives Méditerranéennes*, 31.
Boquet, D., and Nagy, P. (2009), *Le sujet des émotions au moyen âge*, Paris: Beauchesne.
Boquet, D., and Nagy, P. [eds] (2010), *Politiques des émotions au Moyen Âge*, Florence: Sismel.
Boquet, D., and Nagy, P. (2015), *Sensible Moyen Âge: Une histoire des émotions dans l'Occident medieval*, Paris: Seuil.
Boquet, D., and Nagy, P. [eds] (2016), 'Histoire intellectuelle des émotions de l'antiquité à nos jours', special issue of *L'atelier du centre de recherches historiques*, 16.
Boquet, D., Nagy, P., and Moulinier-Brogi, L. [eds] (2011), *La chair des émotions: Pratiques et représentations corporelles de l'affectivité au Moyen Âge*, special issue of *Médiévales*, 61.
Borutta, M., and Verheyen, N. [eds] (2010), *Die Präsenz der Gefühle: Männlichkeit und Emotion in der Moderne*, Bielefeld: transcript-Verlag.
Bound Alberti, F. [ed.] (2006), *Medicine, Emotion and Disease, 1700–1950*, Houndmills: Palgrave.
Bound Alberti, F. (2008), 'Angina pectoris and the Arnolds: Emotions and heart disease in the nineteenth century', *Medical History*, 52: 221–36.
Bound Alberti, F. (2010), *Matters of the Heart: History, Medicine, and Emotion*, Oxford: Oxford University Press.

Boureau, A. (1989), 'Propositions pour une histoire restreinte des mentalités', *Annales*, 44: 1491–509.
Bourke, J. (2003), 'Fear and anxiety: Writing about emotion in modern history', *History Workshop Journal*, 55: 124.
Bourke, J. (2005), *Fear: A Cultural History*, London: Virago.
Bourke, J. (2014), *The Story of Pain: From Prayer to Painkillers*, Oxford: Oxford University Press.
Bracke, M.A. (2012), 'Building a "counter-community of emotions": Feminist encounters and socio-cultural difference in 1970s Turin', *Modern Italy*, 17: 223–36.
Brauer, J. (2012), 'Clashes of emotions: Punk music, youth subculture and authority in the GDR (1978–1983)', *Social Justice*, 38: 53–70.
Brauer, J. (2015), '"Mit neuem Fühlen und neuem Geist": Heimatliebe und Patriotismus in Kinder- und Jugendlieder frühen DDR', in D. Eugster and S. Marti [eds], *Das Imaginäre des kalten Krieges in Europa: Beiträge zu einer Kulturgeschichte des Ost-West-Konfliktes in Europa*, Essen: Klartext-Verlag.
Brauer, J. (2016), '(K)eine Frage der Gefühle? Die Erinnerung an die DDR aus emotionshistorisher Perspektive', in C. Führer [ed.], *Die andere deutscher Erinnerung: Tendenzen literarischen und kulturellen Lernens*, Göttingen: V&R unipress.
Brauer, J., and Lücke, M. [eds] (2013), *Emotionen, Geschichte und historisches Lernen: Geschichtsdidaktische und geschichtskulturelle Perspektiven*, Göttingen: V&R unipress.
Brooke, S. (2017), 'Space, emotions and the everyday: The affective ecology of 1980s London', *20th Century British History*, 28: 110–42.
Brooks, A., and Simpson, R. (2012), *Emotions in Transmigration: Transformation, Movement and Identity*, Houndmills: Palgrave.
Broomhall, S. [ed.] (2008), *Emotions in the Household, 1200–1900*, Houndmills: Palgrave.
Broomhall, S. (2014), 'Emotional encounters: Indigenous peoples in the Dutch East India Company's interactions with the South Lands', *Australian Historical Studies*, 45: 350–67.
Broomhall, S. [ed.] (2015), *Authority, Gender and Emotions in Late Medieval and Early Modern England*, Houndmills: Palgrave.
Broomhall, S. [ed.] (2015), *Spaces for Feeling: Emotions and Sociabilities in Britain, 1650–1850*, London: Routledge.
Broomhall, S. [ed.] (2015), *Ordering Emotions in Europe, 1100–1800*, Leiden: Brill.
Broomhall, S. [ed.] (2015), *Gender and Emotions in Medieval and Early Modern Europe: Destroying Order, Structuring Disorder*, Farnham: Ashgate.
Broomhall, S. [ed.] (2016), *Early Modern Emotions: An Introduction*, New York: Routledge.

Broomhall, S., and Van Gent, J. (2009), 'Corresponding affections: Emotional exchange among siblings in the Nassau family', *Journal of Family History*, 34: 143–65.

Broomhall, S., and Finn, S. [eds] (2015), *Violence and Emotions in Early Modern Europe*, London: Routledge.

Buchner, M. (2016). 'Dosierte Gefühle: Überlegungen zur Trauerkultur im bürgerlichen Italien (1860–1910)', in M. Buchner and A.-M. Götz [eds], *Transmortale: Sterben, Tod und Trauer in der neueren Forschung*, Cologne: Böhlau Verlag.

Bullard, A. (2008), 'Sympathy and denial: A postcolonial re-reading of emotions, race, and hierarchy', *Historical Reflections*, 34: 122–42.

Burdett, C. (2011), 'Is empathy the end of sentimentality?', *Journal of Victorian Culture*, 16: 259–74.

Burman, J.T. (2012), 'History from within? Contextualizing the new neurohistory and seeking its methods', *History of Psychology*, 15: 84–99.

Cabanas, E. (2016), 'Rekindling individualism, consuming emotions: Constructing "psytizens" in the age of happiness', *Culture and Psychology*, 22: 467–80.

Camporesi, P. (1994), *The Anatomy of the Senses: Natural Symbols in Medieval and Early Modern Italy*, trans. Allan Cameron, Cambridge: Polity.

Cannon, W.B. (1915), *Bodily Changes in Pain, Hunger, Fear and Rage: An Account of Recent Researches into the Function of Emotional Excitement*, New York and London: D. Appleton and Co.

Carrera, E. [ed.] (2013), *Emotions and Health, 1200–1700*, Leiden: Brill.

Carter Wood, J. (2011), 'A change of perspective: Integrating evolutionary psychology into the historiography of violence', *British Journal of Criminology*, 51: 479–98.

Caruso M., and Frevert, U. [eds] (2012), *Emotionen in der Bildungsgeschichte*, Bad Heilbrunn: Klinkhardt.

Champion, M., and Lynch, A. [eds] (2015), *Understanding Emotions in Early Europe*, Turnhout: Brepols.

Chaniotis, A. [ed.] (2012), *Unveiling Emotion: Sources and Methods for the Studies of Emotions in the Greek World*, Stuttgart: Franz Steiner Verlag.

Chaniotis, A., and Ducrey, P. [eds] (2014), *Unveiling Emotions II: Emotions in Greece and Rome: Texts, Images, Material Culture*, Stuttgart: Franz Steiner Verlag.

Charcot, J.-M. (1877), *Leçons sur les maladies du système nerveux faites a la Salpêtrière*, Paris: Adrien Delahaye.

Classen, C. (1993), *Worlds of Sense: Exploring the Senses in History and Across Cultures*, London: Routledge.

Classen, C. (2012), *The Deepest Sense: A Cultural History of Touch*, Urbana-Champaign: University of Illinois Press.

Classen, C. [ed.] (2014), *A Cultural History of the Senses*, 6 vols, London: Bloomsbury.
Clifford, R. (2012), 'Emotions and gender in oral history: Narrating Italy's 1968', *Modern Italy*, 17: 209–21.
Coakley, S. [ed.] (2012), *Faith, Rationality and the Passions*, Oxford: Wiley-Blackwell.
Cockcroft, R. (2003), *Rhetorical Affect in Early Modern Writing: Renaissance Passions Reconsidered*, Houndmills: Palgrave.
Cole, J., and Thomas, L.M. [eds] (2009), *Love in Africa*, Chicago: University of Chicago Press.
Conklin, A.L. (2013), *In the Museum of Man: Race, Anthropology, and Empire in France, 1850–1950*, Ithaca: Cornell University Press.
Conway, J. (1972), 'Stereotypes of femininity in a theory of sexual evolution', in M. Vicinus [ed.], *Suffer and Be Still: Women in the Victorian Age*, Bloomington: Indiana University Press.
Cook, H. (2012), 'Emotions, bodies, sexuality and sex education in Edwardian England', *Historical Journal*, 55: 475–95.
Cook, H. (2014), 'From controlling emotion to expressing feelings in mid-twentieth-century England', *Journal of Social History*, 47: 627–46.
Corbin, A. (1995), *Time, Desire and Horror: Towards a History of the Senses*, Cambridge: Polity.
Corbin, A., Courtine, J.-J., and Vigarello, G. [eds] (2016–17), *Histoire des émotions*, 3 vols, Paris: Seuil.
Corrigan, J. (2001), *Business of the Heart: Religion and Emotion in the Nineteenth Century*, Berkeley and Los Angeles: University of California Press.
Crozier-De Rosa, S. (2010), 'Popular fiction and the "emotional turn": The case of women in late Victorian Britain', *History Compass*, 8: 1340–51.
Csengei, I. (2012), *Sympathy, Sensibility and the Literature of Feeling in the Eighteenth Century*, Houndmills: Palgrave.
Cubitt, C. [ed.] (2001), 'The history of the emotions: A debate', special issue of *Early Medieval Europe*, 10.
Damasio, A. (1999), *The Feeling of What Happens: Body and Emotion in the Making of Consciousness*, San Diego: Harcourt.
Darwin, C. (1872), *The Expression of Emotions in Man and Animals*, London: John Murray.
Darwin, C. (1871; 2004), *The Descent of Man, and Selection in Relation to Sex*, London: Penguin.
Daston, L. (1995), 'The moral economy of science', *Osiris*, 2nd series, 10: 2–24.
Daston, L., and Galison, P. (2007), *Objectivity*, New York: Zone Books.
Davidson, J., and Broomhall, S. [eds] (2017), *A Cultural History of the Emotions*, 6 vols, London: Bloomsbury.
Delgado, E., Fernández, P., and Labanyi, J. [eds] (2016), *Engaging the*

Emotions in Spanish Culture and History, Nashville: Vanderbilt University Press.
Delumeau, J. (1978), *Le peur en Occident, XIVe–XVIIIe siècles*, Paris: Fayard.
Delumeau, J. (1990), *Sin and Fear: The Emergence of a Western Guilt Culture, 13th–18th Centuries*, New York: St Martin's Press.
De Boer, W., and Göttler, C. (2013), *Religion and the Senses in Early Modern Europe*, Leiden: Brill.
De Luna, K.M. (2013), 'Affect and society in precolonial Africa', *International Journal of African Historical Studies*, 46: 123–5.
Dixon, T. (2006), *From Passions to Emotions: The Creation of a Secular Psychological Category*, Cambridge: Cambridge University Press.
Dixon, T. (2008), *The Invention of Altruism: Making Moral Meanings in Victorian Britain*, Oxford: Oxford University Press.
Dixon, T. (2012), 'Educating the emotions from Gradgrind to Goleman', *Research Papers in Education*, 27: 481–95.
Dixon, T. (2012), '"Emotion": The history of a keyword in crisis', *Emotion Review*, 4: 338–44.
Dixon, T. (2015), *Weeping Britannia: Portrait of a Nation in Tears*, Oxford: Oxford University Press.
Donauer, S. (2015), *Faktor Freude: Wie die Wirtschaft Arbeitsgefühle erzeugt*, Hamburg: edition Körber-Stiftung.
Downes, S., Lynch, A., and O'Loughlin, K. [eds] (2015), *Emotions and War: Medieval to Romantic Literature*, Houndmills: Palgrave.
Dror, O. (1999), 'The scientific image of emotion: Experience and technologies of inscription', *Configurations*, 7: 355–401.
Dror, O. (1999), 'The affect of experiment: The turn to emotions in Anglo-American physiology, 1900–1940', *Isis*, 90: 205–37.
Dror, O. (2001), 'Techniques of the brain and the paradox of emotions, 1880–1930', *Science in Context*, 14: 643–60.
Dror, O., Hitzer, B., Laukötter, A., and León-Sanz, P. [eds] (2016), 'History of science and the emotions', special issue of *Osiris*, 31.
Duchenne (de Boulogne), G.-B. (1862), *Mécanisme de la physionomie humaine de analyse électro-physiologique de l'expression des passions*, Paris: Jules Renouard.
Eckstein, N.A. (2016), 'Mapping fear: Plague and perception in Florence and Tuscany', in N. Terpstra [cd.], *Mapping Space, Sense, and Movement in Florence: Historical GIS and the Early Modern City*, London: Routledge.
Ekman, P., and Friesen, W.V. (1971), 'Constants across cultures in the face and emotion', *Journal of Personality and Social Psychology*, 17: 124–9.
Eitler, P. (2011), '"Weil sie fühlen, was wir fühlen": Menschen, Tiere und die Genealogie der Emotionen im 19. Jahrhundert', *Historische Anthropologie*, 19: 211–28.
Eitler, P., and Elberfeld, J. [eds] (2015), *Zeitgeschichte des Selbst:*

Therapeutisierung, Politisierung, Emotionalisierung, Bielefeld: transcript-Verlag.

Eitler, P., Hitzer, B., and Scheer, M. [eds] (2014), 'Feeling and faith: Religious emotions in German history', special issue of *German History*, 32.

Elias, N. (1939; 1994), *The Civilizing Process: Sociogenetic and Psychogenetic Investigations*, Oxford: Blackwell.

Ellerbrock, D., and Kesper-Biermann, S. [eds] (2015), 'Between passion and senses? Perspectives on emotions and law', special issue of *InterDisciplines*, 6.

Ellison, J. (1999), *Cato's Tears and the Making of Anglo-American Emotion*, Chicago: University of Chicago Press.

Erichsen, J.E. (1867), *On Railway and Other Injuries of the Nervous System*, Philadelphia: Henry C. Lea.

Essary, K. (2016), 'Fiery heart and fiery tongue: Emotion in Erasmus' Ecclesiastes', *Erasmus Studies*, 36: 5–35.

Eustace, N. (2008), *Passion is the Gale: Emotion, Power, and the Coming of the American Revolution*, Chapel Hill: University of North Carolina Press.

Eustace, N. (2012), *1812: War and the Passions of Patriotism*, Philadelphia: University of Pennsylvania Press.

Fantini, B., Martín Moruno, D., and Moscoso, J. [eds] (2013), *On Resentment: Past and Present*, Newcastle: Cambridge Scholars Publishing.

Febvre, L. (1938; 1992), 'Une vue d'ensemble: Histoire et psychologie', *Combats pour l'Histoire*, Paris: Armand Colin.

Febvre, L. (1941), 'La sensibilité et l'histoire: Comment reconstituer la vie affective d'autrefois?', *Annales d'histoire sociale*, 3: 5–20.

Feldman Barrett, L. (2006), 'Are emotions natural kinds?', *Perspectives on Psychological Science*, 1: 28–58.

Feldman Barrett, L. (2006), 'Solving the emotion paradox: Categorization and the experience of emotion', *Personality and Social Psychology Review*, 10: 20–46.

Feldman Barrett, L., Russell, J.A., and LeDoux, J.E. [eds] (2015), *The Psychological Construction of Emotion*, New York: Guilford Press.

Festa, L. (2006), *Sentimental Figures of Empire in Eighteenth-century Britain and France*, Baltimore: Johns Hopkins University Press.

Flam, H., and Kleres, J. [eds] (2015), *Methods of Exploring Emotions*, London: Routledge.

Flynn, M. (1996), 'The spiritual uses of pain in Spanish mysticism', *Journal of the American Academy of Religion*, 64: 257–78.

Forsa, C.Q. (2015), 'A model heart: Public displays of emotion in Sedgwick's *A New-England Tale*', *Journal of the American Renaissance*, 61: 411–39.

Forum: History of Emotions (2010), *German History*, 28: 67–80.

Francis, M. (2002), 'Tears, tantrums, and bared teeth: The emotional economy of three Conservative prime ministers, 1951–1963', *Journal of British Studies*, 41: 354–87.

Frazer, M. (2012), *The Enlightenment of Sympathy: Justice and the Moral Sentiments in the Eighteenth Century and Today*, Oxford: Oxford University Press.

Freier, M. (2012), 'Cultivating emotions: The Gita Press and its agenda of social and spiritual reform', *South Asian History and Culture*, 3: 397–413.

Freud, S., and Breuer, J. (1893–5; 1974), *Studies on Hysteria*, London: Penguin.

Frevert, U. [ed.] (2009), 'Geschichte der Gefühle', special issue of *Geschichte und Gesellschaft*, 35.

Frevert, U. (2011), *Emotions in History: Lost and Found*, Budapest: Central European University Press.

Frevert, U. (2012), *Gefühlspolitik: Friedrich II. als Herr über die Herzen?*, Göttingen: Wallstein.

Frevert, U. (2013), 'La politique des sentiments au XIXe siè', *Revue d'histoire du XIXe siècle*, 46: 51–72.

Frevert, U. (2013), *Vergängliche Gefühle*, Göttingen: Wallstein.

Frevert, U. (2014), 'Honour and/or/as passion: Historical trajectories of legal defenses', *Rechtsgeschichte – Legal History*, 22: 245–55.

Frevert, U. (2016), 'Vom Schutz religiöser Gefühle: Rechtspraxis und -theorie in der Moderne', in H. Landweer and D. Koppelberg [eds], *Recht und Emotion I: Verkannte Zusammenhänge*, Freiburg: Karl Alber.

Frevert, U., and Schmidt, A. [eds] (2011), 'Geschichte, Emotionen und visuelle Medien', special issue of *Geschichte und Gesellschaft*, 37.

Frevert, U., and Singer, T. (2011), 'Empathie und ihre Blockaden: Über soziale Emotionen', in T. Bonhoeffer and P. Gruss [eds], *Zukunft Gehirn: Neue Erkenntnisse, neue Herausforderungen*, Munich: Beck.

Frevert, U., and Wulf, C. [eds] (2012), *Die Bildung der Gefühle*, Wiesbaden: Springer VS.

Frevert, U., Eitler, P., Olsen, S., et al. (2014), *Learning How to Feel: Children's Literature and the History of Emotional Socialization, 1870–1970*, Oxford: Oxford University Press.

Frevert, U., Scheer, M., Schmidt, A., et al. (2014), *Emotional Lexicons: Continuity and Change in the Vocabulary of Feeling, 1700–2000*, Oxford: Oxford University Press.

Furst, L.R. (2008), *Before Freud: Hysteria and Hypnosis in Later Nineteenth-century Psychiatric Cases*, Lewisburg: Bucknell University Press.

Galton, F. (1878), 'Composite portraits', *Journal of the Anthropological Institute of Great Britain and Ireland*, 8: 132–42.

Gammerl, B. [ed.] (2012), *Emotional Styles – Concepts and Challenges*, special issue of *Rethinking History*, 16.

Gammerl, B., and Herrn, R. [eds] (2015), 'Gefühlsräume – Raumgefühle', special issue of Sub\urban, 3.
Garrido, S., and Davidson, J.W. (2016), 'Emotional regimes reflected in popular ballad: perspectives on gender, love and protest in "Scarborough Fair"', *Musicology Australia*, 38: 65–78.
Gay, P. (1984–98), *The Bourgeois Experience: Victoria to Freud*, 5 vols, Oxford: Oxford University Press.
Gay, P. (1985), *Freud for Historians*, Oxford: Oxford University Press.
Gendron, M., and Feldman Barrett, L. (2009), 'Reconstructing the past: A century of ideas about emotion in psychology', *Emotion Review*, 1: 316–39.
Gertsman, E. [ed.] (2011), *Crying in the Middle Ages: Tears of History*, London: Routledge.
Gienow-Hecht, J.C.E. [ed.] (2010), *Emotions in American History: An International Assessment*, New York: Berghahn.
Gil, D.J. (2002), 'Before intimacy: Modernity and emotion in the early modern discourse of sexuality', *English Literary History*, 69: 861–87.
Gilman, S.L., King, H., Porter, R., Rousseau, G.S., and Showalter, E. [eds], *Hysteria Beyond Freud*, Berkeley and Los Angeles: University of California Press.
Giorgi, K. (2014), *Emotions, Language and Identity on the Margins of Europe*, Houndmills: Palgrave.
Goetschel, P., Granger, C., Richard, N., and Venayre, S. [eds] (2012), *L'ennui: Histoire d'un état d'âme (xixe–xxe siècle)*, Paris: Publications de la Sorbonne.
Goring, P. (2004), *The Rhetoric of Sensibility in Eighteenth-century Culture*, Cambridge: Cambridge University Press.
Gouk, P., and Hills, H. [eds] (2005), *Representing Emotions: New Connections in the Histories of Art, Music and Medicine*, Aldershot: Ashgate.
Gould, S.J. (2008), *The Mismeasure of Man*, New York: W.W. Norton.
Gross, D.M. (2001), 'Early modern emotion and the economy of scarcity', *Philosophy and Rhetoric*, 34: 308–21.
Gross, D.M. (2006), *The Secret History of Emotion: From Aristotle's Rhetoric to Modern Brain Science*, Chicago: University of Chicago Press.
Gross, D.M. (2010), 'Defending the humanities with Charles Darwin's *The Expression of the Emotions in Man and Animals* (1872)', *Critical Inquiry*, 37: 34–59.
Gross, D.M. (2013), 'How can the theory of cognitive and emotional extension alter what we find in 18th-century literature?', in S. Koroliov [ed.], *Emotion und Kognition. Transformationen in der europäischen Literatur des 18. Jahrhunderts*, Berlin: Walter de Gruyter.
Gross, D.M. (2017), *Uncomfortable Situations: Emotion between Science and the Humanities*, Chicago: University of Chicago Press.

SELECT BIBLIOGRAPHY   229

Häberlen, J.C., and Spinney, R.A. [eds] (2014), 'Emotions in protest movements', special issue of *Contemporary European History*, 23.
Hallett, N. (2013), *The Senses in Religious Communities, 1600–1800: Early Modern 'Convents of Pleasure'*, New York: Routledge.
Harris, W.V. (2001), *Restraining Rage: The Ideology of Anger Control in Classical Antinquity*, Cambridge, MA: Harvard University Press.
Harvey, K. (2014), 'Episcopal emotions: Tears in the life of the medieval bishop', *Historical Research*, 87: 591–610.
Harvey, K. (2015), 'What Mary Toft felt: Women's voices, pain, power and the body', *History Workshop Journal*, 80: 31–51.
Harvey, S.A. (2006), *Scenting Salvation: Ancient Christianity and the Olfactory Imagination*, Berkeley and Los Angeles: University of California Press.
Haskell, Y. (2011), 'Lieven de Meyere and early modern anger management: Seneca, Ovid, and Lieven de Meyere's *De ira libri tres* (Antwerp, 1694)', *International Journal of the Classical Tradition*, 18: 36–65.
Haskell, Y. (2016), 'Suppressed emotions: The heroic *Tristia* of Portuguese (ex-) Jesuit, Emanuel de Azevedo', *Journal of Jesuit Studies*, 3: 42–60.
Hayward, R. (2007), 'Desperate housewives and model amoebae: the invention of suburban neurosis in inter-war Britain', in M. Jackson [ed.], *Health and the Modern Home*, London: Routledge.
Hayward, R. (2014), 'Sadness in Camberwell: Imagining stress and constructing history in post-war Britain', in D. Canot and E. Ramsden [eds], *Stress, Shock, and Adaptation in the Twentieth Century*, Rochester: Boydell and Brewer.
Heyd, M. (1995), *Be Sober and Reasonable: The Critique of Enthusiasm in the Seventeenth and Early Eighteenth Centuries*, Leiden: Brill.
Hitzer, B. (2014). 'Angst, Panik?! Eine vergleichende Gefühlsgeschichte von Grippe und Krebs in der Bundesrepublik', in M. Thießen [ed.], *Infiziertes Europa: Seuchen im langen 20. Jahrhundert*, Munich: De Gruyter Oldenbourg.
Hitzer, B., and Scheer, M. (2014), 'Unholy feelings: Questioning evangelical emotions in Wilhelmine Germany', *German History*, 32: 371–92.
Hochschild, A.R. (1979), 'Emotion work, feeling rules, and social structure', *American Journal of Sociology*, 85: 551–75.
Hochschild, A.R. (1983), *The Managed Heart: Commercialization of Human Feeling*, Berkeley and Los Angeles: University of California Press.
Hood, B.M. (2012), *The Self Illusion: How the Social Brain Creates Identity*, Oxford: Oxford University Press.
Howes, D., and Classen, C. (2013), *Ways of Sensing: Understanding the Senses in Society*, New York: Routledge.
Huizinga, J. (1919; 1997), *The Autumn of the Middle Ages*, Chicago: University of Chicago Press.

Hunt, L. (2009), 'The experience of revolution', *French Historical Studies*, 32: 671–8.
Hunt, L., and Jacob, M. (2001), 'The affective revolution in 1790s Britain', *Eighteenth-century Studies*, 23: 491–521.
Hutchison, E. (2014), 'A global politics of pity? Disaster imagery and the emotional construction of solidarity after the 2004 Asian tsunami', *International Political Sociology*, 8: 1–19.
Illouz, E. (2007), *Cold Intimacies: The Making of Emotional Capitalism*, Cambridge: Cambridge University Press.
Illouz, E. (2008), *Saving the Modern Soul: Therapy, Emotions, and the Culture of Self-Help*, Berkeley: University of California Press.
Jaeger, C.S. (1991), 'L'amour des rois: structure sociale d'une forme de sensibilité aristocratiques', *Annales ESC*, 3: 547–71.
Jaeger, C.S. (1999), *Ennobling Love: In Search of a Lost Sensibility*, Philadelphia: University of Pennsylvania Press.
James, W. (1890; 1910), *The Principles of Psychology*, vol. 2, London: MacMillan.
Jarzebowski, C., and Kwaschik, A. [eds] (2013), *Performing Emotions: Interdisziplinäre Perspektiven auf das Verhältnis von Politik und Emotion in der Frühen Neuzeit und in der Moderne*, Göttingen: V&R unipress.
Jarzebowski, C., and Safley, T.M. [eds] (2014), *Childhood and Emotion across Cultures, 1450–1800*, London: Routledge.
Jensen, U., and Schüler-Springorum, S. [eds] (2013), 'Gefühle gegen Juden: Die Emotionsgeschichte des modernen Antisemitismus', special issue of *Geschichte und Gesellschaft*, 39.
Johnston, A.J., Kempf, E., and West-Pavlov, R. [eds] (2016), *Love, History and Emotion in Chaucer and Shakespeare: Troilus and Criseyde and Troilus and Cressida*, Manchester: Manchester University Press.
Jones, C. (2014), *The Smile Revolution in Eighteenth-century Paris*, Oxford: Oxford University Press.
Jorgensen, A., McCormack, F., and Wilcox, J. [eds] (2015), *Anglo-Saxon Emotions: Reading the Heart in Old English Language, Literature and Culture*, Farnham: Ashgate.
Jütte, R. (2005), *A History of the Senses: From Antiquity to Cyberspace*, Cambridge: Polity.
Kagan, J. (2007), *What is Emotion? History, Measures, and Meaning*, New Haven: Yale University Press.
Kambasković, D. [ed.] (2014), *Conjunctions of Mind, Soul and Body from Plato to the Enlightenment*, Dordrecht: Springer.
Karant-Nunn, S.C. (2010), *The Reformation of Feeling: Shaping the Religious Emotions in Early Modern Germany*, Oxford: Oxford University Press.
Kay, A. (2016), '"A reformation so much wanted": Clarissa's glorious shame', *Eighteenth-century Fiction*, 28: 645–66.

Kenny, N. (2015), 'City glow: Streetlights, emotions, and nocturnal life, 1880s–1910s', *Journal of Urban History*, 43.
Kerr, H., Lemmings, D., Phiddian, R. [eds] (2015), *Passions, Sympathy and Print Culture: Public Opinion and Emotional Authenticity in Eighteenth-century Britain*, Houndmills: Palgrave.
Khan, R. (2015), 'The social production of space and emotions in South Asia', *Jounral of the Economic and Social History of the Orient*, 58: 611–33.
Kietäväinen-Sirén, H. (2011), '"The warm water in my heart": The meanings of love among the Finnish country population in the second half of the 17th century', *History of the Family*, 16: 47–61.
Killen, A. (2006), *Berlin Electropolis: Shock, Nerves, and German Modernity*, Berkeley: University of California Press.
Kivimäki, V. (2014), 'Traumatisés par la guerre: Les troubles psychologiques des soldats finlandais en tant que phénomène historique lors de la Guerre d'Hiver de 1939–1940', *Revue d'histoire Nordique*, 17: 123–50.
Kivimäki, V., and Tepora, T. (2009), 'War of hearts: Love and collective attachment as integrating factors in Finland during World War II', *Journal of Social History*, 43: 285–305.
Klothmann, N. (2015), *Gefühlswelten im Zoo: Eine Emotionsgeschichte 1900–1945*, Bielefeld: Transcript.
Konstan, D. (2001), *Pity Transformed*, London: Duckworth.
Konstan, D. (2006), *The Emotions of the Ancient Greeks: Studies in Aristotle and Classical Literature*, Toronto: University of Toronto Press.
Kounine, L., and Ostling, M. [eds] (2016), *Emotions in the History of Witchcraft*, London: Palgrave Macmillan.
Kuijpers, E., and van der Haven, C. [eds] (2016), *Battlefield Emotions, 1500–1800*, Houndmills: Palgrave.
Laffan, M., and Weiss, M. [eds] (2012), *Facing Fear: The History of an Emotion in Global Perspective*, Princeton: Princeton University Press.
Lambert, S., and Nicholson, H. [eds] (2012), *Languages of Love and Hate: Conflict, Communication, and Identity in the Medieval Mediterranean*, Turnhout: Brepols.
Lange, C.G. (1887), *Ueber Gemüthsbewegungen. Eine Psycho-Physiologische Studie*, Leipzig: Theodor Thomas.
Langlotz, A., and Monnet, A.S. [eds] (2014), 'Emotion, affect, sentiment: The language and aesthetics of feeling', special issue of *Swiss Papers in English Language and Literature*, 30.
Langue, F., and Capdeville, L. [eds] (2014), *Le passé des émotions. D'une histoire à vif en Espagne et Amérique Latine*, Rennes: Presses Universitaitres de Rennes.
Lanzoni, S., Brain, R., and Young, A. [eds] (2012), *The Varieties of Empathy in Science, Art, and History*, special issue of *Science in Context*, 25.

Larlham, D. (2012), 'The felt truth of mimetic experience: Motions of the soul and the kinetics of passion in the eighteenth-century theatre', *The Eighteenth Century*, 53: 432–54.

Larrington, C. (2001), 'The psychology of emotion and study of the medieval period', *Early Medieval Europe*, 10: 251–6.

Lateiner, D., and Spatharas, D. [eds] (2016), *The Ancient Emotion of Disgust*, Oxford: Oxford University Press.

Laukötter, A. (2015), 'Vom Ekel zur Empathie: Strategien der Wissensvermittlung im Sexualaufklärungsfilm des 20. Jahrhunderts', *Erkenne Dich selbst! Strategien der Sichtbarmachung des Körpers im 20. Jahrhundert*, Cologne: Böhlau.

Lean, E. (2007), *Public Passions: The Trial of Shi Jianqiao and the Rise of Popular Sympathy in Republican China*, Berkeley and Los Angeles: University of California Press.

Le Bon, G. (1895), *Psychologie des foules*, Paris: Germer Baillière.

Lecuppre-Desjardin, É., and Van Bruaene, A.-L. [eds] (2005), *Emotions in the Heart of the City*, Turnhout: Brepols.

Lemmings, D., and Brooks, A. [eds] (2014), *Emotions and Social Change: Historical and Sociological Perspectives*, London: Routledge.

Leys, R. (2000), *Trauma: A Genealogy*, Chicago: University of Chicago Press.

Leys, R. (2010), 'How did fear become a scientific object and what kind of object is it?', *Representations*, 110: 66–104.

Leys, R. (2011), 'The turn to affect: A critique', *Critical Inquiry*, 37: 434–72.

Liliequist, J. [ed.] (2013), *A History of Emotions, 1200–1800*, London: Routledge.

Lombroso, C. (1897; 2013), 'Affetti e passioni dei delinquenti', *L'uomo delinquent*, 5th edn, Milan: Bompiani.

Lutz, T. (1991), *American Nervousness, 1903: An Anecdotal History*, Ithaca: Cornell University Press.

MacDonald, G., and Jensen-Campbell, L.A. [eds] (2011), *Social Pain: Neuropsychological and Health Implications of Loss and Exclusion*, Washington DC: American Psychological Association.

MacDonald, M. (1992), 'The fearfull estate of Francis Spira: Narrative, identity, and emotion in early modern England', *Journal of British Studies*, 31: 32–61.

Mack, P. (2008), *Heart Religion in the British Enlightenment: Gender and Emotion in Early Methodism*, Cambridge: Cambridge University Press.

MacMullen, R. (2003), *Feelings in History, Ancient and Modern*, Claremont: Regina Books.

Martín Moruno, D., and Pichel, B. [eds] (2018), *Emotional Bodies: Studies on the Historical Performativity of Emotions*, Urbana-Champaign: University of Illinois Press.

Maehle, A.-H. (2009), *Doctors, Honour and the Law: Medical Ethics in Imperial Germany*, Houndmills: Palgrave.
Magnússon, S.G. (2016), 'The love game as expressed in ego-documents: The culture of emotions in late nineteenth century Iceland', *Journal of Social History*, 50: 102–19.
Matt, S. (2011), *Homesickness: An American History*, Oxford: Oxford University Press.
Matt, S. (2011), 'Current emotion research in history: Or doing history from the inside out', *Emotion Review*, 3: 117–24.
McGillivray, G. (2014), 'Motions of the mind: Transacting emotions on the eighteenth-century stage', *Restoration and Eighteenth Century Theatre Research*, 28: 5–24.
McGrath, L.S. (2017), 'Historiography, affect, and the neurosciences', *History of Psychology*, 20: 129–47.
McNamara, R.F., and McIlvenna, U. [eds] (2014), 'Medieval and early modern emotional responses to death and dying', special issue of *Parergon*, 31.
Medick, H., and Sabean, D. [eds] (1984), *Interest and Emotion: Essays on the Study of Family and Kinship*, Cambridge: Cambridge University Press.
Medina-Doménech, R.M. (2013), *Ciencia y sabiduría del amor. Una historia cultural del franquismo (1940–1960)*, Madrid: Iberoamerica Vervuert.
Meek, R., and Sullivan, E. (2015), *Renaissance of Emotion: Understanding Affect in Shakespeare and his Contemporaries*, Manchester: Manchester University Press.
Mellas, A. (2014), '"The passions of his flesh": St Cyril of Alexandria and the emotions of the Logos', *Phronema*, 29: 81–100.
Menin, M. (2014), '"Who will write the history of tears?" History of ideas and history of emotions from eighteenth-century France to the present', *History of European Ideas*, 40: 516–32.
Mercer, P. (1972), *Sympathy and Ethics: A Study of the Relationship between Sympathy and Morality with Special Reference to Hume's Treatise*, Oxford: Clarendon Press.
Micale, M.S. (1995), *Approaching Hysteria: Disease and Its Interpretations*, New Jersey: Princeton University Press.
Micale, M.S. (2008), *Hysterical Men: The Hidden History of Male Nervous Illness*, Cambridge, MA: Harvard University Press.
Millar, C. (2016), 'Rebecca West's demonic marriage: Exploring emotions, ritual and women's agency in seventeenth-century England', *Women's History*, 2: 4–11.
Milner, M. (2011), *The Senses and the English Reformation*, Farnham: Ashgate.
Mitchell, T. (1990), *Passional Culture: Emotion, Religion, and Society in Southern Spain*, Philadelphia: University of Pennsylvania Press.

More, H. (1834), 'On the danger of sentimental or romantic connexions' [1778], *Works*, vol. 6, London: Fisher, Fisher and Jackson.

Morgan, C.L. (1894), *An Introduction to Comparative Psychology*, London: W. Scott.

Moscoso, J. (2012), *Pain: A Cultural History*, Houndmills: Palgrave.

Moscoso, J. (2014), 'Celos románticos. Celos mórbidos. Un capítulo en la historia de la patologización de las pasiones', *IBERICAL. Revue d'études ibériques et ibéro-américaines*, 6: 13–22.

Moscoso, J. (2015), 'Politics of pain and the history of passions: A good subject for eminent amateurs", *Rúbrica de Historia Contemporánea*, 4: 67–77.

Moscoso, J. (2015), 'La historia de las emociones, ¿de qué es historia?', *Vínculos de Historia Contemporánea*, 4: 15–27.

Moscoso, J., and Zaragoza, J.M. (2014), 'Historias del Bienestar. Desde la historia de las emociones a las políticas de la experiencia', *Cuadernos de Historia Contemporánea*, 36: 73–89.

Moshenska, J. (2014), *Feeling Pleasures: The Sense of Touch in Renaissance England*, Oxford: Oxford University Press.

Mosso, A. (1896), *Fear*, London and New York: Longmans, Green, and Co.

Muchembled, R. (2007), 'Pour une histoire des émotions au XVIe siècle', in J.-F. Chauvard and I. La Boulais [eds], *Les Fruits de la récolte. Etudes offertes à Jean-Michel Boehler*, Strasbourg: Presses Universitaires de Strasbourg.

Mullaney, S. [ed.] (2015), *The Reformation of Emotions in the Age of Shakespeare*, Chicago: University of Chicago Press.

Musumeci, E. (2015), *Emozioni, crimine, giustizia. Un'indagine storico-giurdica tra Otto e Novecento*, Milan: FrancoAngeli.

Myllykangas, M., and Parhi, K. (2016), 'The unjustified emotions: Child suicide in Finnish psychiatry from the 1930s until the 1970s', *Journal of the History of Childhood and Youth*, 9: 489–508.

Nagy, P. (2000), *Le Don des larmes au Moyen Âge. Un instrument en quête d'institution*, Paris: Albin Michel.

Nagy, P. [ed.] (2007), 'Émotions médiévales', special issue of *Critique*, 716–17.

Naphy, W.G., and Roberts, P. [eds] (1997), *Fear in Early Modern Society*, Manchester: Manchester University Press.

Nielsen, P. (2015), 'Disgust, compassion or tolerance: Law and emotions in the debate on § 175 in West Germany', *InterDisciplines*, 6: 159–86.

Nielsen, P. (2015), 'Politik und Emotionen aus der Perspektive der Geschichtswissenschaft', in T.B. Müller and A. Tooze [eds], *Normalität und Fragilität: Demokratie nach dem Ersten Weltkrieg*, Hamburg: Hamburger Edition HIS.

Oatley, K. (2004), *Emotions: A Brief History*, Oxford: Wiley-Blackwell.

Olsen, S. (2014), *Juvenile Nation: Youth, Emotions and the Making of the Modern British Citizen, 1880–1914*, London: Bloomsbury.

Olsen, S. [ed.] (2015), *Childhood, Youth and Emotions in Modern History: National, Colonial and Global Perspectives*, Houndmills: Palgrave.

Olsen, S., '"Happy Home" and "Happy Land": Informal emotional education in British bands of hope, 1880–1914', *Historia y Memoria de la Educación*, 2: 195–218.

Parisot, E. (2014), 'Suicide notes and popular sensibility in the eighteenth-century British press', *Eighteenth-century Studies*, 47: 277–91.

Paster, G.K., Rowe, K., and Floyd-Wilson, M. [eds] (2004), *Reading the Early Modern Passions: Essays in the Cultural History of Emotion*, Philadelphia: University of Pennsylvania Press.

Pernau, M. (2011), 'Male anger and female malice: Emotions in Indo-Muslim advice literature', *History Compass*, 10: 119–28.

Pernau, M. (2014), 'Space and emotion: Building to feel', *History Compass*, 12: 541–9.

Pernau, M. (2016), 'From morality to psychology: Emotion concepts in Urdu, 1870–1920', *Contributions to the History of Concepts*, 11: 38–57.

Pernau, M., and Rajamani, I. (2016), 'Emotional translations: Conceptual history beyond language', *History and Theory*, 55: 46–65.

Pernau, M., Jordheim, H., et al. (2015), *Civilizing Emotions: Concepts in Nineteenth-century Asia and Europe*, Oxford: Oxford University Press.

Pfister, J., and Schnog, N. [eds] (1997), *Inventing the Psychological: Toward a Cultural History of Emotional Life in America*, New Haven: Yale University Press.

Pichel, B. (2016), 'From facial expressions to bodily gestures: Passions, photography and movement in French 19th-century sciences', *History of the Human Sciences*, 29: 27–48.

Pick, D. (1993), *Faces of Degeneration: A European Disorder, c.1848–c.1918*, Cambridge: Cambridge University Press.

Plamper, J. [ed.] (2009), 'Emotional turn? Feelings in Russian history and culture', special issue of *Slavic Review*, 68.

Plamper, J. (2010), 'The history of emotions: An interview with William Reddy, Barbara Rosenwein, and Peter Stearns', *History and Theory*, 49: 237–65.

Plamper, J. (2013), 'Vergangene Gefühle: Emotionen als historische Quellen', *Aus Politik und Zeitgeschichte*, 63: 12–19.

Plamper, J. (2015), *The History of Emotions: An Introduction*, Oxford: Oxford University Press.

Plamper, J., and Lazier, B. [eds] (2012), *Fear: Across the Disciplines*, Pittsburgh: Pittsburgh University Press.

Prestel, J.B. (2015), 'Hierarchies of happiness: Railway infrastructure and suburban subject formation in Berlin and Cairo around 1900', *City: Analysis of Urban Trends, Culture, Theory, Policy, Action*, 19: 322–31.

Prinz, J. (2007), *The Emotional Construction of Morals*, Oxford: Oxford University Press.
Reddy, W. (1997), 'Against constructionism: The historical ethnography of emotions', *Current Anthropology*, 38: 327–51.
Reddy, W. (1997), *The Invisible Code: Honor and Sentiment in Postrevolutionary France, 1814–1848*, Berkeley and Los Angeles: University of California Press.
Reddy, W. (2000), 'Sentimentalism and its erasure: The role of emotions in the era of the French Revolution', *Journal of Modern History*, 72: 109–52.
Reddy, W. (2001), *The Navigation of Feeling: A Framework for the History of Emotions*, Cambridge: Cambridge University Press.
Reddy, W. (2008), 'Emotional styles and modern forms of life', in N. Karafyllis and G. Ulshöfer [eds], *Sexualized Brains: Scientific Modelling of Emotional Intelligence from a Cultural Perspective*, Cambridge, MA: MIT Press.
Reddy, W. (2009), 'Historical research on the self and emotions', *Emotion Review*, 1: 302–15.
Reddy, W. (2009), 'Saying something new: Practice theory and cognitive neuroscience', *Arcadia*, 44: 8–23.
Reddy, W. (2010), 'Neuroscience and the fallacies of functionalism', *History and Theory*, 49: 412–25.
Reddy, W. (2012), *The Making of Romantic Love: Longing and Sexuality in Europe, South Asia, and Japan, 900–1200 CE*, Chicago: University of Chicago Press.
Redlin, J., and Neuland-Kitzerow, D. (2014), *Der gefühlte Krieg: Emotionen im Ersten Weltkrieg*, Husum: Verlag der Kunst.
Ribot, T.A. (1896), *La psychologie des sentiments*, Paris: Germer Baillière.
Richards, R.J. (1989), *Darwin and the Emergence of Evolutionary Theories of Mind and Behaviour*, Chicago: University of Chicago Press.
Richardson, A. (2003), *Love and Eugenics in the Late Nineteenth Century: Rational Reproduction and the New Woman*, Oxford: Oxford University Press.
Richardson, A. [ed.] (2013), *After Darwin: Animals, Emotions, and the Mind*, Amsterdam: Rodopi.
Rieber, R.W., and Robinson, D.K. [eds] (2001), *Wilhelm Wundt in History: The Making of a Scientific Psychology*, New York: Kluwer Academic.
Risse, G.B. (2016), *Driven by Fear: Epidemics and Isolation in San Francisco's House of Pestilence*, Urbana-Champaign: University of Illinois Press.
Rizzolatti, G., and Sinigaglia, C. (2006), *Mirrors in the Brain: How Our Minds Share Actions and Emotions*, Oxford: Oxford University Press.
Robinson, E. (2010), 'Touching the void: Affective history and the impossible', *Rethinking History*, 14: 503–20.
Rodman, M.C. (2003), 'The heart in the archives: Colonial contestation

of desire and fear in the New Hebrides', *Journal of Pacific History*, 38: 291–312.
Romanes, G.J. (1882; 1883), *Animal Intelligence*, 3rd edn, London: Kegan Paul, Trench & Co.
Romanes, G.J. (1883), *Mental Evolution in Animals*, London: Kegan Paul, Trench & Co.
Romanes, G.J. (1888), *Mental Evolution in Man: Origin of Human Faculty*, London: Kegan Paul, Trench & Co.
Romano, T.M. (2002), *Making Medicine Scientific: John Burdon Sanderson and the Culture of Victorian Science*, Baltimore: Johns Hopkins University Press.
Roper, M. (2005), 'Between manliness and masculinity: The "war generation" and the psychology of fear in Britain, 1914–1950', *Journal of British Studies*, 44: 343–62.
Roper, M. (2009), *The Secret Battle: Emotional Survival in the Great War*, Manchester: Manchester University Press.
Rosenfeld, S. (2009), 'Thinking about feeling, 1789–1799', *French Historical Studies*, 32: 697–706.
Rosenwein, B. [ed.] (1998), *Anger's Past: The Social Use of an Emotion in the Middle Ages*, Ithaca: Cornell University Press.
Rosenwein, B. (2002), 'Worrying about emotions in history', *American Historical Review*, 107: 821–45.
Rosenwein, B. (2006), *Emotional Communities in the Early Middle Ages*, Ithaca: Cornell University Press.
Rosenwein, B. (2007), 'The uses of biology: A response to J. Carter Wood's "The Limits of Culture"', *Cultural and Social History*, 4: 553–8.
Rosenwein, B. (2010), 'Problems and methods in the history of emotions', *Passions in Context*, 1: 1–32.
Rosenwein, B. (2010), 'Thinking historically about medieval emotions', *History Compass*, 8: 828–42.
Rosenwein, B. (2016), *Generations of Feeling: A History of Emotions, 600–1700*, Cambridge: Cambridge University Press.
Rubin, M. (2009), *Emotion and Devotion: The Meaning of Mary in Medieval Religious Cultures*, Budapest: Central European University Press.
Ruys, J.F. (2012), 'Love in the time of demons: Thirteenth-century approaches to the capacity for love in fallen angels', *Mirabilia*, 15: 28–46.
Rylance, R. (2000), *Victorian Psychology and British Culture, 1850–1880*, Oxford: Oxford University Press.
Sánchez, G.J. (2004), *Pity in Fin-de-siècle French Culture: liberté, égalité, pitié*, Westport, CT: Praeger.
Sanders, E., and Johncock, M. [eds] (2016), *Emotion and Persuasion in Classical Antiquity*, Stuttgart: Franz Steiner Verlag.
Santangelo, P. (1994), 'Emotions in late imperial China: Evolution and

continuity in Ming-Qing perception of passions', in V. Alleton and A. Volkov [eds], *Notions et perceptions du changement en Chine*, Paris: IHEC.

Santangelo, P. (1999), 'Emotions and the origin of evil in Neo-Confucian thought', in H. Eifring [ed.], *Minds and Mentalities in Traditional Chinese Literature*, Beijing: Culture and Art Publishing House.

Santangelo, P. (1999), 'The myths of love-passion in late imperial China', *Ming Qing Yanjiu*, 8: 131–95.

Santangelo, P. (2005), 'Evaluation of emotions in European and Chinese traditions: Differences and analogies', *Monumenta Serica*, 53: 401–27.

Santangelo, P. [ed.] (2007), 'Passioni d'Oriente. Eros ed emozioni nelle civiltà asiatiche', supplement no. 2, *Rivista di Studi Orientali*, 78.

Santangelo, P. (2011), *Pubblico e privato, visibile e invisibile Ideologia, religione, morale e passioni. L'impero cinese agli inizi della storia globale*, Rome: Aracne.

Santangelo, P. (2011), *Laughing in Chinese. Emotions behind smiles and laughter: from facial expression to literary descriptions*, Rome: Aracne.

Santangelo, P. (2014), *La rappresentazione delle emozioni nella Cina tradizionale*, Carpi: Festival Filosofia.

Santangelo, P., and Guida, D. [eds] (2006), *Love, Hatred, and Other Passions: Questions and Themes on Emotions in Chinese Civilization*, Leiden: Brill.

Santangelo, P., and Middendorf, U. [eds] (2006), *From Skin to Heart: Perceptions of Emotions and Bodily Sensations in Traditional Chinese Culture*, Wiesbaden: Harrassowtiz.

Santangelo, P., and Tan, T.Y. (2015), *Passion, Romance, and Qing*, 3 vols, Leiden: Brill.

Scheer, M. (2011), 'Welchen Nutzen hat die Feldforschung für eine Geschichte religiöser Gefühle?', *VOKUS – Volkskundlich-Kulturwissenschaftliche Schriften*, 21: 65–77.

Scheer, M. (2012), 'Are emotions a kind of practice (and is that what makes them have a history)? A Bourdieuian approach to understanding emotion', *History and Theory*, 51: 193–220.

Scorpo, A.L. (2016), 'Emotional memory and medieval autobiography: King James I of Aragon (r. 1213–76)'s *Libre dels fets*', *Journal of Medieval Iberian Studies*.

Scull, A. (2009), *Hysteria: The Biography*, Oxford: Oxford University Press.

Seymour, M. (2012), 'Emotional arenas: From provincial circus to national courtroom in late nineteenth-century Italy', *Rethinking History*, 16: 177–97.

Sherrington, C.S. (1899–1900), 'Experiments on the value of vascular and visceral factors for the genesis of emotion', *Proceedings of the Royal Society of London*, 66: 390–403.

Showalter, E. (1985), *The Female Malady: Women, Madness and English Culture, 1830–1980*, London: Virago.

Shryock, A., and Smail, D.L. [eds] (2011), *Deep History: The Architecture*

of Past and Present, Berkeley and Los Angeles: University of California Press.
Smail, D.L. (2003), *The Consumption of Justice: Emotions, Publicity, and Legal Culture in Marseille, 1264–1423*, Ithaca: Cornell University Press.
Smail, D.L. (2005), 'Emotions and somatic gestures in medieval narratives: The case of Raoul de Cambrai', *Zeitschrift für Literaturwissenschaft und Linguistik*, 138: 34–47.
Smail, D.L. (2008), *On Deep History and the Brain*, Berkeley and Los Angeles: University of California Press.
Smith, A. (1759; 2009), *The Theory of Moral Sentiments*, London: Penguin.
Smith, M.M. (2008), *Sensing the Past: Seeing, Hearing, Smelling, Tasting, and Touching in History*, Los Angeles and Berkeley: University of California Press.
Soyer, F. (2013), 'Faith, culture and fear: Comparing Islamophobia in early modern Spain and twenty-first-century Europe', *Ethnic and Racial Studies*, 36: 399–416.
Spinks, J., and Zika, C. [eds] (2016), *Disaster, Death and the Emotions in the Shadow of the Apocalypse, 1400–1700*, Houndmills: Palgrave.
Stalfort, J. (2014), *Die Erfindung der Gefühle: Eine Studie über den historischen Wandel menschlicher Emotionalität*, Bielefeld: Transcript.
Starling, E.H. (1905), 'The Croonian Lectures. I. On the chemical correlation of the functions of the body', *Lancet*, 166: 339–41.
Stearns, C.Z., and Stearns, P.N. (1986), *Anger: The Struggle for Emotional Control in America's History*, Chicago: University of Chicago Press.
Stearns, C.Z., and Stearns, P.N. [eds] (1988), *Emotion and Social Change: Toward a New Psychohistory*, New York: Holmes & Meier.
Stearns, P.N. (1989), *Jealousy: The Evolution of an Emotion in American History*, New York: New York University Press.
Stearns, P.N. (1994), *American Cool: Constructing a Twentieth-century Emotional Style*, New York and London: New York University Press.
Stearns, P.N. (1999), *Battleground of Desire: The Struggle for Self-Control in Modern America*, New York: New York University Press.
Stearns, P.N. (2006), *American Fear: The Causes and Consequences of High Anxiety*, New York: Routledge.
Stearns, P.N., and Lewis, J. [eds] (1998), *An Emotional History of the United States*, New York: New York University Press.
Stearns, P.N., and Matt, S. [eds] (2014), *Doing Emotions History*, Urbana-Champaign: University of Illinois Press.
Stearns, P.N., and Stearns, C.Z. (1985), 'Emotionology: Clarifying the history of emotions and emotional standards', *American Historical Review*, 90: 813–36.
Stedman, G. (2002), *Stemming the Torrent: Expression and Control in the Victorian Discourses on Emotion, 1830–1872*, Aldershot: Ashgate.

Stirling, J. (2010), 'Hystericity and hauntings: The female and the feminised', *Representing Epilepsy: Myth and Matter*, Liverpool: Liverpool University Press.

Strange, C., Cripp, R., and Forth, C.E. [eds] (2014), *Honour, Violence and Emotions in History*, London: Bloomsbury.

Styles, J. (2014), 'Objects of emotion: The London Foundling Hospital tokens, 1741–60', in A. Gerritsen and G. Riello [eds], *Writing Material Culture History*, London: Bloomsbury.

Sullivan, E. (2016), *Beyond Melancholy: Sadness and Selfhood in Renaissance England*, Oxford: Oxford University Press.

Sykes, I. (2015), *Society, Culture and the Auditory Imagination in Modern France: The Humanity of Hearing*, Houndmills: Palgrave.

Thomson, M. (1998), *The Problem of Mental Deficiency: Eugenics, Democracy, and Social Policy in Britain, c. 1870–1959*, Oxford: Oxford University Press.

Toivo, M.R., and Van Gent, J. [eds] (2016), 'Gender, material culture and emotions in Scandinavian history', special issue of *Scandinavian Journal of History*, 41.

Trigg, S. (2012), *Shame and Honor: A Vulgar History of the Order of the Garter*, Philadelphia: University of Pennsylvania Press.

Trigg, S. [ed.] (2014), 'Pre-modern emotions', special issue of *Exemplaria*, 26.

Turner R., and Whitehead, C. (2008), 'How collective representations can change the structure of the brain', *Journal of Consciousness Studies*, 15: 43–57

Tyson, A.M. (2013), *The Wages of History: Emotional Labor on Public History's Front Lines*, Amherst: University of Massachusetts Press.

Vallgårda, K., and Bjerre, C. (2016), 'Childhood, divorce, and emotions: Danish custody and visitation rights battles in the 1920s, *Journal of the History of Childhood and Youth*, 9: 470–88.

Vallgårda, K., McLisky, C., and Medena, D. [eds] (2015), *Emotions and Christian Missions*, Houndmills: Palgrave.

Van Gent, J. (2014), 'Sarah and her sisters: Identity, letters and emotions in the early modern Atlantic world', *Journal of Religious History*, 38: 71–90.

Van Gent, J., and Young, S. [eds] (2015), 'Emotions and conversion', special issue of *Journal of Religious History*, 39.

Vidor, G.M. (2014), 'Satisfying the mind and inflaming the heart: Emotions and funerary epigraphy in nineteenth-century Italy', *Mortality*, 19: 342–60.

Vidor, G.M. (2015), 'Emotions and writing the history of death: An interview with Michel Vovelle, Régis Bertrand and Anne Carol', *Morality*, 20: 36–47.

Vincent-Buffault, A. (1991), *The History of Tears: Sensibility and Sentimentality in France*, Houndmills: MacMillan.

Waldow, A. [ed.] (2016), *Sensibility in the Early Modern Era: From Living Machines to Affective Morality*, London: Routledge.
Wassmann, C. (2009), 'Physiological optics, cognition and emotion: A novel look at the early work of Wilhelm Wundt', *Journal of the History of Medicine and Allied Sciences*, 64: 213–49.
Wassmann, C. (2014), '"Picturesque incisiveness": Explaining the celebrity of James' theory of emotion', *Journal of the History of the Behavioral Sciences*, 50: 166–88.
Wassmann, C. (2017), 'Forgotten origins, occluded meanings: Translation of emotion terms', *Emotion Review*, 9: 163–71.
White, P. [ed.] (2009), 'Focus: The emotional economy of science', *Isis*, 100.
White, R.S. (2013), 'Emotional landscapes: Romantic travels in Scotland', *Keats-Shelley Review*, 27: 76–90.
Wierzbicka, A. (1986), 'Human emotions: Universal or culture-specific?', *American Anthropologist*, 88: 584–94
Wierzbicka, A. (1999), *Emotions across Languages and Cultures: Diversity and Universals*, Cambridge: Cambridge University Press.
Wolfgang, M.E. (1961), 'Pioneers in criminology: Cesare Lombroso (1825–1909)', *Journal of Law and Criminology*, 52: 361–91.
Woodward, W.R., and Ash, M.G. [eds] (1982), *The Problematic Science: Psychology in Nineteenth-century Thought*, New York: Praeger.
Wundt, W. (1864), *Vorlesungen über die Menschen und Tierseele*, Leipzig: Voss.
Wundt, W. (1874), *Grundzüge der physiologischen Psychologie*, Leipzig: Engelmann.
Young, A. (2009), 'Mirror neurons and the rationality problem', in S. Watanabe, L. Huber, A. Young and A. Blaidsel [eds], *Rational Animals, Irrational Humans*, Tokyo: Science University Press.
Young, A. (2011), 'Empathy, evolution, and human nature', in J. Decety, D. Zahavi and S. Overgaard [eds], *Empathy: From Bench to Bedside*, Cambridge, MA: MIT Press.
Young, A. (2012), 'Empathic cruelty and the origins of the social brain', in S. Choudhury and J. Slaby [eds], *Critical Neuroscience: A Handbook of the Social and Cultural Contexts of Neuroscience*, Oxford: Blackwell.
Zeldin, T. (1982), 'Personal history and the history of emotions', *Journal of Social History*, 15: 339–47.

INDEX

Note: an *n* after a page reference indicates a footnote number

acting 37, 110, 116–17
Aelred of Rievaulx 160
aesthetics 56, 172, 175
affect 20, 41–3, 46, 61, 63, 85–7,
 90, 96–7, 101, 111–13, 115–16,
 120–2, 125, 127, 129, 132–3,
 138, 140–1, 148, 150–1,
 154, 161–3, 174–5, 179–80,
 195–204
Affect Theory 25, 111–13, 115
Ahmed, Sara 67, 82–3, 121, 152,
 183–7
Alexander, Amir 200
Alexander, Kristine 177
anachronism 43, 46, 89, 194
anger 12, 24, 42, 50, 58, 61, 64–5,
 102, 111, 114, 116, 172
animal (animality) 19, 25–6, 33,
 98, 100–5, 109, 134, 139–40,
 188–9
animal behaviour (see 'ethology')
anthropology 1–4, 10, 14, 32, 34–5,
 47–8, 60, 62–4, 74, 85, 103,
 106, 113, 118, 134, 136, 198
anthropomorphism 100–4, 134
anxiety 145, 152, 166, 168, 180
Aquinas, Thomas 139
architecture 7, 38, 169–73
Aristophanes 96–7
Aristotle 44, 138, 194*n*4
art 36, 56, 108, 129–30, 169, 172,
 181–2

association 7, 20, 97, 134, 166, 171,
 179–87, 203
Athens 11–14, 97, 173
atmospheres 170, 174–5, 186,
 201
Austen, Jane 54
authenticity 37, 54, 63–4, 78, 81,
 91, 116, 129–30, 153, 206–7

Bain, Alexander 18–24, 26
basic emotions 36–7, 62, 107–8,
 113–16, 118, 156, 158–9, 192,
 207–8
Baxandall, Michael 130–1
behaviourism 103*n*48, 109
belief 86–7, 123, 140, 154, 184
Bell, Charles 108–11, 114, 129
Berlant, Lauren 185
Bernard of Clairvaux 137
bioculture 2, 6–7, 10, 28, 34, 59,
 63, 69, 113, 118, 124, 135, 156,
 165, 167, 192, 208, 212
biology 6, 10, 21–2, 26, 49, 53, 62,
 111–12, 154, 156–7, 162–7,
 192
Bloch, Marc 27
blood 25, 57, 139, 181–2
 blood pressure 24–5
 blush 68–70
body 2, 6, 9–10, 22, 24–5, 38, 53,
 62–3, 65, 92–7, 106, 111–14,
 117–19, 121–4, 131, 144–54,

INDEX

157, 163–4, 166, 172–3, 180, 201, 203, 208, 212–13
body-mind 7, 19, 112n11, 138, 192
  history of 6, 27, 133, 190
body language 36–7
  see also gesture
Böhme, Gernot 174
Boquet, Damien 206–7
Bourdieu, Pierre 69, 121, 123, 174
Bourke, Joanna 88
Bourke, Julia 160
brain 7, 19, 22, 28–9, 34, 39–40, 48, 50, 56, 75, 92, 96, 102, 111–12, 118–19, 121, 125, 133–5, 138, 142–51, 155–7, 159, 161–3, 192, 201–3, 212–13
Broomhall, Susan 82
Burman, J.T. 162

callousness 139–40
Camporesi, Piero 134
caritas 161
Catholicism 77, 130, 203
causation 2, 13, 155n57, 180
Centres for the History of Emotions 1
  Australia 1n2, 216
  Berlin 1n2, 48, 198
  London 1n2
childhood (children) 30, 39, 48, 82, 84, 99–100, 139–40, 172, 176–8, 213
Christ 130
Christian martyrs 129–30
Cicero 42
citizenship 82, 100, 172, 176–7, 189
civilisation 20–2, 28, 99, 105, 129, 140, 165, 173, 181, 209, 211, 214
civility 19, 104, 140, 184, 206
class 2, 27, 30–1, 38, 54, 92, 97–9, 190, 198
Classen, Constance 134, 137, 142, 202

cogmotion 85, 96, 98
compassion 55, 119, 128, 140, 161
consciousness 19–21, 27, 32, 64, 68–9, 75, 81, 112–13n12, 121–21, 131, 153, 157, 159, 161–2, 207
constructionism 10, 24, 62, 68, 74–5, 114
Corbin, Alain 27, 29, 38–9, 133, 141
cortisol 145, 166
courage 11–14, 57
cruelty 128, 139–41, 188–9
customs 12, 24, 40, 68, 108, 118, 177

Damasio, Antonio 112, 113n12, 119
Darwin, Charles 21, 36, 69, 108–10, 114, 115–17
Darwinism 18, 113–14, 126, 197
  Descent of Man 35, 109
  Expression of Emotions 109–10, 113–14
  Origin of Species 18
Daston, Lorraine 85, 195–200
Dawkins, Richard 213
democracy 53, 73–4, 172, 188, 206
depression 102, 145
Descartes, René 19, 104n52, 137–8, 142, 146
disability 9
disease 9, 25, 40, 58, 127, 145, 152
disgust 38, 111, 114, 116, 139, 158–9, 175, 183
Dixon, Thomas 46, 48–9, 120
DNA 164, 166, 213
domesticity 77, 97
Don Quixote 57
Dror, Otniel 25
Duchenne de Boulogne, Guillaume-Benjamin-Amand 110, 114, 117
Dunning, Eric 28

Eakins, Thomas 181
Eisenberger, Naomi 151
Ekman, Paul 36–7, 49, 107–8, 111, 113–17, 119, 124, 207
  Inside Out 36–7
  Lie to Me 36–7, 115
  Pictures of Facial Affect 116–17
Elias, Norbert 28–9, 72, 87, 134, 208–11
  Civilizing Process 28, 209, 211
  psychogenesis 28, 87
  sociogenesis 28, 87
emotion work *see* emotional effort
emotional communities 6, 30, 77–83, 176–9, 192, 194–5, 209–11
emotional control (restraint) 61–2, 104–5, 209
emotional crisis 66, 178
emotional effort 54, 60, 63–7, 73, 75–6, 81, 95, 104, 107, 117, 159, 161, 192, 197, 211
emotional formation 176–7, 179, 212
emotional frontiers 177–9, 184
emotional improvisation 66
emotional liberty 74–5, 101
emotional navigation 63, 74, 78, 178–80
emotional practice 6, 76, 121, 179, 184, 194–5, 207–8, 211
emotional prescription 6–7, 11, 13, 29, 31, 38, 54, 64–7, 70, 72–7, 81–2, 87–9, 94–9, 101, 104, 123, 148, 158, 169–71, 178–80, 186, 188–9, 192, 196, 210–11, 213
emotional refuges 76–7, 171
emotional regimes 6, 29, 70–7, 79–81, 87–8, 96, 98, 101, 170, 175, 177–8, 186–8, 192, 194–7, 209–11
emotional styles (emotionology) 6, 30, 38, 59–62, 67, 72–3, 76, 78, 80–2, 87–8, 94–5, 101, 126, 130, 169, 177, 188, 196, 200, 210

emotional suffering 63, 67, 72–5, 88
emotional turn 1
emotionology *see* emotional styles (emotionology)
emotives 62–73, 75–7, 80–1, 88, 90, 95–6, 99, 101, 104, 120, 124, 126, 153, 169–71, 175, 177–8, 187, 192, 195, 197, 201, 212–13
empathy 6, 55–6, 101, 124–8, 139–40, 161–2, 182, 184–5
empathy wall 131, 184
epigenetics 112, 166–7, 213
epistemic virtue 199–200
ethics 2, 175, 188–9, 193–4, 199
ethology (animal behaviour) 25, 103
Eustace, Nicole 41–2, 54–5, 91
Evans, Richard 84
evolution (theory/science of) 21–2, 24–5, 33, 100, 109–13, 118–19, 124, 128, 154–5, 157, 164–5, 213
exaptation 154, 163, 165
experience (history of) 86, 142, 167, 212
expression 4, 6, 11, 15, 19–20, 23–4, 28, 36–7, 39, 42, 51, 54, 60–70, 72–3, 78–9, 86, 88, 96, 99, 106–11, 120–1, 123–6, 129–30, 153, 158–9, 169–70, 196–7, 200, 206, 209, 212
  facial 33, 36–7, 52, 67–8, 79, 106–11, 113–18, 125, 129
Extended Mind Theory 121

fear 11–13, 18, 23–5, 27, 33, 50, 57, 61, 71, 102, 111, 114, 116, 130, 133–4, 146–9, 152, 164–5, 172, 180, 183, 186, 188, 210
Febvre, Lucien 26–9, 134, 163, 207
Feldman-Barrett, Lisa 146
Foucault, Michel 170
French Revolution 15–18, 131, 161–2

Freud, Sigmund (Freudianism) 28, 30–2, 59
Frevert, Ute 57, 89–90, 92
Fridlund, Alan 52
Friesen, Wallace 36, 107
Fukuyama, Francis 53
functional magnetic resonance imaging (fMRI) 143, 146, 150

Galen of Pergamon 37, 57–8, 93
Galison, Peter 85, 199–200
Galton, Francis 75
Gay, Peter 27, 30–2, 80
Geertz, Clifford 16, 116
Gefühle 44–5, 55
gender 2, 38, 77, 91–6, 98–9, 180, 190, 202, 212
genetics 4, 48, 148, 164–7, 192, 205, 213
gesture 36–7, 61, 64, 66–8, 71, 86, 88, 106, 116–18, 120–1, 123–4, 129, 148, 163, 212
Giorgi, Kyra 176
global history 2, 175, 179
Grahek, Nikola 150
grief 34, 38, 42, 52–3, 110, 116–17, 127, 160, 182, 184
Gross, Daniel 113n12, 119–20

habitus 69, 81, 174–5, 199
Hallett, Nicky 120, 202
happiness 12, 33, 56, 65, 106–7, 114, 116, 186–8
Harvey, Susan Ashbrook 203
Haskell, Thomas 120, 188–9
heart 17, 27, 57, 96, 114, 138
Hippocrates 93
history of medicine 150
history of science 22, 84–6, 197–8, 200
Hochschild, Arlie Russel 60, 65–7, 107, 184
Hogarth, William 139–40
Holocaust 9, 168, 213
honour 12–13, 57, 90, 92
hope 12, 18, 33, 134, 153, 182, 185, 198
hormones 24, 145, 157, 159
Howes, David 132
human–animal relations 100, 104
humanity 15, 22, 31, 100, 104, 124, 140
Hume, David 21, 180–1
humours 37, 57–8
Hunt, Lynn 131, 161–3
Hutton, Richard 45
Huxley, Aldous 186
hysteria 93–5, 152–3

intelligent design 109, 114
irrationality 18, 27, 59–60, 89, 93–7, 173, 191, 206–7

Jaeger, C. Stephen 35, 89–91
James, William 23–4, 26, 111, 122
jealousy 61
Jewish Museum, Berlin 168–9
justice 53, 67, 72–5, 189, 193, 202–4
Jütte, Robert 134–5

Kant, Immanuel 139
Kivimäki, Ville 191
Kleinginna, P.R. and Kleinginna, A.M. 43
knowledge 8, 21, 51, 57, 77, 83–7, 121–2, 126, 137–9, 142, 173–4, 184, 195–6, 199
Konstan, David 92
Kozlovsky, Roy 171–2
Kuhn, Thomas 201

LaCapra, Dominick 99
Lamarckism 109, 165–6
language/linguistics 5–6, 20, 35–6, 41–6, 49–51, 53–8, 61, 66, 68, 108, 142, 163, 177, 205, 211, 213–15
Lanzoni, Susan 55
Latour, Bruno 201
Lefebvre, George 27
Lehman, Geoff 173–4
Lewes, George Henry 21–2
Libeskind, Daniel 168

love 12–13, 15–17, 33, 35, 42, 54–5, 71, 73, 87, 89–91, 102, 136–7, 160, 182, 186, 191
Lutheranism 77

Maehle, Andreas Holger 92
manners 68, 134, 209
Manning, Erin 138
Marx, Karl (Marxism) 31–2, 97, 135–7
McGrath, Larry 125, 154–6, 159, 162
melancholy 57
mentalités 26–7, 29, 134
Michelet, Jules 15–18
Milner, Matthew 123, 179, 203
mirror neurons 125, 128
moral economy 153, 192, 195–203, 211–13
moral sense 7, 21, 192, 199, 201–4
Moscoso, Javier 153, 198

Nagy, Piroska 206–7
nature/nurture debates 10, 47–8, 62–3, 118–19, 192
neurobiology 33, 112, 119, 143–4, 155, 162, 200, 216
neurohistory 7, 22, 75, 122, 139, 143, 154–65, 212
neuromatrix 148–9
neuroscience 1, 3–5, 7, 10, 34, 39, 46–8, 50, 56, 67, 106, 112–13, 112–13n12, 118, 125–8, 135–6, 142–52, 161, 167, 201, 205, 208, 212–13
Newhauser, Richard G. 137
Nielsen, Philipp 172
nociception 146–7

objectivity 11, 14, 24–5, 85–6, 89, 111, 121, 134, 136–7, 147, 155, 193, 199–200
objects 7, 20, 24, 38–9, 103, 134–6, 140, 142–3, 147–9, 152, 158–9, 162, 169, 179–87, 191, 196–7
Olsen, Stephanie 176–7

pain 34, 44, 55, 73, 109, 121, 127–8, 130, 132, 138–9, 144–54, 157, 161, 166, 180–1, 186, 202
Parrott, W. Gerrod 207
Parthenon 173–5
passions 11–14, 24, 37, 41, 44, 49, 91, 109, 133, 152–3, 181, 211
pathos 44, 182
performance 37, 64–6, 78–9, 90, 206
Pericles 12–14, 22
period eye 130–1
periodisation 206–14
Pernau, Margrit 173
personhood 100
phantom limb 149
phenomenology 85, 99n39
philosophy 3, 9, 21, 34, 49, 51, 54, 85, 100, 104, 121, 192–4, 200
photography 36, 40, 115–18, 124, 129
physiology 9, 19, 21–6, 32, 68, 101–2, 106, 112, 145, 151–2, 157–61, 166, 175, 207, 213
pity 92, 99, 119, 180
place 38–9, 76, 169–79
Plamper, Jan 2, 43–6, 74
plasticity (neuro) 10, 34, 112, 122, 142, 146, 148–9, 155, 157, 159
Plato 30, 104
politics 2, 10, 45, 51, 54, 79–80, 84, 91–2, 97, 100, 106, 118, 177, 183, 188, 190, 192
post-modernism 16, 32, 74, 165n87, 193
power 6, 28, 37, 70, 72, 77, 80–1, 83, 86–99, 104, 137, 170, 172, 186–7, 190–3, 195–8, 200–2, 209–11
practice theory 67, 120–2
psychiatry 94
psychoanalysis 30–1, 37, 47, 94
psychohistory 5, 29–32, 59
psychology 2–3, 5, 18–28, 33–4, 37, 47, 49, 59, 96, 101, 103, 106, 108, 118, 121, 144, 157, 163–5, 179, 191, 195–6, 207–9, 212

psychotropics 39, 156, 160, 162, 164, 186

race 2, 30, 38, 54, 98–9, 158, 190, 212
Ranke, Leopold von 14–15, 84
reason (rationality) 21, 26–8, 60, 84–6, 89, 95–9, 123, 161–2, 173, 190–1, 193, 195, 200, 202, 204, 206
Reckwitz, Andreas 174–5
Reddy, William 6, 48, 54, 62–5, 67–8, 70, 72–4, 76, 78–82, 88, 101, 107, 113–14, 122, 158, 171, 176, 178, 192, 197, 209, 211–12
Reformation 123, 130, 179
religion 30, 38, 87, 127, 177, 203
Ribot, Théodule 26
Rimé, Bernard 207
Riskin, Jessica 200
ritual 37, 70, 76, 137, 179, 203–4, 206–7
Romanes, George John 126–7
Roper, Lyndal 32
Rosenwein, Barbara 6, 30, 41–2, 46, 77–83, 178, 206, 208–11

sadness 114, 116, 127, 142
Sartre, Jean-Paul 118
satisfaction 57, 101, 185–9
Schadenfreude 128
Scheer, Monique 121–4, 131, 143
Scheler, Max 55
Scottish Enlightenment 194
self 8, 55, 91, 122–6, 137, 161, 182, 198–9
senses 6–7, 29, 45, 120, 123–4, 131–42, 144, 150, 152–3, 173, 183, 201–3
sensibility 6, 29, 50, 93, 136, 139
separate spheres 97
sex 9, 31, 90–3, 97, 153–5, 174, 190
Seymour, Mark 81
Shakespeare, William 112
sight 125, 131–3, 137, 141, 146, 148, 181–2, 203

slavery 9, 51, 189
Smail, Daniel Lord 63, 156–60, 164–5, 214
smell 111, 132–4, 137, 141, 203
smile 52–3, 65, 67, 106–7
Smith, Adam 21, 180–1
social exclusion 9–10, 80, 86, 92, 98–101, 104, 128, 150–1, 185
soul 19, 41, 106, 108, 137–8, 173
sources 34–40
Sparta 14
spatial theory 168–75
Spinoza, Baruch 49
Stearns, Carol Z. 32, 47, 59–61, 67, 78, 81, 97, 196, 200
Stearns, Peter 6, 30, 32, 47, 59–61, 67, 78, 81, 95n28, 96–7, 115, 196, 200
Strange, Julie-Marie 180
Styles, John 182
suffering 44, 55–6, 63, 127, 130, 140, 144, 149, 181, 189
see also emotional suffering
Sullivan, Erin 66
surgery 180–2
sympathy 21, 35, 42, 55, 63, 128, 140, 162, 181, 184, 207

taste 134, 137, 142, 203
teaching 205, 216–17
Tepora, Tuomas 191
terror 117, 180–1
Thompson, E.P. 31, 195, 196n6, 198
Thucydides 11–14
Tomkins, Silvan 111–13, 119
Toner, Jerry 152
touch 134, 142, 145, 150, 153
translation 42, 44–6, 58, 63, 66, 83, 122, 138, 147, 159, 176, 179, 203, 214–16

unconsciousness 37, 67–9, 75, 80–1, 113n12, 121–2, 131, 161–2

Vallgårda, Karen 177
violence 28, 72, 87, 104, 140, 191, 193, 209
virtue 2, 11, 16, 57, 61, 90–1, 199–200, 211

Weimar Germany 77
Weinman, Michael 173–4
White, Hayden 15–17

White, Paul 120, 197
Wierzbicka, Anna 49–53, 106
women's history 9
World War I 176, 213–14
World War II 172, 191
Wundt, Wilhelm 19

Young, Allan 128